2.12.80

COMPUTER ESSENTIALS FOR BUSINESS

COMPUTER
FOR

McGRAW-HILL

New York □ St. Louis □ San Francisco □ Auckland
Madrid □ Mexico □ Montreal □ New Delhi □ Panama

ESSENTIALS
BUSINESS

DONALD H. SANDERS

M. J. Neeley School of Business
Texas Christian University

BOOK COMPANY

Bogotá □ Düsseldorf □ Johannesburg □ London
Paris □ São Paulo □ Singapore □ Sydney □ Tokyo □ Toronto

COMPUTER ESSENTIALS FOR BUSINESS

34567890   VHVH   7832109

This book was set in Helvetica Light by University Graphics, Inc.
The editors were Peter D. Nalle and Annette Hall;
the designer was Jo Jones;
the production supervisor was Leroy A. Young.
The drawings were done by J & R Services, Inc.
The cover was designed by John Hite.
Von Hoffmann Press, Inc., was printer and binder.

Cartoon Acknowledgments

The cartoons found in this text are taken from *Educational Technology* and *Datamation* magazines and are reprinted with the permission of the publishers of these periodicals. More specifically, cartoons on pages 5, 22, 63, 64, 71, 74, 81, 99, 131, 152, 171, 179, 211, 217, 234, 237, 242, 250, 268, 286, 301, and 324 are from *Educational Technology* and are reprinted by permission of Educational Technology Publications, Inc., 140 Sylvan Avenue, Englewood Cliffs, New Jersey 07632. And cartoons on pages 15, 40, 55, 79, 113, 125, 154, 173, 188, 254, 269, 273, 291, 294, 323, and 328 are from *Datamation* and are reprinted with permission of *Datamation*®, copyright © 1966, 1967, 1968, 1969, 1970, 1972, 1973, 1974, 1975, and 1976 by Technical Publishing Company, Greenwich, Connecticut 06830.

Library of Congress Cataloging in Publication Data

Sanders, Donald H
    Computer essentials for business.

    Includes index.
      1. Business—Data processing. I. Title.
HF5548.2.S219   001.6′4′02465   77-22697
ISBN 0-07-054647-9

CONTENTS

THREE SOLVING PROBLEMS: THE SYSTEM DEVELOPMENT/PROGRAMMING PROCESS

FOUR   COMPUTER IMPLICATIONS FOR MANAGEMENT

FIVE   COMPUTERS AND THE FUTURE

Although most students for whom this book was written probably accept the fact that in their future work they will need a basic understanding of computerized information processing and a familiarity with computers, they have not chosen to become computer scientists or information systems specialists. Rather, these students are preparing for management or staff positions in such functional areas of business as accounting, finance, marketing, personnel, and production, or they are planning to become administrators in government, health, or educational organizations that make use of business procedures. Thus, as *end-users* (rather than as designers) of information systems, these students have needs and objectives that differ from those of students who expect to work more closely with computers. The purpose of this book, therefore, is to introduce these students, at an early stage in a college program, to many of the important topics that are likely to be most relevant to them in their future careers.

Objectives and Organization

More specifically, the *objectives of this book* are to provide these future users of information system output with (1) some of the fundamental concepts of computerized information processing; (2) a general orientation to the computer—what it is, what it can and cannot do, how it operates, and how it may be instructed to solve problems; and (3) some insights into the broad impact that computers are having on businesspeople, on the environment in which they work, and on the society in which they live.

To achieve these objectives, *the book is divided into five parts.* The first objective is considered in the two chapters of Part One. The four chapters in Part Two (dealing with computer capabilities, limitations, and hardware) and the four chapters in Part Three (emphasizing the system development/programming process for solving problems) focus attention on the second objective, and the chapters in Parts Four and Five deal with the final objective.

Distinctive Characteristics of This Text

Some of the main differences between this text and many others are

A balanced presentation of topics.   An attempt has been made to avoid hardware/software details that are beyond the needs of information system users, and to balance these topics with the managerial and social implications of computer use.

The use of humor to maintain student interest.   Cartoons are liberally inserted at the correct places in the text to reinforce important points that are presented. This approach differs from some

books where cartoons and inserts are randomly placed in such a way as to cause distraction rather than reinforcement. In addition to cartoons, humorous quotes are occasionally used.

The use of learning objectives.   Learning objectives and chapter outlines are presented at the beginning of each chapter. The review and discussion questions at the end of each chapter support these learning objectives.

The availability of support materials.   A student *Study Guide* and an *Instructor's Manual* are available.

Use of This Book

This book is designed to be used in a one-semester (quarter) course taken by business and administration students. No mathematical or data processing background is required or assumed.

An issue that has yet to be resolved concerns the depth of programming instruction that the users of computer output should receive. For many introductory courses, the limited programming language emphasis contained in this book will be quite sufficient. However, when considerable emphasis is to be placed on the writing of programs in a specific language for a specific make and model of machine, two types of instructional materials are frequently required: (1) a basic text to add breadth to the course and (2) programming manuals available from equipment manufacturers and publishers and/or notes and materials prepared by the instructor. In such situations, this book is well suited for use as the basic text.

The organization of the book into five parts permits some *modular flexibility*. For example, if a number of programs are to be written, the first three chapters can be quickly covered, and then the chapters in Part Three may be considered early in the course to provide background and support for the problem-solving process.

Since this is an introductory text dealing with the general uses, operations, and implications of computers, and since the author has written other volumes that deal with many of the same basic subjects, there are a number of similarities between this book and the other works. In general, however, the material presented here is *much less detailed* than in the author's other texts. For example, the material on computer hardware and software does not have the depth of coverage of the same topics found in *Computers in Business,* 3d ed., McGraw-Hill Book Company, 1975. And the chapter dealing with the broader social implications of the use of computers is greatly abridged when compared with similar material presented in *Computers in Society,* 2d ed., McGraw-Hill Book Company, 1977.

Of course, the organizational structure and many of the sections in this book differ from either of those earlier volumes.

It is customary at about this point in a preface (although there is always the question of whether anyone is reading a preface at this point) to acknowledge the contributions and suggestions received from numerous sources. A special tribute must go to those equipment manufacturers and magazine publishers who furnished technical materials, cartoons, photographs, and other visual aids. Their individual contributions are generally acknowledged in the body of the book. Several amusing quotations were found in *InROL II,* the clever student handbook of Texas A & M University. Finally, I appreciate the encouragement and support received from Dean Gilbert Whitaker and from the faculty of the M. J. Neeley School of Business, Texas Christian University.

Donald H. Sanders

COMPUTER ESSENTIALS FOR BUSINESS

COMPUTERIZED INFORMATION PROCESSING: SOME FUNDAMENTALS

Computers are used in business because they can produce necessary information. Therefore, the purpose of the chapters in this first Part is to (1) develop some fundamental concepts about the subject of information, (2) study the evolution of information processing, and (3) examine the setting for, and a few of the developments and issues associated with, the information revolution that business is currently experiencing. At the conclusion of this Part, you will then have a background for the orientation to computers that is the subject of Part Two.

1

INFORMATION AND INFORMATION PROCESSING: CONCEPTS AND EVOLUTION

LEARNING OBJECTIVES

After studying this chapter and answering the discussion questions, you should be able to:

Identify the sources of data and the activities associated with data processing.

Discuss the information needs of managers and the properties that management information should possess.

Identify the pressures responsible for the current efforts to improve management information.

Outline some major developments in the evolution of information processing.

Dictionaries assign to the word *awful* such meanings as "monstrous, filling with awe, inspiring dread, and commanding solemn wonder or reverential fear." In recent years you may have found support for each of these meanings—i.e., you may have concluded that "computers are awful"—from computer-related articles and television shows that you have read and watched. Perhaps in one article the computer was pictured as having *human* characteristics, e.g., as being a device that can play checkers and form verbal answers to inquiries. Or perhaps in another account the computer was presented as *subhuman;* stupid errors in billing, for example, could have been cited, such as the case of the woman who was charged for the purchase of 4,000 new tires instead of 4. And at the opposite extreme, the computer may have been placed in a *superhuman* role. In an article in *Smithsonian,* for example, it is estimated that in about the year 1986 a self-programming machine will be developed that will usher in a "new form of intelligent life" on this planet—a form of intelligence similar to HAL, the superhuman computer which was featured in the science fiction film *2001: A Space Odyssey.*[1] Finally, you may have watched a television program that depicted the computer as an *inhuman* instrument that could be used to invade your privacy or to make heartless decisions affecting you without regard for your feelings.

Such contradictory characterizations of computers and their uses may have left you with feelings of excitement, frustration, amazement, awe, or even fear. Although there may be elements of truth in each of these characterizations, they seldom lead to the understanding of computer capabilities and limitations that you will need in the future.

OBJECTIVES AND APPROACH OF THIS BOOK

To do is to be—*J. P. Sartre*

To be is to do—*I. Kant*

Do be do be do—*F. Sinatra*[2]

---

[1]See Gregory Benford and David Book, "Promise-Child in the Land of the Humans," *Smithsonian,* pp. 58–65, April 1971. HAL is an *acronym*—i.e., a term formed from the first letters of related words—which means Heuristically programmed ALgorithmic computer. Acronyms are frequently used in the jargon of computing and information processing.

[2]Have you ever noticed that chapters and sections of chapters in learned books and academic treatises are often preceded by quotations such as these that are selected by the author for some reason? In some cases the quotation is intended to emphasize a point to be presented; in other cases (often in the more eruidite sources)

"It's happened! . . . It's happened!!"

It is probable that your future career and private life will be greatly affected by the computer. As a potential leader, you must prepare for a successful working relationship with computerized information processing. And as a well-educated citizen, you must acquire an understanding of this processing so that you will be prepared to cope with the expanding uses of computers in our society. Therefore, to lay the foundation for the *continuing study* that will provide you with such a working relationship and understanding, *the objectives of this book are* to (1) introduce you to some of the fundamental concepts of (and developments associated with) computerized information processing; (2) provide you with a general orientation to the computer—what it is, what it can and cannot do, how it operates, and how it may be instructed to solve problems; and (3) furnish you with some insights into the broad impact that computers have had, are having, and may be expected to have on managers, the environment in which managers work, and the society in which we live.

To achieve these overall objectives, the book is divided into five

---

there appears to be no discernible reason for the message, and it forever remains a mystery to the reader. In this particular case, the quotations from the above philosophers unfortunately fall into the *latter category!* However, we will from time to time throughout the book attempt to use quotations (from such authorities as Aldous Huxley and Winnie-the-Pooh) for the more valid purpose of emphasizing a point.

parts. The first objective is considered in the two chapters of Part One, the chapters in Parts Two and Three focus attention on the second goal, and the chapters in Parts Four and Five deal with the final goal. On a more detailed level, at the beginning of each chapter you will find (1) a summary of what you should learn in that chapter, and (2) an outline of the major topics that are presented in the chapter. In total, of course, these chapter learning objectives achieve the overall goals of the book.

In addition to these goals and the approach taken to achieve them, a further purpose of this book is to attempt to reduce the communications gap that currently exists between computer specialists and those who use (or are affected by) the machine's output. Of course, there is nothing new about the problem of lack of communication.[3] In ancient Babylon, a vast public works program was started by the leaders with the objective of building a tower reaching to the heavens. Obviously, a project of such magnitude required a considerable amount of managerial skill as well as the labor of thousands of workers. The book of Genesis tells us that this ambitious project was never completed. Displeased with the haughty conduct of the people, God confused their language. Supervisors could not communicate with workers; workers could not even understand each other. The project came to a standstill, and the episode has been used for centuries as an example of the consequences of a communications breakdown.

A whole new language has developed in the past decade in information processing—a language that might be labeled "Computerese" and that must be mastered to some extent by the future manager. New concepts in the design and use of computers are announced with mind-boggling frequency, and these concepts are often described with newly coined words or phrases. Thousands of new computers are installed each year; understanding suffers because it sometimes seems that the number of new terms and acronyms are increasing at about the same rate.

In the following section and throughout the book, words are defined as they are introduced. *A glossary of commonly used tech-*

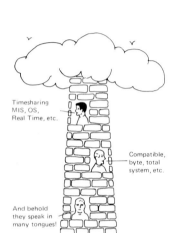

Timesharing MIS, OS, Real Time, etc.

Compatible, byte, total system, etc.

And behold they speak in many tongues!

---

[3]Nor is this communications gap unique to the computing field. Representative Ben Grant, in arguing for plain language in a proposed new Texas constitution, pointed out that if one person were to give another an orange, he or she would simply say, "Have an orange." But if a lawyer were the donor, the gift might be accompanied with these words: "I hereby give and convey to you, all and singular, my estate and interests, right, title, claim, and advantages of and in said orange, together with its rind, juice, pulp, and pips, and all rights and advantages therein, with full power to bite, cut, suck, and otherwise eat same. . . ."

nical terms is included at the back of the book. You will find that although some Computerese terms sound quite impressive and forbidding—as is often the case with technical jargon—closer inspection will prove them to be relatively simple.

The above remarks have served to introduce you to the objectives of this book. In later chapters we will examine computer systems in some detail. At this point, however, we should place the role of computers in proper perspective. Computers are used *because they produce information;* were this not so, the machines would be merely expensive curiosities. Therefore, in the pages of this chapter that follow, let us examine the subject of information. After first explaining some *information concepts,* we will then consider the *need for management information,* the *pressures bringing about management information improvement,* and the *evolution of information processing.*

INFORMATION CONCEPTS

Three elements fundamental to human activities are information, energy, and materials. The harnessing of energy brought about the industrial revolution, and the attempt to harness and transform information is bringing about another revolution at the present time.[4]

Information Defined

The word *data* is the plural of *datum,* which means *fact.* Data, then, are facts, unevaluated messages, or informational raw materials, but they are not information except in a constricted and detailed sense.

As used in this text, the term *information* is generally considered to designate data arranged in ordered and useful form. Thus, information will usually be thought of as relevant knowledge, produced as output of processing operations, and acquired to provide insight in order to (1) achieve specific purposes or (2) enhance understanding. From this definition, we see that information is the result of a transformation process. Just as raw materials are transformed into finished products by a manufacturing process [Figure 1-1(a)], so too are raw data transformed into information by the data processing operation [Figure 1-1(b)].

---

[4]This information revolution is the subject of the next chapter. An indication of the scope and importance of information is found in the estimate of the director of the President's Office of Telecommunications Policy that during 1975 "more than 50 percent of the US labor force and more than 50 percent of the gross national product were expected to be devoted to the production, processing, or distribution of information. . . ." See "Washington Info," *Infosystems,* p. 14, January 1976.

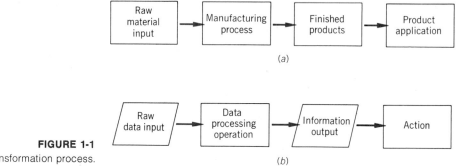

FIGURE 1-1
Transformation process.

The purpose of data processing is to evaluate and bring order to data and place them in proper perspective or context so that meaningful information will be produced. The primary distinction between data and information, therefore, is that while all information consists of data, not all data produce specific and meaningful information that will reduce uncertainty and lead to greater insight (and better decisions).

Sources of Data

The input data used to produce information originate from internal and external sources. *Internal sources* consist of individuals and departments located within an organization. These sources may furnish facts on a regular and planned basis (i.e., on a formal basis) to support decisions if the potential user is aware that the facts are available. Internal data gathered on a formal basis typically relate to events that have already happened; they often represent feedback to managers of the effectiveness and accuracy of earlier plans. Of course, in addition to what might be called "planned data gathering," data may also be received from internal sources on an informal basis through casual contacts and discussions.

External, or *environmental,* sources are the generators and distributors of data located outside the organization. These sources include such categories as customers, suppliers, competitors, business publications, industry associations, and government agencies. Such sources provide the organization with environmental and/or competitive data that may give managers important clues on what is likely to happen.

Data Processing

All data processing, whether it is done by hand or by the latest electronic methods, consists of an *originating-recording* (input) activity, *transformation* (processing) operations, and *output/records-management* activities.

Originating-recording activity   Data must be originated or captured in some form for processing. Data may be initially recorded on paper *source documents* such as sales tickets or deposit slips, and they then may be converted into a machine-usable form for processing. Alternatively, they may be initially captured directly in a paperless machine-usable form.

Transformation operations   One or more of the following operations may then need to be performed on the gathered data:

Classifying   Identifying and arranging items with like characteristics into groups or classes is called *classifying.* Sales data taken from a sales ticket may be classified by product sold, location of sales point, customer, sales clerk, or any other classification that the processing cycle may require.

Classifying is usually done by a shortened, predetermined method of abbreviation known as *coding.* The three types of codes used are *numeric, alphabetic,* and *alphanumeric.*

Sorting   After the data are classified, it is usually necessary to arrange or rearrange them in a predetermined sequence to facilitate processing. This arranging procedure is called *sorting.* Sorting is done by number as well as by letter. Sales invoices may be sorted by invoice number or by customer name. Numeric sorting usually requires less time than alphabetic sorting in machine-based processing systems and is therefore generally used.

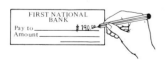

Calculating   Arithmetic manipulation of the data is known as *calculating.* In the calculation of an employee's pay, for example, the total of hours worked multiplied by the hourly wage rate would give the taxable gross earnings. Payroll deductions such as taxes and insurance are then computed and subtracted from gross earnings to leave net or take-home earnings.

Summarizing   To be of value, data must often be condensed or sifted so that the resulting output reports will be concise and effective. Reducing masses of data to a more usable form is called *summarizing.* Sales managers may be interested only in the total

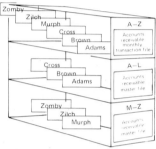

sales of a particular store. Thus, it would be wasteful in time and resources if they were given a report that broke sales down by department, product, and sales clerk.

Output/records-management activities Once the data have been transformed into information, one or more of the following activities may be required:

Communicating The information, in a usable form, must be *communicated* to the user. Output information may be in the form of a vital printed report; but output can also be in the form of a gas bill on a punched card or an updated reel of magnetic tape.

Storing Placing similar data into files for future reference is *storing*. Obviously, facts should be stored only if the value of having them in the future exceeds the storage cost. Storage may take a variety of forms. Storage *media* that are frequently used include paper documents, microfilm, magnetizable media and devices, and punched paper media.

Retrieving Recovering stored data and/or information when needed is the *retrieving* step. Retrieval methods range from searches made by file clerks to the use of quick-responding inquiry terminals that are connected directly (i.e., they are *online*) to a computer. The computer, in turn, is connected directly to a mass-storage device that contains the information.

Reproducing It is sometimes necessary or desirable to copy or duplicate data. This operation is known as data *reproduction* and may be done by hand or by machine.

These, then, are the basic steps in data processing. Figure 1-2 presents these steps and indicates some of the ways in which they are accomplished. The means of performing the steps vary according to whether *manual, electromechanical,* or *electronic* processing methods are used.

The above brief remarks on the sources of data and the nature of data processing now make it possible to expand Figure 1-1(*b*). In Figure 1-3 we see that data input is divided into sources and that data processing is broken down into operational steps. The solid lines represent the possible communication of data and information in a single processing cycle; the dashed lines represent the feed-back communication required to obtain additional data (either retrieved and reproduced stored data or new data) and recycle the data base for further processing.

NEED FOR MANAGEMENT INFORMATION

When a man kens, he can—*Thomas Carlyle*

Information is needed in virtually every field of human thought and action. Compared with information "have nots," individuals who have relevant information may have better career opportunities and may be better equipped to make personal decisions.

Besides being essential to individuals who use it to achieve personal ends, however, information is also needed by decision makers in organizations. All managers must perform certain basic management tasks or functions in order to achieve goals. The objectives pursued differ, of course, but the basic tasks are common to all. In other words, the functions of *planning, organizing, staffing,* and *controlling* are performed by all managers.[5] The success of any business is determined by how well its executives perform these activities. And how well these functions are carried out is dependent, in part, upon how well the information needs of managers are being met. Why is this? It is because each function involves decision making, and decision making must be supported by information that is accurate, timely, complete, concise, and relevant. If a manager's information does not possess these characteristics, the quality of the decisions that are made will probably suffer and the business (at best) will not achieve the success it might otherwise have had.

In summary, as shown in Figure 1-4, quality information in the hands of those who can effectively use it will support good decisions; good decisions will lead to effective performance of managerial activities; and effective managerial performance will lead to successful attainment of organizational goals. Thus, information is the bonding agent that holds an organization together.

What Information Is Needed?

What information is needed to manage effectively? A common need basic to all managers is an understanding of the purpose of the organization, i.e., its policies, its programs, its plans, and its goals. But beyond these basic informational requirements, the question of what information is needed can be answered only in broad, general terms because individual managers differ in the ways in which they view information, in their analytical approaches in using it, and in their conceptual organization of relevant facts. An additional factor

---

[5]We will look at how computer usage affects the performance of these functions in Chapters 11 and 12.

Steps in the Data Processing Operation

Processing Methods	Originating-Recording	Classifying	Sorting	Calculating
Manual methods	Human observation; handwritten records; pegboards	Hand posting; pegboards	Hand posting; pegboards; edge-notched cards	Human brain
Manual with machine assistance	Typewriter; cash register; manual	Cash register; bookkeeping machine	Mechanical collators	Adding machines; calculators; cash registers
Electrome-chanical punched card methods	Prepunched cards; keypunched cards; mark-sensed cards; manual	Determined by card field design; sorter; collator	Card sorter	Accounting machines (tabulators); calculating punch
Electronic methods	Magnetic tape encoder; magnetic and optical character readers; card and tape punches; online terminals; manual; key-to-disk encoder	Determined by systems design; computer	Computer sorting	Computer

FIGURE 1-2

Tools and techniques for data processing.

that complicates the subject of the information needed by managers is the organizational level of the managerial job. Managers at the lower operating levels need information to help them make the day-to-day operating decisions. At the top levels, however, information is needed to support long-range policy decisions.

In Figure 1-5(a) we see that at the lower managerial levels more time is generally spent in performing control activities (e.g., checking to make sure that production schedules are being met) while at the upper levels more time is spent on planning (e.g., determining

Summarizing	Communicating	Storing	Retrieving	Reproducing
Pegboards; hand calculations	Written reports; hand-carried messages; telephone	Paper in files, journals, ledgers, etc.	File clerk; bookkeeper	Clerical; carbon paper
Accounting machines; adding machines; cash registers	Documents prepared by machines; message conveyors	Motorized rotary files Microfilm	Motorized rotary files; Microfilm	Photocopying machines; duplicators; addressing machines
Accounting machines (tabulators); calculating punch	Printed documents; interpreter	Trays of cards	Manual tray movement	Reproducing punch
Computer	Online data transmission; printed output; visual display; voice output	Magnetizable media and devices; punched media; computer; microfilm	Online inquiry with direct-access devices; manual movement of storage media to computer	Multiple copies from printers; microfilm copies

the location and specifications of a new production plant). Figure 1-5(*b*) shows that although lower-level managers need detailed information relating to daily operations of specific departments, top executives are best served with information that summarizes trends and indicates exceptions to what was expected. A final generalization is that the higher one is in the organization, the more one needs and is likely to use information obtained from external sources [see Figure 1-5(*c*)]. A supervisor uses internally generated feedback information to control production processes, but a president study-

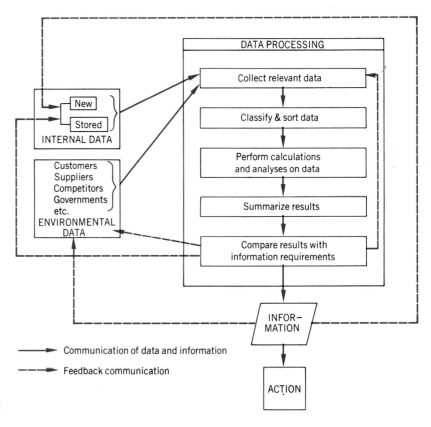

FIGURE 1-3

FIGURE 1-4

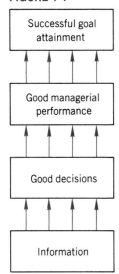

ing the feasibility of a new plant needs information about customer product acceptance, availability of labor and suppliers, etc., and this information is environmental in nature.

In summary, the types of decisions made by managers vary, and so information needs also vary. Thus, it is unlikely that we shall soon see (if, indeed, we ever do) an information system that is uniformly suitable and desirable for all managers in an organization.

Desired Properties of Management Information

As a general rule, the more information serves to reduce the element of uncertainty in decision making, the greater is its value (Figure 1-6). But information is a resource, and like other resources it is usually not free. It is therefore necessary that the cost of acquiring the resource be compared with the value to be obtained from its availa-

"Miss Dennison, send in some reports, charts, programs, files, data, indices, facts, figures, totals, actuaries, systems analyses, projections, printouts, breakdowns, summaries, rates, records, statements, memorandums, graphs, requisitions . . ."

© DATAMATION ®

FIGURE 1-5

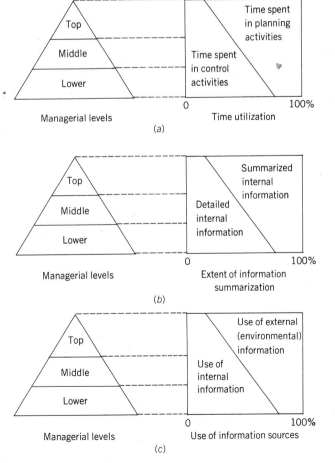

(a)

(b)

(c)

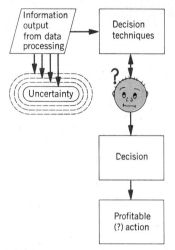

FIGURE 1-6

bility. Information should be prepared if (1) its cost is less than the additional *tangible revenues* produced by its use, (2) it serves to reduce *tangible expenses* by a more than proportionate amount, or (3) it provides such *intangible* benefits as insight, understanding, better customer service, etc., which the information-user considers to be worth the costs involved.

You should keep in mind these brief comments on information economics as we look at the desirability of information that possesses the characteristics of *accuracy, timeliness, completeness, conciseness,* and *relevancy.* Up to a certain point, information that possesses these properties may be expected to be more valuable than information lacking one or more of these characteristics.

Accuracy Accuracy may be defined as the ratio of correct information to the total amount of information produced over a period of time. If, for example, 1,000 items of information are produced and 950 of these items give a correct report of the actual situation, then the level of accuracy is 0.95. Whether or not this level is high enough depends upon the information being produced. Fifty incorrect bank balances in a mailing of 1,000 bank statements would hardly be acceptable to depositors or to the bank. On the other hand, if physical inventory records kept on large quantities of inexpensive parts achieve an accuracy level of 0.95, this might be acceptable. Inaccuracies are the result of *human errors* and/or *machine malfunctions.* Human error (in system design, machine operation, the preparation of input data, and other ways) is the primary cause of inaccuracy.

Timeliness Timeliness is another important information characteristic. It is of little consolation to a manager to know that information that arrived too late to be of use was accurate. Accuracy alone is not enough.

How fast must be the *response time* of the information system? Unfortunately, it is once again impossible to give an answer which will satisfy all situations. In the case of *regular reports,* a compromise is often required. The response interval should be short enough so that the information does not lose its freshness and value, but the interval should be long enough to reduce report volume (and associated costs) and reveal important trends that signal the need for action. Thus, the most appropriate regular report interval is a matter that must be determined by each organization. However, as we shall see in the next chapter, computer-based systems have been designed to enable managers to obtain in seconds the answers to nonrecurring questions that are not available from regular reports.

Completeness Most managers faced with a decision to make have been frustrated at some time by having supporting information that is accurate, timely—and *incomplete.* An example of the consequences of failure to consolidate related pieces of information occurred at Pearl Harbor in 1941. Historians tell us that data available, in bits and pieces and at scattered points, if integrated, would have signaled the danger of a Japanese attack. Better integration of the facts available at scattered points in a business is a goal of information systems designers.

Conciseness Important information, along with relatively useless data, is often buried in stacks of detailed reports. Managers are then faced with the problem of extracting those items that they need. Concise information that summarizes the relevant facts and that points out areas of exception to normal or planned activities is what is often needed by—but less often supplied to—today's managers.

Relevancy Relevant information is "need-to-know" information that leads to action or provides new knowledge and understanding. Reports that were once valuable but that are no longer relevant should be discontinued.

INFORMATION IMPROVEMENT AND COMPUTER PROCESSING

Most of the information processing developments occurring today are aimed at obtaining information with more of the desirable properties discussed above. A number of pressures are responsible for current information improvement efforts, and as these pressures have built managers have often turned to the use of the computer for relief. Included among these pressures are:

1 *Increased paperwork volume* Processing capability in many organizations has been strained by (a) the growth in size and complexity of the organization, (b) the increased demand for data from external sources, and (c) the demand of managers for more information. Fortunately, the greater the volume of data that must be processed, the more economical computer processing becomes relative to other processing methods.

2 *Demand for accuracy* If a processing system has gone beyond the capacity for which it was designed, inaccuracies will begin to appear and the control of organizational activities will suffer. Computer processing, however, will be quite accurate *if* the tasks performed have been properly prepared.

3 *Demand for timeliness* With an increase in processing volume, there is often a delay in report preparation. Thus, many firms

have turned to the use of computers to speed up their processing.

4 *Increased costs* The increasing labor and materials costs associated with a noncomputer-processing operation have often caused managers to look to computer usage for economic relief. Managers know, of course, that a business must earn a sufficient profit to continue to exist. Simply defined, *profit* is the difference between revenue and costs or expenses (that is, profit = revenue − expenses). Therefore, one way to increase profit is to reduce information processing expenses while other costs and revenue remain stable. In some organizations, computer usage has led to this tangible benefit. Another way that the profit outlook may be improved is by increasing revenue at a faster rate than expenses. Many businesses have achieved this result by using computers to give old customers better service and to expand their marketing efforts to include new customers.

EVOLUTION OF INFORMATION PROCESSING

Earlier in the chapter (in Figure 1-2), we classified processing methods into *manual, machine-assisted manual, electromechanical punched card,* and *electronic computer* categories. In the remaining pages of this chapter, let us use these categories to look briefly at the history of information processing.

The Manual Stage

For centuries, people lived on earth without keeping records. But as social organizations such as tribes began to form, adjustments became necessary. The complexities of tribal life required that more details be remembered. Methods of counting, based on the biological fact that people have fingers, were thus developed. However, the limited number of digits combined with the need to remember more facts posed problems. For example, if a shepherd were tending a large tribal flock and if he had a short memory, how was he to keep control of his inventory? Problems bring solutions, and the shepherd's solution might have been to let a stone, a stick, a scratch on a rock, or a knot in a string represent each sheep in the flock.

As tribes grew into nations, trade and commerce developed. Stones and sticks, however, were not satisfactory for early traders. In 3500 B.C., the ancient Babylonian merchants were keeping records on clay tablets.

Manual record-keeping techniques continued to develop through the centuries, with such innovations as record audits (the Greeks) and banking systems and budgets (the Romans). In the United

States, in the 20 years following the Civil War, the main tools of data processing were pencils, pens, rulers, work sheets (for classifying, calculating, and summarizing), journals (for storing), and ledgers (for storing and communicating).

The volume of business and government processing during this period was expanding rapidly, and, as might be expected, such complete reliance upon manual methods resulted in information that was relatively inaccurate and often late. To the consternation of the Census Bureau, for example, the 1880 census was not finished until it was almost time to begin the 1890 count! In spite of accuracy and timeliness limitations, however, *manual processing methods have the following advantages:* (1) information is in a humanly readable form; (2) changes and corrections are easily accomplished; (3) no minimum economic processing volume is generally required; and (4) manual methods are easily adapted to changing conditions.

Machine-assisted
Manual Development

The evolution of machine-assisted processing methods has gone through several phases. In the *first phase,* machines were produced which improved the performance of a *single* processing step. In 1642, for example, the first mechanical calculating machine (see Figure 1-7) was developed by Blaise Pascal, a brilliant young Frenchman. And in the 1880s, the typewriter was introduced as a recording aid that improved legibility and doubled writing speeds.

In the *second phase* of machine-assisted methods, equipment was invented which could *combine* certain processing steps in a single operation. Machines that calculate and print the results were first produced around 1890. They combine calculating, summarizing, and recording steps and produce a printed tape record suitable

FIGURE 1-7

Pascal's adding machine (courtesy IBM Corporation).

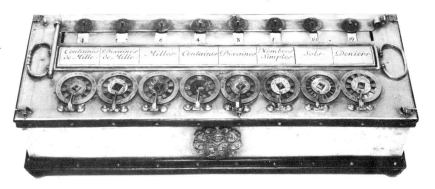

for storing data. After World War I, accounting machines designed for special purposes (e.g., billing, retail sales, etc.) began to appear. These machines also combine steps and often contain several adding *registers* or *counters* to permit the accumulation of totals (calculation and summarization) for different classifications. For example, the supermarket cash register has separate registers to sort and total the day's sales of health items, hardware, meats, produce, and groceries.

A *third phase* has emerged in recent years. Equipment manufacturers have taken steps to ensure that small calculators and accounting machines are not made obsolete by the computer. Features of these machines are being combined with features taken from computers to create new electronic pocket-size and desk-size hardware. Many of these new calculators (computers?) have data-storage capability and can be programmed to perform processing steps in sequence just like computers. However, programmable calculators usually cannot match a computer in the speed with which both alphabetic and numeric data can be processed.

When compared with the manual processing of the late 1800s, machine-assisted manual methods have the advantages of greater speed and accuracy. However, a higher processing volume is generally required to justify equipment costs, there is some reduction in the flexibility of the processing techniques, and it is relatively more difficult to (1) correct or change data once they have entered the processing system and (2) implement changes in machine-assisted procedures.

Electromechanical
Punched Card Development

Punched card methods have been in *widespread* business use only since the 1930s, but the history of the punched card dates back to about the end of the American Revolution when a French weaver named Jacquard used them to control his looms.

Although punched cards continued to be used in process control, it was not until the use of manual methods resulted in the problem of completing the 1880 census count that they began to be considered as a medium for data processing. The inventor of modern punched card techniques was Dr. Herman Hollerith, a statistician. He was hired by the Census Bureau as a special agent to help find a solution to the census problem. In 1887, Hollerith developed his machine-readable card concept and designed a device known as the *"census machine.''* Tabulating time with Hollerith's methods was only one-eighth of that previously required, and so his techniques were adopted for use in the 1890 count. Although population had increased from 50 to 63 million people in the decade after 1880, the 1890 count was completed in less than 3 years. (Of course, this would be considered intolerably slow by today's standards,[6] but the alternative in 1890 would have been to continue the count beyond 1900 and violate the constitutional provision that congressional seats be reapportioned every 10 years on the basis of census data.)

Following the 1890 census, Hollerith converted his equipment to business use and set up freight statistics systems for two railroads. In 1896 he founded the Tabulating Machine Company to make and sell his invention. Later, this firm merged with others to form what is now known as International Business Machines Corporation (IBM).

Punched card processing is based on a simple idea: Input data are initially recorded in a coded form by punching holes into cards, and these cards are then fed into machines that perform processing steps—e.g., sorting, calculating, and summarizing. The early Hollerith cards measured 3 by 5 inches; different sizes are used today and different coding schemes are employed with modern cards containing either 80 or 96 columns.

The 80-column card Figure 1-8 shows the typical 80-column punched card. One corner is usually trimmed to help maintain proper positioning during processing. The card is divided into 80 consecutively numbered vertical *columns.* These columns, in turn, have 12 horizontal positions or *rows.* By appropriate coding, each column can record one character of information, i.e., a digit, a letter, or a special character. Columns 5 to 14 in Figure 1-8 illustrate the numeric punches.

When *letters* of the alphabet are recorded, *two* holes must be punched. Along the top of the card are three *zone* punching positions—the 0 row and the blank area at the top of the card, which is designated as punching positions 11 and 12 (or as areas X and Y). A logical combination of zone and digit punches is required for letters in the Hollerith code. For example, letters A to I are coded by using a 12-zone punch and digit punches 1 to 9. Special characters are coded by using one, two, or three holes.

---

[6]The 1950 census, using punched card equipment, took about 2 years to produce; the 1970 census yielded figures in a few months.

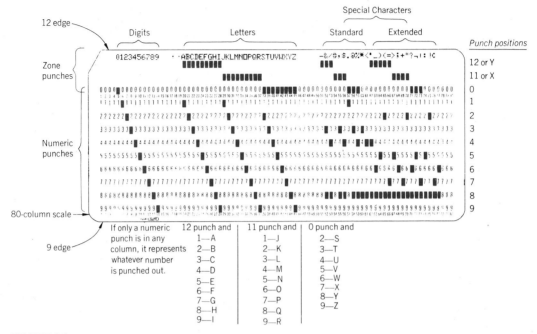

FIGURE 1-8
The punched card and Hollerith code.

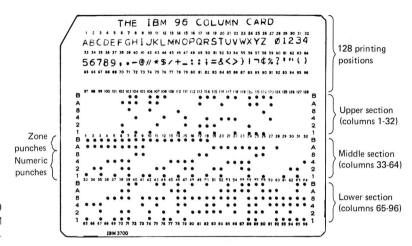

FIGURE 1-9
IBM 96-column card (courtesy IBM Corporation).

The 96-column card The card in Figure 1-9 is actually only one-third the size of the 80-column card. The 96 columns are separated into three 32-column sections or tiers. The upper third of the card contains positions for the printing of characters.

In addition to using round rather than rectangular holes, the 96-column card also differs from the 80-column card in the coding method employed. The rows of the small card are divided into A and B zone positions and 1, 2, 4, and 8 numeric positions. Columns 60 to 69 in Figure 1-9 illustrate the coding of digits. The numeral 1 is represented by a single hole punched in the 1 row of column 61. Column 62 codes the numeral 2. But in columns 63, 65, 66, 67, and 69, the numerals are represented by the *sum* of the rows punched; e.g., in column 67 the digit 7 is represented by holes punched in the 4, 2, and 1 rows.

Alphabetic characters are represented by combinations of holes punched in the zone and numeric rows. The nine letters A to I, for example, are coded by holes punched in the A and B rows plus the combination of holes used to represent the numerals 1 to 9. To illustrate, the seventh letter G is coded by holes in the A and B zone positions plus the combination of holes in rows 1, 2, and 4, which add to seven (see column 39 in Figure 1-9). The special characters represented in columns 70 to 96 are coded by various combinations of holes punched in the six rows.

How are 80- and 96-column cards used? Thank you for asking. Card columns are laid out for specific purposes in consecutive groups called *fields*. Fields are carefully planned by the application

designer and may be of any width from 1 to 80 (or 96) columns.[7] To
illustrate, Figure 1-10 shows the use of a card and fields in a
business application. In this example, a customer invoice (the
detailed description of what has been shipped) serves as the source
document for the sales accounting card. The card is divided into 11
fields. The *item amount* field is seven columns wide, which means

---

[7]It should be emphasized that judgment and compromises are required in determining field width. For example, a 15-column employee name field would be satisfactory in most cases—until the personnel department hires Agamemnon
Southwesterfield.

FIGURE 1-10

Data fields (courtesy IBM Corporation).

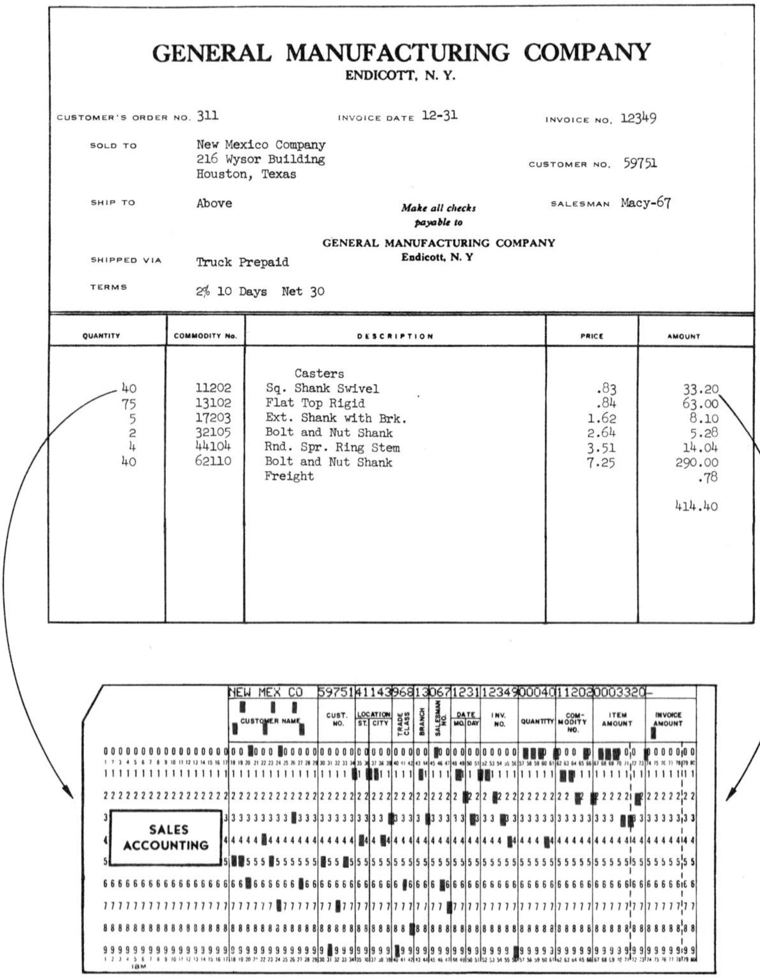

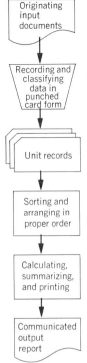

FIGURE 1-11

that the maximum amount that can be recorded is $99,999.99 (columns are not used to punch the dollar sign, comma, and decimal point). Of course, in addition to the card shown in Figure 1-10, five other cards would be required to capture all the invoice data. These cards could then be used to update inventory records and to prepare reports giving such information as total sales to the particular customer and total sales credited to the salesperson and sales branch during a specified time period.

Punched card equipment   Several punched card machines are needed to perform the typical processing steps shown in Figure 1-11. The most common way of *recording* data in cards is through the use of a keypunch or *card punch* machine. When a key is depressed, the correct combination of holes is produced in the card. The operation of a card punch machine is discussed in Appendix A. To check keypunching accuracy, *verifiers* are used. The verifier is similar to the keypunch, but instead of punching holes, it merely senses whether or not the holes in the card being tested correspond with the key being depressed. In some machines keypunching and verifying are combined.

Sorters and *collators,* as you might expect, are devices for *sorting and arranging* cards. Putting the cards in some desired order or sequence is the job of the sorter. There are as many pockets in the sorter as there are rows in the card being processed; there may also be a reject pocket for cards that do not belong in any other pocket. Sorting (which generally moves from the right column to the left column of the data field) is done *one* column at a time in each sorting *pass.* Thus, the sorting procedure in a data field of five digits would take five passes before the cards would be in the proper numerical *sequence.*

The collator is a machine that can combine two decks of sequenced cards into a single sequenced deck (*merging*). It can also compare agreement between two sets of cards without combining them (*matching*). Other manipulations are possible with two decks of sequenced cards. The collator can check a tray of cards to determine correct ascending or descending order. After the arrangement of the cards in the proper order, they are usually then taken to a machine that can perform calculations on the data.

The *calculator* is directed in its operation by an externally wired control panel. It reads data from input cards, performs (according to the wiring arrangements in the control panel) the arithmetic operations of addition, subtraction, multiplication, and division, and punches the results into (1) the input card that supplied the data or (2) a following card.

The *accounting machine or tabulator* is used to *summarize* data from input cards and print the desired reports. It can add and subtract during summarization and has several registers or counters for this purpose. Finally, the *reproducer* is used to duplicate the data found in a large number of cards; it is also used for gangpunching, i.e., copying data from a master card into any number of blank cards, and for punching the holes in mark-sensed cards.

From this very brief survey of punched card data processing, it is obvious that significant improvement was possible over manual methods previously used. Gains in speed and accuracy were made. Punched card equipment proved effective in performing many of the individual steps necessary, e.g., sorting, calculating, and summarizing. But it is still necessary to have people handle trays of cards between each step. Separate machines must be fed, started, and stopped. *This limited intercommunication between processing stages requiring manual intervention is a major disadvantage.* With the computer this disadvantage is eliminated; no manual interference between data input and information output is required. What sets the computer apart from any other type of data processing machine is the concept of storing, within the machine itself, alterable instructions that will direct the machine to perform automatically the necessary processing steps. Let us now, in the remainder of this chapter, look at the history and development of the computer.

Computer Development

In 1833, Charles Babbage, Lucasian Professor of Mathematics at Cambridge University in England, proposed a machine, which he named the *Analytical Engine.* Babbage was an eccentric and colorful individual[8] who spent much of his life working in vain to build his machine. Babbage's dream—to many others it was "Babbage's folly"—would have included many of the features found in modern computers. In short, Babbage had designed a prototype computer which was 100 years ahead of its time. Following Babbage's death in 1871, little progress was made until 1937.

Beginning in 1937, Harvard professor Howard Aiken set out to build an automatic calculating machine that would combine estab-

---

[8]He was also something of a literary critic. In "The Vision of Sin," Tennyson wrote: "Every moment dies a man/Every moment one is born." Babbage wrote Tennyson and pointed out to the poet that since the population of the world was increasing, it would be more accurate to have the verse read: "Every moment dies a man, Every moment one and one-sixteenth is born." What he lacked in aesthetic taste he compensated for with mathematical precision!

lished technology with the punched cards of Hollerith. With the help of graduate students and IBM engineers, the project was completed in 1944. The completed device was known as the Mark I digital computer. (A *digital* computer is one that essentially does counting operations.) Internal operations were controlled automatically with electromagnetic relays; arithmetic counters were mechanical. The Mark I was thus not an *electronic* computer but was rather an *electromechanical* one. In many respects the Mark I was the realization of Babbage's dream.

The first *electronic* digital computer to be put into full operation was built as a secret wartime project between 1939 and 1946 at the University of Pennsylvania's Moore School of Electrical Engineering. The team of J. Presper Eckert, Jr., and John W. Mauchly was responsible for its construction. However, as was later determined by a federal judge in an important patent suit, "Eckert and Mauchly did not themselves first invent the automatic electronic digital computer, but instead derived that subject matter from one Dr. John Vincent Atanasoff." (Atanasoff was a professor of physics and mathematics at Iowa State College, and did his most important computer work between 1935 and 1942, at which time he stopped work on his prototype and left Iowa State to work at the Naval Ordnance Laboratory.)

Vacuum tubes (19,000 of them!) were used in place of relays in the Eckert-Mauchly machine. This computer was called "ENIAC" and could do 300 multiplications per second (making it 300 times faster than any other device of the day).[9] Operating instructions for ENIAC were not stored internally; rather, they were fed through externally located plugboards and switches. In 1959, ENIAC was placed in the Smithsonian Institution.

In 1946, in collaboration with H. H. Goldstine and A. W. Burks, John von Neumann, a mathematical genius and member of the Institute for Advanced Study in Princeton, New Jersey, suggested in a paper that (1) *binary* numbering systems be used in building computers and (2) computer *instructions* as well as the *data* being manipulated could be stored internally in the machine. These suggestions became a basic part of the philosophy of computer design. The binary numbering system is represented by only two digits (0 and 1) rather than the 10 digits (0 to 9) of the familiar decimal

---

[9]William Shanks, an Englishman, spent 20 years of his life computing π to 707 decimal places. In 1949, ENIAC computed π to 2,000 places in just over 70 hours and showed that Shanks had made an error in the 528th decimal place. Fortunately, Shanks was spared the knowledge that he had been both slow and inaccurate, for he preceded ENIAC by 100 years.

system. Since electronic components are typically in one of two conditions (on or off, conducting or not conducting, magnetized or not magnetized), the binary concept facilitated equipment design.

These design concepts came too late to be incorporated in ENIAC, but Mauchly, Eckert, and others at the University of Pennsylvania set out to build a machine with stored program capability. This machine—the EDVAC—was not completed until several years later. To the EDSAC, finished in 1949 at Cambridge University, must go the distinction of being the first *stored program electronic* computer.

One reason for the delay in EDVAC was that Eckert and Mauchly founded their own company in 1946 and began to work on the UNIVAC. In 1949, Remington Rand acquired the Eckert-Mauchly Computer Corporation, and in early 1951, the first UNIVAC-I became operational at the Census Bureau. In 1963, it too was retired to the Smithsonian Institution—a historical relic after just 12 years! The first computer acquired for data processing and record keeping by a business organization was another UNIVAC-I, which was installed in 1954 at General Electric's Appliance Park in Louisville, Kentucky.[10]

In the period from 1954 to 1959, many businesses acquired computers for data processing purposes even though these *first-generation* machines had been designed for scientific uses. Managers generally considered the computer to be an accounting tool, and the first applications were designed to process routine tasks such as payrolls and customer billing. Unfortunately, in most cases little or no attempt was made to modify and redesign existing accounting procedures in order to produce more effective managerial information. The potential of the computer was consistently underestimated; more than a few were acquired for no other reason than prestige.

But we should not judge the early users of electronic data processing too harshly. They were pioneering in the use of a new tool not designed specifically for their needs; they had to staff their computer installations with a new breed of workers; and they initially had to cope with the necessity of preparing programs in a tedious machine language. In spite of these obstacles, the computer was found to be a fast, accurate, and untiring processor of mountains of paper.

The computers of the *second generation* were introduced around 1959 to 1960 and were made smaller, faster, and with greater computing capacity. The vacuum tube, with its relatively short life,

---

[10]The IBM 650 first saw service in Boston in December 1954. It was an all-purpose machine, comparatively inexpensive, and it was widely accepted. It gave IBM the leadership in computer production in 1955.

gave way to compact *solid state* components such as diodes and transistors. Unlike earlier computers, some second-generation machines were designed from the beginning with business processing requirements in mind.

In 1964, IBM ushered in the *third generation* of computing hardware when it announced its System/360 family of computers. And during the early 1970s, several manufacturers introduced new equipment lines. For example, IBM announced the first models of its System/370 line of computers. These machines continued the trend toward miniaturization of circuit components. Further improvements in speed, cost, and storage capacity were realized. In the next chapter we shall look in more detail at some of the recent developments in computer technology.

Size and scope of computer industry In 1956 there were only about 600 computers installed in the United States; today, they are numbered in the hundreds of thousands. In 1956 the installed computers had a total value of about $350 million; today, the cumulative value probably exceeds $50 *billion.*

There are several dozen computer manufacturers, many of whom specialize in scientific, process control, and very small general-purpose machines. Of the larger firms, most were initially business machine manufacturers (e.g., IBM, Sperry UNIVAC, Burroughs Corporation, and NCR Corporation), or they manufactured electronic equipment (e.g., Honeywell). Exceptions are such firms as Control Data Corporation (CDC) and Digital Equipment Corporation (DEC) which were founded to produce computers. The industry leader is IBM, with over 60 percent of the market.

In spite of the economic health of the computer industry as a whole, more than a few firms were unable to compete profitably in the 1970s. Some of the more notable "dropouts" were General Electric, Xerox, and RCA. There have also been numerous antitrust suits and countersuits involving various manufacturers, IBM, and the federal government in the 1970s.

Computer size categories Although the first computers were all large enough to store grain in, today's machines vary in size from the large to those that are smaller than this book. Thus, in terms of relative computing power and cost, today's systems may be classified as *micro-sized, mini-sized, small, medium,* or *large.*

Microcomputers are tiny processors (see Figure 1-12); they began to appear in quantity in 1973. Although they are relatively slow in operation and have relatively limited data-handling capabilities, these computers are being used in a rapidly expanding number

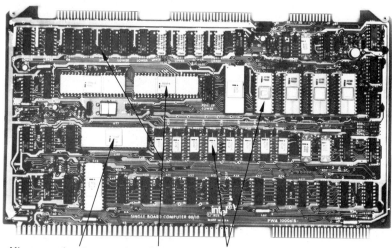

FIGURE 1-12

Complete microcomputer on a single board (courtesy of Intel Corporation).

Microprocessing element (see Figure 2-2 for a magnified view of the circuitry)

Input/output connections and components

Computer storage elements

of applications. Perhaps their most common use at this writing is to provide control and intelligence functions for some of the peripheral devices used with larger computer systems.

Minicomputers (see Figure 1-13) are, naturally, very small machines that perform the same arithmetic and logic functions, use several of the same programming languages, and have many of the

FIGURE 1-13

Minicomputer (courtesy Digital Equipment Corporation).

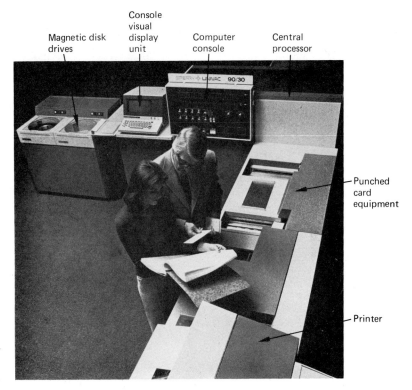

Magnetic disk drives   Console visual display unit   Computer console   Central processor

Punched card equipment

Printer

FIGURE 1-14

Small-scale business computer (courtesy Sperry UNIVAC Division, Sperry Rand Corporation).

same circuitry features of larger computers. Although they are general-purpose devices, some are used for special or dedicated purposes such as controlling a machine tool or a process. Others are (1) used for business data processing purposes, (2) connected to larger computers to act as input/output (I/O) and message-switching devices, (3) used in school systems for educational purposes, and (4) used in laboratories for scientific computation purposes. The versatility of minicomputers, combined with their low cost (from about $2,500 to $25,000), accounts for their rapid acceptance.

Small computers may be the punched-card–oriented successors to electromechanical punched card installations, or they may substitute magnetic tapes or magnetic disks for cards as data-storage media (see Figure 1-14). Small tape and disk systems are generally faster than card processors, have greater internal data-storage capacity, and are thus more expensive (they sell in the $25,000 to $200,000 range).

Medium-size computers sell for $200,000 to $1 million, and

Magnetic disk drives

Magnetic tape drives

Consoles of central processors

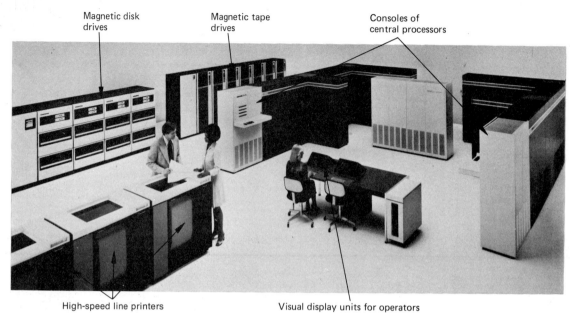

High-speed line printers

Visual display units for operators

FIGURE 1-15
Large-scale computer installation
(courtesy Burroughs Corporation).

larger systems (see Figure 1-15) exceed this price range. In return for higher prices, users receive faster processing speeds, greater data-storage capacity, wider selection of optional equipment from which to choose, and a lower cost-per-calculation figure.[11]

SUMMARY Data are the input from which information is produced, and they are obtained in an organization from internal and external sources. The data processing operation, in its entirety, consists of nine steps; however, some steps may be omitted in specific situations. Manual, machine-assisted manual, electromechanical punched card, and computer methods may be used to perform these steps.

---

[11]This assumes that the volume of work is sufficient to keep a large machine occupied. If a human being can compute the answer to a multiplication problem in 1 minute, and there are 125 million such problems to be solved, the total cost to do the calculations manually would exceed $10 million. The UNIVAC-I (which in terms of computing power is a very small machine by today's standards) could have done the job for $4,300. However, the CDC 6600, which rents for over $100,000 per month, could do the job for $4.

Although information is needed for decision making, it is usually impossible to state specifically what information a manager will need. Regardless of the information needed, however, it should possess the characteristics of accuracy, timeliness, completeness, conciseness, and relevancy. In recent years, the receipt of information lacking one or more of these characteristics has motivated managers to look at the possible use of computerized information systems.

Data processing techniques have been undergoing evolutionary change since the beginning of the human race. This evolution has advanced through four stages, from manual methods to the development of the computer. However, none of these stages should be considered obsolete, for each has its place.

There can be little doubt that the computer is responsible in large measure for the significant and sweeping change that is now taking place in the field of information processing. The next chapter examines some of the causes and effects of this revolution.

REVIEW AND DISCUSSION QUESTIONS

1 (a) What is management information? (b) What is the difference between data and information? (c) Compare the manufacturing process with the information-producing process.

2 Identify and explain the sources of business data.

3 (a) Identify and explain the basic data processing steps. (b) What processing methods may be used to perform these steps?

4 "Beyond certain basic informational requirements, the question of what information is needed by managers can be answered only in broad, general terms." Discuss this statement.

5 (a) Why does the organizational level of the managerial job affect the information needed? (b) How do informational needs differ?

6 Identify and discuss the desired properties of management information.

7 What factors have focused attention on the need for management information improvement in recent years?

8 Describe the 80-column punched card and the Hollerith code.

9 Describe the 96-column punched card and the coding employed.

10 What is a field?

11 (a) What was the Analytical Engine? (b) What features would it have had in common with modern computers?

12 After a survey of a computer center available to you, identify:
(**a**) The hardware generation of the equipment (**b**) The approximate value of the center equipment (**c**) The names of firms
supplying equipment, programs, and supplies to the center (**d**)
The size category of the center's computer (or computers) (**e**)
The services offered by the center to its customers.

THE INFORMATION REVOLUTION

2086846

35

History records, in a relatively unfavorable light, periods such as the Dark Ages following the fall of the Roman Empire when European political and religious leaders reduced the tempo of change. But it can hardly be said today that the tempo of change has diminished. Rather, we are witnessing rapid technological[1] changes taking place more quickly and over a broader front than ever before in history. And these changes are threatening to sweep aside many current (and sometimes comfortable) practices, open many new opportunities, and create new problems for business organizations. Such results are possible because contemporary technology is producing tools that are more powerful than any heretofore developed, and the use of these new tools often leads to pervasive social and economic changes—and problems. Even those who develop the new tools are often surprised (and sometimes dismayed) at the effects of their work. In 1950, for example, top executives of data processing firms agreed that 8 or 10 of the "big" computers of that day would satisfy the entire demand for such devices! Obviously, the present effects of computer usage were completely unforeseen.

A basic challenge to managers and educated citizens in the next few years will be to foresee and manage (and not be swept along by) the flood of technologically induced change that will face organizations and individuals, and to do this within a democratic framework for the benefit of society. Of course, if we are to control these forces of change, we must have high-quality information for decision making. Thus, in the following pages of this chapter, we will first briefly consider the *environmental setting* in which decision makers must function. We will then examine the *revolutionary developments* in *computer technology* and in *management information systems* that may produce better information. Finally, we will conclude with a brief summary of some of the *problems of adjustment* that are accompanying the information revolution.

THE ENVIRONMENTAL SETTING

It was the best of times, it was the worst of times, it was the age of wisdom, it was the age of foolishness, it was the epoch of belief, it was the epoch of incredulity, it was the season of Light, it was the season of Darkness, it was the spring of hope, it was the winter of despair. . . .

Charles Dickens

---

[1]*Technology* may be defined as the organization and application of knowledge to achieve practical purposes.

Some people today may view rapid technological change as an unblemished blessing that will lead us to "the best of times"; and others may see it as an unbridled curse that is leading us to "the worst of times." The truth, of course, usually lies somewhere between these extreme opinions.

A new technological development may create the opportunity in business to improve on a production process or to do something that was previously not possible. When such a development occurs, there will usually be those who will seek to take advantage of the new opportunity, even though changes in the ways individuals and groups are organized may then be necessary. And these newly organized groups may then compete for resources with established units. Thus, gains achieved by new groups in utilizing the new technology may create problems and losses for those that are using older tools and techniques. The development of the automobile, for example, created a new industry and millions of new jobs, but buggy manufacturing organizations were virtually eliminated and their employees were displaced; automobiles have increased individual mobility and suburbs have sprung up, but many older central cities are in decay and their public transportation facilities have deteriorated; and automobiles have been responsible for the construction of convenient new shopping centers, but urban streets are congested, the air is polluted, and the world's oil reserves are being depleted at a rapid rate. In short, as the development of the automobile has illustrated, both positive and negative social effects may be expected when significant technological changes occur.

One implication of significant technological change is clear: Managers must be prepared to make continuous readjustments in their plans. They must make more and better decisions about new products and existing products because of their shorter profitable life span; and they must constantly reevaluate decisions about product prices, new markets, and the channels of distribution to use. Furthermore, they must make these decisions within a time span that is constantly shrinking. To compete profitably in the future will require information of the highest possible quality. The computer, which is undergoing rapid technological improvement, is a tool that can provide the needed information to managers who must operate in a dynamic environment.

REVOLUTION IN COMPUTER TECHNOLOGY

The computer is a tool that is *contributing* to advances in virtually all fields. Computer-hardware technology is also benefiting from new discoveries in the fields of electronics and physics. Computer *hardware* consists of all the machines that make up a functioning computer system. Basically, these machines accept data input, store data, perform calculations and other processing steps, and prepare information output.

Hardware alone, however, is merely one or more boxes of electronic parts that represent an expense; an equally important (perhaps more important) consideration in the effective use of computers is the *software.* Software is the name given to the multitude of instructions, i.e., the name given to *programs* and *routines,* that have been written to cause the hardware to function in a desired way. Let us now briefly look at the technological advances in computer hardware and software.

Hardware Developments

Hardware technological development has been incredibly rapid, as may be seen by an examination of the factors of (1) *size,* (2) *speed,* (3) *cost,* (4) *information storage capacity,* and (5) *reliability.* And as Figure 2-1 shows, the past trends in these factors are likely to continue through the 1980s.

Size Second-generation computers were much smaller than their predecessors because transistors and other smaller components were substituted for tubes. And as you can see in Figure 2-1, this size reduction continues today. It is now possible, through *large-scale integration* (LSI) of electronic circuits (see Figure 2-2), to pack well over 100,000 components on a square-inch chip of silicon. These LSI chips may then be sealed and arranged on compact boards as we saw earlier in Figure 1-2, page 30.

Has the end to the feasible size reduction of computer circuitry been reached? Hardly. The boards of today will become the tiny chips of tomorrow. One scientist has speculated that by about the early 1980s it may be possible to achieve the packing density currently obtained on a square inch *throughout a cubic inch* of material. The density of electronic components would then be "about a fourth the density of nerve cells in the human brain."[2] Thus, it is expected that in the 1980s central processors with the power of today's large computers will occupy the space of a shoebox!

---

[2]F. G. Heath, "Large-Scale Integration in Electronics," *Scientific American,* p. 22, February 1970.

Hardware Development Factors	1950	1960	1970	1975	1980
Size factor Number of circuits per cubic foot	1,000	100,000	10 million	1 billion	Many billions
Speed factor Time to execute an instruction in the central processor	300 microseconds	5 microseconds	80 nanoseconds	25 nanoseconds	5 nanoseconds or less
Cost factors Cost (in dollars) to process 1 million basic computer instructions	28	1	0.02	0.001	Less than 0.001
Cost (in dollars) to provide storage for one binary number in the central processor	2.61	0.85	0.05	0.001	Less than 0.001
Storage capacity Primary storage capacity (in characters) of the central processor	20,000	120,000	1 million	10 million	Much greater than 10 million
Characters of secondary online storage	—	20 million	Over 100 billion	Virtually unlimited	Virtually unlimited
Reliability factor Mean (average) time between failures of some central processors	Hours	Tens of hours	Hundreds of hours	Thousands of hours	Tens of thousands of hours (years)

FIGURE 2-1
Summary of hardware developments.

Speed Circuit miniaturization has brought increased speed of operation to the latest computers. Why is this? It is because size reduction means shorter distances for electric pulses to travel, and thus processor speed has increased.

Early computer speed was expressed in *milliseconds* (thousandths of a second); second-generation speed was measured in *microseconds* (millionths of a second); third- and fourth-generation hardware has internal operating speeds measured in *nanoseconds* (billionths of a second). Since circuit speeds are likely to increase by

FIGURE 2-2

A greatly magnified view of the
Intel 8080 microprocessor shown
as one element on the board in
Figure 1-12 (courtesy of Intel
Corporation).

© DATAMATION ®

"That's a great innovation . . . microprocessors so small they're invisible . . . unless, of course, you're putting me on."

five times between 1975 and 1985, future machines may have speeds measured in *picoseconds* (trillionths of a second).[3]

Cost   A significant cause of the growth in the number of computer installations is the dramatic reduction in the cost of performing a specific number of operations (see Figure 2-1). If automobile costs were reduced to the same degree that computation costs have been, you would now be able to buy for less than $1 a luxury car costing $5,000 in 1950. Nor does it appear that the end is in sight in computational cost reduction. The cost of certain basic components will continue to decline while their speed and performance increases.

Information storage capacity   Information may be stored for use by a computer in a number of ways. The central processing unit (CPU) of the computer holds data and the instructions needed to manipulate the data internally in its *primary storage,* or *main memory,* section. Figure 2-1 summarizes the trend in primary storage capacity. Perhaps even more impressive has been the improvement in mass *external online* (or *secondary*) storage devices (see Figure 2-1). These devices are connected directly to, i.e., they are *online* to, the CPU, and they serve as *reference libraries* by accepting data directly from and returning data directly to the CPU without human intervention. Of course, data which the computer may use are also stored outside the CPU in the form of punched cards and magnetic tape, but these facts are *offline* since the CPU does not have direct and unassisted access to them (see Figure 2-3).

---

[3]Such speeds are difficult to comprehend. A space ship traveling toward the moon at 100,000 miles per hour would move less than 2 *inches* in 1 microsecond; it would move only the length of 10 fat germs in a nanosecond. More antiseptically speaking, there are as many nanoseconds in 1 second as there are seconds in 30 years, or as many nanoseconds in a minute as there are minutes in 1,100 *centuries*. Electricity travels about 1 foot per nanosecond, and this fact imposes an ultimate limit to internal computer speed.

FIGURE 2-3
Computer information storage.

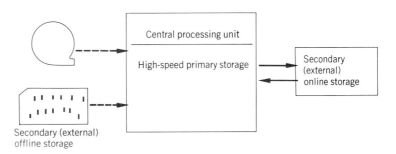

Reliability The reliability of hardware has improved substantially with the substitution of long-life solid state components for the early vacuum tubes. Much of the research effort directed toward achieving greater reliability has been sponsored by the United States government for space and missile programs. For example, scientists have been working on self-repairing computers that would remain in operation during unmanned space missions lasting many years. The self-repairing concept essentially involves partitioning the computer into functional blocks and building identical components into each block. Some of the parts are used for processing immediately; others serve as standby spares. A failure occurring in one component or subsystem would be detected by a status-sensing device, and the faulty part would be electronically and automatically replaced with a spare.

The down-to-earth benefits of increased reliability are great; for example, self-repairing computers could be incorporated into the intensive-care monitoring and control systems of hospitals where a failure could result in a death. If those sections of future earthbound computers with a reduced number of standby spares were replaced during periodic preventive maintenance, the mean (average) time between failures would probably be measured in years rather than in weeks or months. The self-repairing *commercial* computer is still on the drawing boards because of the additional cost of redundant parts. However, as LSI circuit technology produces lower costs, this obstacle may be overcome in the not-too-distant future.

Software Developments

Software is the name given to all the programs and routines associated with the use of computer hardware. The production of good software is a costly and time-consuming process that generally determines the speed with which computer-based projects to supply management information are completed. In most computer installations, the investment in programming and systems personnel and in the software they create now far exceeds the investment in hardware. And as Figure 2-4 shows, this trend will undoubtedly continue because hardware production is automated and increasingly complex software must generally be prepared on an artisan basis.

Yet there have been significant gains in the development of software. The three basic software categories are (1) *translation programs,* (2) *applications programs,* and (3) *operating-system programs.* Let us look at the developments in each of these categories.

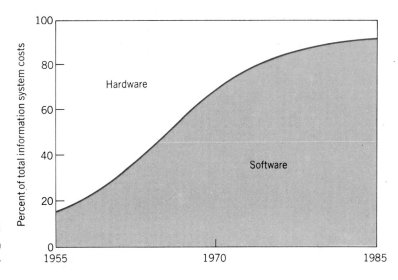

FIGURE 2-4

Total cost trends for information systems.

Translation programs In the early 1950s, users had to translate problem-solving instructions into special machine codes for each computer. Such instructions typically consisted of strings of numbers (sometimes in a binary form), which were quite tedious to prepare. In addition to remembering the code numbers for dozens of machine operations (21 might mean "add"), the employee performing the task of instructing the computer (a *programmer*) was also required to keep track of the locations in the central processor where the instructions and data items were stored. Thus, initial program coding often took many months.

To ease the programmer's burden, a compromise approach between people and machine was developed which resulted in the introduction of special coding *languages* that save time and are more convenient to use. In using these languages, the programmer writes instructions in a form that is easier to understand—e.g., the programmer may print the word ADD or use the plus symbol rather than use the number 21. Unfortunately, this code is not in the machine's language, and so it does not directly understand the orders. How, then, can the machine execute instructions if they are in a language that it cannot understand? Just as an American and a German can communicate if one of them uses a translating dictionary, so, too, can the programmer and computer communicate if a separate translation program is employed. Briefly, this translating program is loaded into the computer where it controls the translation procedure. The instructions written by the programmer (called the *source program*) are then fed into the computer where they are translated. The result of this operation is a set of machine instructions (called the *object program*) that may then be used to control the processing of problem data.[4]

Almost all problem-solving programs prepared today are first written in languages preferred by programmers and are then translated by special software into the equivalent machine language codes. Continuing efforts are being made to produce software that will permit easier human/machine communication. For example, efforts are being made to develop software that will give the ultimate users of the processed information the ability to prepare programs in languages that are more familiar to them.

Application programs   The programs written for the purpose of solving particular processing jobs also come under the heading of software. These programs are commonly prepared by each using organization to process such applications as payroll, inventory control, and other tasks. Many applications programs must, of course, be prepared by users to process tasks that are unique to their particular needs. In the past, however, much programmer time has been spent in duplicating programs prepared in other companies. Recognizing the wastefulness of such duplication, equipment manufacturers and independent software companies have prepared generalized *applications packages* (or *packaged programs*) for widely used applications. Retail stores, for example, sell on credit and thus maintain credit records and perform billing operations. Since many retail firms employ essentially the same accounting procedures in such cases, a billing and accounts-receivable application package may often be purchased by a retailer from an outside source and used with good results. But although a packaged program prepared by an excellent programmer specialist may be implemented quicker and may be more efficient and less expensive than a run-of-the-mill program prepared by the user, there is also the possibility that an available package may not fit the needs of the user without extensive modification—a potentially difficult task for user programmers who may be unfamiliar with the package.

Operating-system programs   As the name implies, the *operating system* (OS) was initially a set of programs prepared by equipment manufacturers and users to assist the computer operator. It is the function of the operator to load data input devices with cards and

---

[4]Further details of this translation procedure are presented in Chapter 9.

tapes, to set switches on the computer console, to start the process-ing run, and to prepare and unload output devices. It should not be the operator's job, however, to waste time (both human and machine) doing things that the computer could do more quickly and reliably. Housekeeping duties such as loading and unloading I/O equipment, and loading into storage the next job program and data from the jobs stacked up in a waiting queue are now controlled by the software. Shifting control to specially prepared operating programs thus reduced the operator's work, cut down on the programmer's drudg-ery (by eliminating the need to rewrite certain input and output instructions for each program), provided relatively nonstop opera-tion, and therefore speeded up the amount of processing that could be accomplished.

The objective of current operating systems is still to operate the computer with a minimum of idle time and in the most efficient and economical way. But the operating software is now vastly more complex. More sophisticated software has been required to keep faster and more powerful hardware occupied. An example is the development of *multiprogramming,* the name given to the *inter-leaved* execution of two or more different and independent programs by the same computer.[5]

Multiprogramming *is not* generally defined to mean that the com-puter is executing instructions from several programs at the *same instant* in time;[6] instead, it *does* mean that there are a number of programs stored in primary and/or online storage and that a portion of one is executed, then a segment of another, etc. The processor switches from one program to another almost instantaneously. Since internal operating speeds of CPUs are much faster than are the means of getting data into and out of the processor, the CPU can allocate time to several programs instead of remaining idle while one is bringing in data or printing out information. With multipro-gramming, it is thus possible for several user stations to share the time of the CPU (see Figure 2-5). This *timesharing* feature may permit more efficient use of the capacity of the processor.

FIGURE 2-5

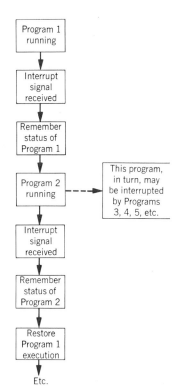

This program, in turn, may be interrupted by Programs 3, 4, 5, etc.

[5]If you are mechanically inclined, you may know that the automobile distributor head rotates, makes electrical contact with, and zaps a pulse of electricity to each spark plug in one revolution. Similarly, the computer may allocate a small amount, or *slice,* of time—say, 150 milliseconds per second—to each program being executed. Fifteen-hundredths of a second may not seem like much time to you, but that is enough to calculate the amounts owed to hundreds of employees for a given pay period. The result of such speed is that each user has the illusion that he or she has the undivided attention of the computer.

[6]The term *multiprocessing* is used to describe interconnected computer configura-tions or computers with multiple arithmetic-logic units that have the ability to *simulta-neously* execute several programs.

In recent years, operating-system development (and specialized hardware) has also made possible the widespread[7] introduction of computers with *virtual storage* capability. Prior to this development, the size of an application program was effectively limited by the size of the computer's primary storage section. This was because the complete program was typically held in primary storage during its entire execution. If the program size did not exceed the limited primary storage capacity, then there was no problem; if, on the other hand, the task required several thousand instructions, then the programmer might be forced to write two or more programs to complete the job. With virtual storage capability, however, the computer can divide total programs into small sequences of instructions called *pages*. Then, only those program pages that are actually required at a particular time in the processing need be in primary storage. The remaining segments may be kept temporarily in online storage, from which they can be rapidly retrieved as needed (see Figure 2-6). Thus, from the programmer's point of view, the effective (or "virtual") size of the available primary storage may appear to be unlimited.

The incorporation of multiprogramming and virtual storage capabilities into the OS has, of course, complicated matters. For example, software must keep track of the locations in primary and secondary

---

[7]The virtual storage concept was being used in the 1950s in Europe, and Burroughs Corporation introduced the concept in the United States in 1962. But *widespread* acceptance of virtual storage did not occur until IBM announced its intention to employ the technique 10 years later.

FIGURE 2-6
Virtual storage capability.

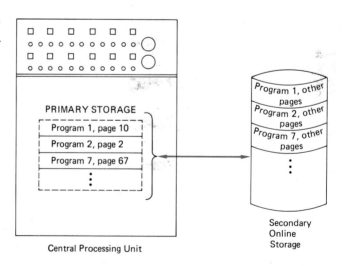

storage of each of the several programs and program segments, must remember at what point it should return to an interrupted program, and must, perhaps, assign job priorities to the several tasks waiting to be completed. The operating systems of many of today's computers are, in short, integrated collections of processing programs and a master control program that are expected to perform the *scheduling, control, loading,* and *program call-up* functions described below:

1 The *scheduling* function involves the selection of jobs to be run on a priority basis from a table or list of jobs to be processed. Available storage space and the most suitable peripheral hardware to use is allocated to the job or jobs being processed. Whenever possible, jobs are selected to balance I/O and processing requirements.

2 The *control* function consists of a number of activities including (*a*) the control of input and output housekeeping operations, (*b*) the proper handling, shifting, and protection of data, instructions, and intermediate processing results when a high-priority program interrupts the processing of a lower-priority program, (*c*) the timing of each job processed and the allocation of processor time to user stations, and (*d*) the communication of error and control messages to human operators.

3 The *loading* function includes reading in and assigning storage locations to object programs and data. Checks are also made to prevent the loading and processing of incorrect files.

4 The *program call-up* function emphasizes the overall control of the OS master program (referred to by such names as *monitor, executive routine,* and *supervisor*) over other software elements. The monitor integrates this assorted software into a single consistent system. The system monitor generally remains in primary storage where it may occupy 25 to 60 percent of the available space; in installations with online storage capability, many of the other programs and routines are kept online and are called up and temporarily stored in the CPU as needed.

Figure 2-7 summarizes the relationship existing between the hardware and software categories discussed in the above pages.

Technological advances in computer hardware and software have both contributed to, and been stimulated by, a dynamic environment. And as we will see in the next section, managers have sought to implement computer-oriented management information systems that will enable them to cope with rapidly changing conditions.

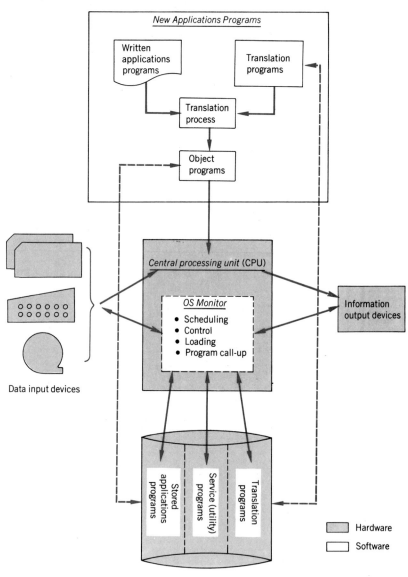

FIGURE 2-7   Operating system elements

**DEVELOPMENTS
IN MANAGEMENT
INFORMATION
SYSTEMS**

Traditional information systems have often been found wanting because they do not provide information with the desired properties mentioned in Chapter 1—that is, the information they produce may be too costly and is not (1) timely, (2) properly integrated, (3) concise, (4) available in the proper format, or (5) relevant. To reduce the difficulties experienced with traditional approaches, new computer-oriented management information system concepts have been developed (and are now emerging).

An MIS Definition

What is a management information system (MIS)? Strangely enough, it is not easy to pin down these words for they are defined in dozens of different ways. For our purposes, however, an MIS is a network of computer-based data processing procedures developed in an organization and integrated as necessary with other manual and/or mechanical procedures for the purpose of providing information to support decision making and other necessary management functions. Of course, running a business is a complicated process which, in larger organizations, takes place on at least three levels. As we saw in Figure 1-5, page 15, top executives plan and make policy decisions of *strategic* importance. These strategic decisions are then used by middle-level managers who devise the *tactics* to allocate resources and establish controls to implement the top-level plans. And finally, lower-level *operating* managers make the necessary day-to-day scheduling and control decisions to accomplish specific tasks (see Figure 2-8).

Although the development of new information systems is a challenging assignment, many organizations have now adopted an MIS orientation and are moving toward the implementation of new systems utilizing concepts that are *quicker responding* and *broader in scope* than those employed with traditional systems.[8] Let us now look at systems possessing these characteristics.

Quick-Response Systems

All that is not eternal is eternally out of date
C. S. Lewis

Quick-response systems, as the name implies, have been developed to increase the timeliness, effectiveness, and availability of

---

[8]Many concerns have not yet moved beyond the creation of computer-based procedures that are designed primarily to provide lower-level operating managers with the information they need. But other organizations have advanced beyond this stage to incorporate planning and decision models that enable middle and top managers to evaluate the possible results of different courses of action. We will consider the subject of planning with computers in Chapter 11.

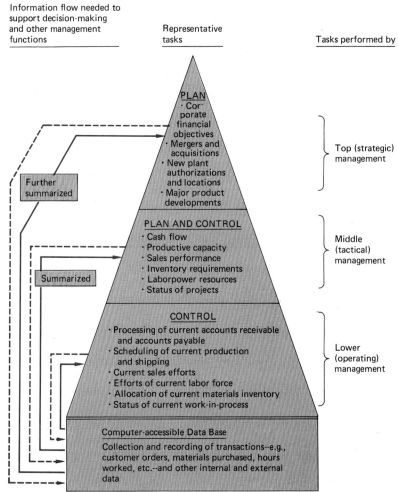

FIGURE 2-8

An MIS orientation.

information. They may allow users to react more rapidly to changing conditions, reduce waste in the use of time and other resources, and permit quick follow-up on creative ideas. They may also be described by a bewildering variety of Computerese terms. A glance through a few current data processing periodicals shows the subject to be a veritable semantic jungle with many "experts" swinging from different definition vines (Figure 2-9). We will try to cut through this foliage by examining the concepts of (1) *online processing,* (2) *real time processing,* and (3) *timesharing and distributed networks.*

FIGURE 2-9

Online processing The term *online* is used in different ways. We have seen that a peripheral machine connected directly to and capable of unassisted communication with the central processor is said to be an online device. *Online* also describes the status of a person who is communicating directly with (i.e., having *direct access* to) the central processor without the use of media such as punched cards or magnetic tape. Finally, *online* refers to a *method of processing data.* However, before looking at the concept of *online processing,* we should pause to describe the characteristics of the *batch processing* approach.

Perhaps an illustration will best explain batch methods. Let us trace the activities that follow Zelda Zilch's credit purchase of a zither in a department store. The sales slip for this *transaction* is routed to the accounting office where it and others are collected for several days until a large batch accumulates. The data on the slips may be recorded on a machine input medium such as punched cards. The cards are then sorted by customer name or charge-account number into the proper sequence for processing. Processing consists of adding the item description and price of all the recent transactions to the customer's other purchases for the month. Thus, a customer accounts-receivable master file, perhaps in the form of magnetic tape, must be updated to reflect the additional charges. The sequence in which the new transactions are sorted is an ordered one and corresponds to the sequence on the master file. Figure 2-10 illustrates this batch processing procedure. At the end of the accounting period, the master file is used to prepare the customer statements.

Other files are periodically updated in similar fashion. A *file,* then, is a collection of related records and items treated as a unit. In our example, the zither purchase was one *item* on Zelda's bill; Zelda's

FIGURE 2-10

Batch processing.

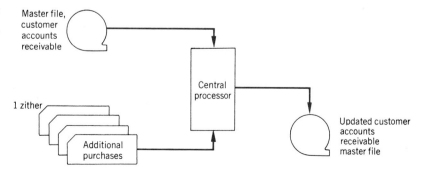

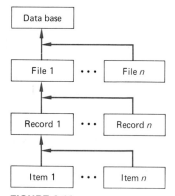

FIGURE 2-11

Data hierarchy.

bill would represent one charge-account *record;* and the purchase records of all credit customers would comprise the accounts-receivable *file.* Furthermore, a set of integrated files may be organized into a *data base* (see Figure 2-11).

Batches may be collected at a central computer site or at other locations. In some cases, *remote stations* at distant locations may employ telephone circuits to transmit data directly into the central computer system. *Although batch processing is economical* when a large volume of data must be processed, *it* (1) *requires sorting,* (2) *reduces timeliness* in some situations, and (3) *requires sequential file organization*—and this may prove to be a handicap.

Online processing has been developed for certain uses as an answer to the batch processing deficiencies noted above. In contrast to batching, online (or *direct access* or *random*) processing permits transaction data to be fed under CPU control directly into secondary online storage devices from the point of origin without first being sorted. These data may be keyed in by the use of a terminal (see Figure 2-12), or they may be produced by a variety of other data-collection and transaction-recording devices. Information contained in any record is accessible to the user without the necessity of a sequential search of the file and within a fraction of a second after the inquiry message has been transmitted. Thus, online processing systems may feature *random* and rapid input of transactions and immediate and *direct access* to record contents as needed (see Figure 2-13).

FIGURE 2-12

(Courtesy Teletype Corporation).

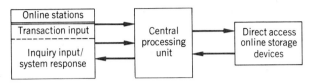

FIGURE 2-13

Online processing.

Online processing and direct access to records *require unique hardware and software.* For example, the capacity of the primary storage unit of the CPU must be adequate to (1) handle the complex online operating-system control program and (2) serve a variety of other storage uses. Also, since many online users may have access to stored records, software security provisions are necessary to (1) prevent confidential information from falling into unauthorized hands and (2) prevent deliberate or accidental tampering with data and program files. Finally, data transmission facilities must be provided to communicate with online terminals located in the next room, on the next block, or thousands of miles away.

The speed of processing *needed* by a business varies with the particular application. As we have seen, batch processing is appropriate for many jobs. Online processing, although quicker responding than traditional methods, may involve different degrees of quickness in the needed response. For example, a system may combine immediate access to records for inquiry purposes with *periodic* (perhaps daily) transaction input and updating of records from a central collecting source. Such a system would meet many needs and would be simpler and less expensive than an online real time system.

Real time processing   The words *real time* represent a semantic bucket of worms—you can choose from dozens of definitions that have surfaced. The consensus of opinion is, however, that a real time processing operation is (1) in a parallel time relationship with an ongoing activity and (2) producing information quickly enough to be useful in controlling this current live and dynamic activity. Thus, we shall use the words *real time* to describe an online processing system with severe time limitations. A real time system is generally considered to be online; an online processing system, however, *need not* be operating in real time.

Real time processing requires *immediate* (not periodic) transaction input from all input-originating terminals. Many remote stations may be tied directly by high-speed communications equipment into the central processor; several stations may be operating simultaneously. Files may be updated each minute, and inquiries may be answered by split-second access to up-to-the-minute records.

Among the examples of real time processing are the systems designed to keep track of the availability of motel and hotel rooms, the systems that provide for immediate updating of customer records in savings banks, and the reservation systems used by airlines to control the inventory of available seats. In the airline systems, central computers receive transaction data and inquiries from remote terminals located at hundreds of reservation and ticket sales desks across the nation. In seconds, a customer may request and receive information about flights and available seats. If a reservation is made, the transaction is fed into the computer immediately and the inventory of available seats is reduced. The reverse, of course, occurs in the event of a cancellation. What if a flight is fully booked? If the customer desires to be placed on a waiting list, data such as customer name and telephone number are maintained by the computer. If cancellations occur, waiting-list customers are notified by agents. In addition, the reservation systems of competing airlines are tied together to provide an exchange of information on seat availability. Thus, an agent for any of the participating companies may sell space on *any* of the airlines if the system shows it is available.

Real time processing is required and cooperation is necessary among airlines because of the perishability of the service sold—when an airplane takes off, vacant seats have no value until the next landing. It would be a mistake, however, to assume that real time processing should be universally applied to all data processing applications. A quick-response system can be designed to fit the needs of the business. Some applications can be processed on a lower-priority, or "background," basis using batch methods (e.g., payroll); some can be online with periodic (not immediate) updating of records; and some can utilize real time methods.

Timesharing and distributed networks *Timesharing* is a term used to describe a processing system with a number of independent, relatively low-speed, online, *simultaneously usable* stations. Each station provides direct access to the central processor. The speed of the system and the use of multiprogramming allow the central processor to switch from one using station to another and to do a part of each job in the allocated "time slice" until the work is completed. The speed is frequently such that the user has the illusion that no one else is using the computer. Timesharing systems vary from those that are designed for a *single* organization to those that are intended to provide services to a *multitude* of different organizations seeking to process a broad range of business and scientific jobs.

"The Accounting Department helped us design our
new time-sharing system."   ©DATAMATION

The number of timesharing systems dedicated to the use of a *single* organization is growing rapidly. For example, timesharing systems utilizing minicomputers are popular with managers and engineers who must solve problems that are too large for calculators, but may not be large enough to receive a high priority at the organization's large computer center.

In addition, firms that offer general-purpose data processing resources to *many* organizations are also achieving significant growth. In this type of service, transactions are initiated from, and output is delivered to, the premises of the user at electronic speeds. The subscriber pays for the processing service in much the same way he or she pays for telephone service: There is an initial installation charge; there are certain basic monthly charges; and, perhaps largest of all, there are transaction charges (like long-distance calls), which vary according to usage. These variable charges are generally based on the time the terminal is connected to the central processing system and/or on the seconds of CPU time used.

In earlier paragraphs we have used the word *timesharing* because it is commonly applied to the interleaved use of the time of a computer. When *one* or *two* processors handle the workload of several outlying terminals, then the term timesharing is probably still appropriately descriptive. But when *many* dispersed or *distributed* independent computer systems are connected by a communications network, and when messages, processing tasks, programs, data, and other information-processing resources are transmitted between processors and terminals, then the term *timesharing* may no longer be adequate. Such a distributed computer-communications network is similar in some respects to public utilities such as telephone and electric companies—e.g., electric power plants are geographically dispersed and the energy resources generated are transmitted through a coordinating regional network or grid to the places where the energy resources are needed. (In the past, in fact, timeshared networks were called *information utilities* and *computing utilities.*)

The term *distributed network* is now frequently used to describe this extension of timesharing, which may result in a large number of computers and significant software resources being shared among a large number of users. Figure 2-14 shows some of the possible network configurations, and Figure 2-15 shows the network of a firm offering resource-sharing services to customers.

Distributed networks, like smaller timesharing systems, may be for the use of a single organization or for many organizations, and they may be designed with special-purpose or general-purpose applications in mind (see Figure 2-16).

As you might expect, there are both advantages and disadvantages at present to the sharing of computing resources. Some of the *advantages of resource sharing* are that it can (1) reduce central processor idle time, (2) offer sophisticated computing capability to small users, (3) offer the quick-response benefits noted earlier in this chapter, and (4) make libraries of applications programs available to users. Unfortunately, however, some of the *possible limitations of resource sharing* at present are that (1) the reliability and cost of the data communications and computing services may be disappointing in some cases, (2) input and output terminals are often rather slow and inefficient, and (3) provisions for protecting the confidentiality and integrity of user programs and data files maintained in online storage are generally ineffective against a skilled penetrator.

The quick-response-system concepts that we have now considered are improving the timeliness, effectiveness, and availability of information. In addition, many of these emerging quick-response systems are taking a broader data-base approach to the needs of organizations by attempting to provide better integration of information-producing activities. In the following section we shall briefly examine this trend.

FIGURE 2-14

Possible network configurations.

Star network

Ring or loop network

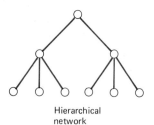

Hierarchical network

○ = dispersed processors

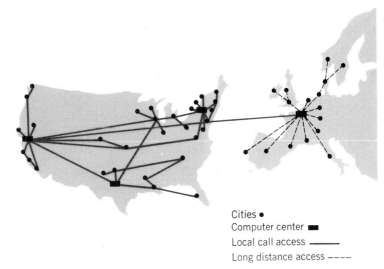

Cities •
Computer center ▬
Local call access ───────
Long distance access ─ ─ ─ ─

FIGURE 2-15

TYMNET network of Tymshare, Inc.

Data-Base Systems

Better integration of information-producing activities can lead to information that is more complete and relevant. Traditionally, data processing activities have been organized by departments and by applications. Many computers were originally installed to process a large-volume job. Other applications, treated independently, followed, but it soon became clear that this approach was unsatisfactory. In some cases, basic data were defined and organized differently for each application; thus, the data were often expensively

FIGURE 2-16

Features of selected networks.

Special-Purpose Distributed Networks	General-Purpose Distributed Networks
1 *OCTOPUS:* Connects 1,000 researchers at the Lawrence Livermore Laboratory of the University of California with five very large computers. Work is performed for the federal government.	1 *TYMNET:* Connects over 70 cities on two continents with 40 large-scale computers. Offers network resources to customers in business, government, education, etc.
2 *Eastern Airlines:* Over 2,300 ticket agent terminals are connected to two very large computers in Miami; over 350 flight operations terminals are connected to three large computers in Charlotte, N.C.; and other terminals used for business purposes are connected to four large processors in Miami. The computers are all linked together.	2 *ARPA Net:* Connects over 30 universities and research institutes throughout the nation and Europe with 50 processors ranging in size from minicomputers to the giant ILLIAC IV.
	3 *General Electric Net:* Has over 100 computers in operation, serving over 100,000 users in more than 20 countries.

duplicated (with an increase in the possibility of error) because it was impossible to integrate these facts in meaningful ways. For example, information from the payroll file and the personnel file could not be combined because of different methods of classifying employees.

Dissatisfied with such conditions, some organizations began looking for ways to consolidate activities using a data-base approach. Although there are some differences of opinion about what constitutes a data-base system, the most prevalent view is that such systems are designed around an integrated information file or *data bank*. This file is located in directly accessible online storage. Transactions are introduced into the system only once; all data-base records that these transactions affect are updated at the time of input. The total file may not be subdivided into applications. The data-base concept requires that input data be commonly defined and consistently organized and presented throughout the business.

Why the interest in data-base systems? One reason is that a data-base system, combined with *data management software* that will organize, process, and present the necessary data elements, will enable managers to search, probe, and query file contents in order to extract answers to nonrecurring and unplanned questions that are not available in regular reports. These questions might initially be vague and/or poorly defined, but managers can "browse" through the data base until they have the needed information. In short, the data management software will "manage" the stored data items and assemble the needed items from a common data base in response to the queries of managers who are not programming specialists. In the past, if managers wished to have a special report prepared using information stored in the data base, they would probably communicate their needs to a programmer, who, when time permitted, would write one or more programs to prepare the report. The availability of data management software,[9] however, offers the user a much faster alternative communications path (see Figure 2-17).

Perhaps an illustration of the possible use of a data-base system is in order here. Suppose, for example, a personnel manager of a large multinational corporation has just received an urgent request to send an employee to a foreign country to effect an emergency repair of a hydraulic pump that the company stopped making 6 years

---

[9]Data management software can be purchased or rented from a computer vendor or a software house. Among the most popular of the packages now in use are IBM's "Information Management System," Informatics' "Mark IV," Honeywell's "Integrated Data Store," and CinCom Systems' "Total."

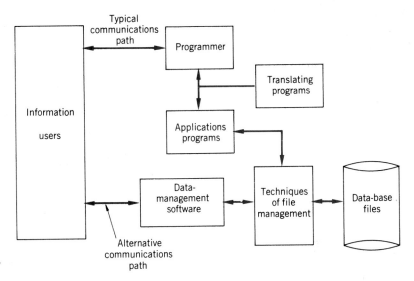

FIGURE 2-17

ago. The employee needed must be a mechanical engineer, must have knowledge of the particular pump (and therefore, let us assume, must have been with the corporation for at least 8 years), must be able to speak French, and must be willing to accept an overseas assignment. Obviously, there is not likely to be a report available that will have the names of engineers with just these characteristics. However, the records on each employee in the corporate personnel file stored in the data base do contain information on educational background, date of employment, work experience, and language capability. Although in the past it might have been necessary for the manager to request that a time-consuming program be prepared that would locate employees who match the requirements, with data management software it is now possible for the manager to use an online terminal to search through the personnel file and sort out the records of French-speaking mechanical engineers with 8 or more years of company experience. Armed with such information, obtained in a few minutes, the manager can then contact the employees named to fill the overseas assignment.

In addition to having direct access to data generated *within* the organization, a decision maker may also have *externally produced* data readily available in the data base. Marketing, financial, and economic data are currently being sold in machine-sensible form by such organizations as *Sales Management* magazine, Dun and Bradstreet, Standard & Poor's Corp., the Bureau of the Census, and the Department of Commerce.

In summary, as you have probably anticipated, *there are both benefits and limitations* at present *to the use of data-base systems.* Among the *possible benefits* are (1) fewer applications programs and lengthy regular reports containing reference data may be needed when managers can directly access the data base, (2) better integration (and less duplication) of data originating at different points is feasible, and (3) faster preparation of information to support nonrecurring tasks is likely. But some of the *possible limitations* are (1) more complex and expensive hardware and software are needed, and (2) the integrity of sensitive data in the data base may be endangered by hardware/software malfunctions or by other breakdowns in systems security.

In this chapter we have now seen some of the revolutionary changes taking place in technology and in the uses of this technology for information processing purposes. As might be expected, however, rapid change is often accompanied by problems of adjustment.

SELECTED PROBLEMS OF ADJUSTMENT

Take heart among the deepening gloom that your dog is finally getting enough cheese; and reflect that whatever misfortune may be your lot, it could only be worse in Milwaukee.

Anonymous in Deteriorata

The growth in the development and use of computers in the last decade has made it possible for computer-users to obtain more timely and more complete information. But this growth has brought adjustment problems which affect *organizations* and *individuals* and which must be dealt with in the future. Some of these issues are briefly outlined in the following sections; in later chapters several of them are considered in more detail.

Organizational Issues

Computer usage may enhance the efficiency of an organization by providing information that can lead to better planning, decision making, and control of organizational activities. But, as we have seen, technological change may also be harmful as well as helpful in some cases. The following listing focuses on challenges and issues that are currently the subject of concerned study and debate:

1 *The challenges in information systems design* As implied in earlier pages (and in Figure 2-8), systems design is a complex

and challenging task that has often produced disappointing internal results, a bad public image, and/or economic losses. Designers are currently grappling with the following questions: (*a*) Can a single data base be created to satisfy the differing information needs of administrators at different organizational levels? (*b*) Can decision makers with different job specialties share the same data base? (*c*) How can externally produced data be most effectively incorporated into the data base? and (*d*) How can suitable flexibility and adaptability to human needs be built into the system?

2 *The systems security issue* Lack of computer control and problems with the security of information systems have threatened the very existence of some organizations. Assets have been stolen through computer manipulation; trade secrets have been copied and sold to competitors; systems penetrators have repeatedly broken through the security controls and gained access to sensitive information; and fire, flood, accidents, and sabotage have destroyed irreplaceable computer files.

3 *Computer industry issues* Some organizations that have tried to compete in the computer industry have gone bankrupt; other giant corporations have suffered large losses trying to compete with IBM (at this writing, several antitrust suits are pending against this industry leader); and the problem of adequate legal software protection (an attempt to patent software was killed by the Supreme Court in 1972) has created headaches for software-producing organizations.

4 *Data communications uncertainties* There is considerable uncertainty about the governmental regulatory status of organizations that offer *both* computing and communications services. An *unregulated* legal status currently applies to organizations whose communications services are only incidental to their computing services, and a *regulated* legal status currently applies to organizations whose data processing services are only incidental to the furnishing of communications. But between these defined areas are a growing number of hybrid organizations that offer significant services in both communications and data processing. It is in this middle area that the regulatory status is unclear (see Figure 2-18).

5 *Organizational structure questions* Will the structure of a particular organization be drastically altered in the future as a result of the introduction and use of advanced computer systems? Will work groups need to be realigned, and should existing departments be eliminated?

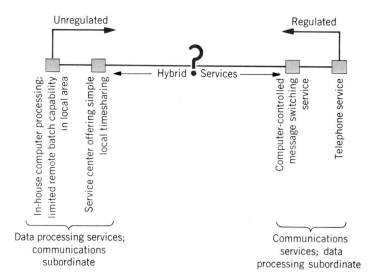

FIGURE 2-18

The uncertainty of governmental regulation.

6 *Concentration of power issue* Organizations with limited computing resources may have difficulty competing against those with much greater sophistication in the use of computers for planning and decision making.

7 *The electronic funds transfer systems (EFTS) issue* The EFTS concept may reduce the need for cash and checks and may permit the future widespread nationwide transfer of "electronic money" between organizations and individuals. Although legal and regulatory confusion currently exists, commercial banks anticipate using EFTS to improve efficiency and preserve their dominant position in the nation's payments system; other savings institutions see the use of EFTS as both a commercial bank competitive threat and as an opportunity to play a larger role in the funds transfer system; small retailers see EFTS as a means of reducing bad check losses; and large retailers may view the concept as a threat to their own credit-card business. In short, powerful organizations have a vital stake in the ways that computers are permitted to influence how "money" is transmitted and accounted for.

Individual Issues

The computer has perhaps the greatest potential to improve the quality of life and well-being of individuals of any tool ever invented. Certainly, there are examples all around us of the many positive benefits that individuals have received from computer usage. Thus,

It's the office. They want to hire you back. The computer can't figure out what you were doing.

it is probably unfortunate that most of the adjustment issues affecting people that are prominently discussed focus attention on the possible negative aspects of computer use. But there *are* some possible dangers as the following listing briefly outlines:

1 *Employment concerns* The greater efficiency made possible by computer usage in an organization may result in job obsolescence and displacement for some employees and disruptive changes in the compatible work groups in which others work.

2 *Systems-design issues* Faulty systems design has sometimes led to an out-of-control situation in the *originating* and *recording* of input data. That is, data may be gathered about individuals when there is no real need to know; errors of omission and commission may distort the records kept on an individual, and these errors are difficult to correct; and documents and procedures designed for processing convenience may lead to individual confusion and bewilderment. Also, data must be in a standardized form for computer system *classification* and *sorting,* and faulty systems design has often led to a depersonalized treatment of individuals—i.e., the individual has been made to feel like an insignificant number rather than like a human being. Finally, computer system *miscalculations* have resulted in individuals being harassed and inconvenienced.

"The University may be a large, sometimes cold and seemingly unfeeling place—but let me assure you that you have not lost your identity, Number 17932."

3 *Data security distress* The lack of control over data security in a computer system has resulted in the destruction of an individual's records, and in both the accidental and intentional disclosure to unauthorized persons of confidential information of a very personal nature.

4 *Privacy peril* Lack of control over data storage, retrieval, and communication has led to abuses of an individual's legitimate right to privacy—i.e., the right to keep private (or have kept on a confidential basis) those facts, beliefs, thoughts, and feelings that one does not wish to divulge publicly.

5 *Human self-understanding questions* As developmental work continues, and as computer programs become better able to solve relatively ill-structured problems and perform tasks that have heretofore been assumed to require human intelligence, will we as individuals alter the way we look at ourselves? Will we think less highly of ourselves if we see computers "outthinking" us?

SUMMARY   Technological changes are occurring rapidly today and are creating new opportunities and problems. Rapid reductions in size and cost (and significant inreases in speed and storage capacity) of computer hardware, combined with advances in computer software, are contributing to the development of quicker-responding and more integrated MIS concepts to meet the informational need of decision makers.

Quick-response systems utilizing online processing techniques enable managers to react more rapidly and to reduce waste in the use of economic resources. In some cases immediate updating of records from all online transaction-originating terminals is required, and so a real time system must be installed. *Timesharing* is a term that describes a quick-response system with a number of online, simultaneously usable terminals that are connected to the central processor. A *distributed computer network* is an extension of the original timesharing concept that may result in a large number of computers and significant software resources being shared among a large group of users.

Many quick-response systems are taking a broader approach to the needs of organizations by attempting to provide better integration of information-producing activities. *Data-base systems,* utilizing data management software, are being designed to help managers find answers to nonrecurring questions.

Difficult problems and challenges face individuals and organizations as they attempt to adapt to changes brought about by the information revolution. A few of these issues have been introduced in this chapter.

REVIEW AND DISCUSSION QUESTIONS

1 Discuss this statement: "The basic challenge to the leaders of today is to foresee and manage (and not be swept along by) the flood of changes facing their organizations, and to do this within a democratic framework, for the benefit of society."

2 Why does a technological change simultaneously create new opportunities and problems?

3 (**a**) What changes have taken place in computer hardware? (**b**) In computer software?

4 (**a**) What are the three basic software categories? (**b**) Discuss the developments in each of these categories.

5 What functions are performed by operating systems?

6 What is the purpose and orientation of an MIS? (Hint: see Figure 2-8.)

7 (**a**) Why have quick-response systems been developed? (**b**) What are the advantages of such systems? (**c**) What is the distinction between online processing and real time processing?

8 (**a**) What is batch processing? (**b**) How does it differ from online processing? (**c**) What are the advantages and disadvantages of batch processing?

9 "Online processing and direct access to records require unique hardware and software." Discuss this statement.

10   (**a**) What is meant by *timesharing?* (**b**) What is a *distributed
network?* (**c**) What do you think the long-term implications of
computer networks will be?

11   Identify and discuss the data-base approach to information
systems design.

12   (**a**) Will data management software have any effect on applications programmers? (**b**) Defend your answer to 12(**a**).

13   "Difficult problems and challenges face individuals and organizations as they attempt to adapt to changes brought about by
the information revolution." Discuss this statement from the
viewpoint of (**a**) a systems designer, (**b**) a law enforcement
officer, (**c**) a civil liberties advocate, (**d**) a spy or saboteur, (**e**) a
junior business executive, (**f**) a college student, (**g**) a competitor of IBM, (**h**) a telephone company executive, (**i**) a bookkeep-
ing machine operator, (**j**) an individual with social security
number 350-26-5840, and (**k**) a politician.

ORIENTATION
TO COMPUTERS

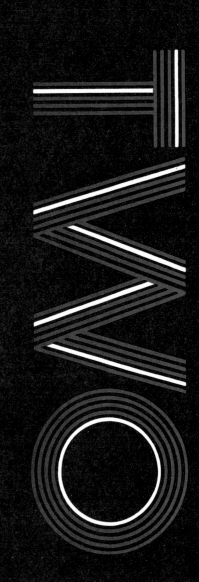

The chapters in Part One have now provided you with a background for the study of computer concepts. One of the objectives of this book is to provide you with an orientation to the computer (what it is, what it can and cannot do, and how it operates). The chapters in Parts Two and Three are directed toward this objective. Computer capabilities and limitations are examined, and basic computer *hardware* topics are presented, in the four chapters of this Part; the process involved in developing computer *software* to solve business problems is considered in the four chapters of Part Three.

INTRODUCTORY COMPUTER CONCEPTS

LEARNING OBJECTIVES After studying this chapter and answering the discussion questions, you should be able to:

Explain the various ways in which computers may be classified.

Identify and discuss some of the important capabilities of computers.

Identify and discuss some of the important limitations of computers.

Outline the five basic functions performed by computers.

69

In earlier pages we have dealt with computers in general terms. In this chapter, however, we begin the closer examination of this exciting tool. More specifically, in the next few pages we shall consider: (a) the *classes* of computers, (2) their *capabilities,* (3) their *limitations,* (4) their *learning* ability, and (5) their *functional* organization.

COMPUTER CLASSIFICATIONS

As you know, some firms offer tours of their facilities to interested parties. Let us assume that you are in a group visiting an insurance company. In the course of your visit, the tour guide asks you to identify the equipment located in a large room. Because you are an intelligent person, you respond that this is the firm's computer. The guide replies, "Yes, this is our medium-sized, fourth-generation, electronic, stored program, digital (a gasp for breath), general-purpose computer used for business purposes."

You recognize what the guide meant by the terms *medium-sized, fourth-generation, electronic,* and *stored program.* Computers are sometimes classified by size into large, medium, small, mini, and micro categories on the basis of computing power and cost. The fourth-generation age classification is arbitrary and may refer to equipment produced in the 1970s. The stored program concept refers to the ability of the machine to store internally a list of sequenced instructions that will guide it automatically through a series of operations leading to a completion of the task. We will come back to this concept in later chapters.

But what about the other classifying terms used by the guide—what do *digital, general-purpose,* and *business purposes* mean? Let us look at each of these items.

Analog and Digital Computers

There are two broad classes of computing devices—the analog and the digital. The *analog* machine does not compute directly with numbers; rather, it measures continuous physical magnitudes (e.g., pressure, temperature, voltage, current, shaft rotations, length), which represent, or are *analogous* to, the numbers under consideration. The service station gasoline pump, for example, contains an analog computer that converts the flow of pumped fuel into two measurements—the price of the delivered gas to the nearest penny and the quantity of pumped fuel to the nearest tenth or hundredth of a gallon. Another example of an analog device is the automobile speedometer which converts drive-shaft rotational motion into a numerical indication by the speedometer pointer.

Analog computers are used for scientific, engineering, and process-control purposes. Because they deal with quantities that are continuously variable, they give only approximate results. The speedometer pointer, for example, might give a reading of 45 miles per hour. But if the pointer were lengthened and sharpened, if the speedometer were calibrated more precisely, and if the cable were given closer attention, the reading might then be 44 miles per hour. Further refinements might give a reading of 44.5 miles per hour. A well-known soap product has claimed for years to be "99 and 44/100 percent pure." Under the best circumstances, an analog computer can achieve a somewhat higher degree of precision than this figure. But in a problem involving $1 million, an analog device might give answers only to the nearest hundred or thousand dollars.

The *digital* computer operates by *counting* numbers. It operates directly on numbers expressed as digits in the familiar decimal system or some other numbering system. The ancient shepherd, it will be recalled, used stones to represent sheep, and these were counted one by one to determine the total number of sheep in the flock. Nothing was measured as an analogous representation of the number of sheep; they were counted directly, and their total was exact. Stones have been replaced by adding machines, desk calculators, and digital computers, but all employ the same counting rules we learned in grade school.

Digital computation results in greater accuracy. While analog

"MY COMPUTER CALCULATIONS SHOW THAT YOUR
SLEIGH IS AERODYNAMICALLY UNSOUND..."

computers may, under ideal conditions, be accurate to within 0.1 percent of the correct value, digital computers can obtain whatever degree of accuracy is required simply by adding *places* to the right of the reference or decimal point. Every youngster who has worked arithmetic problems dealing with circles knows that pi (π) has a value of 3.1416. Actually, however, the value is 3.14159. . . . In 1959, a digital computer worked the value of π out to 10,000 decimal places in a short period of time.[1]

Digital computers, unlike analog machines, are used for both business data processing and scientific purposes. In special situations (e.g., to simulate a guided missile system or a new aircraft design), desirable features of analog and digital machines have been combined to create a *hybrid* computer.

Special-Purpose and General-Purpose Computers

Digital computers may be produced for either special or general uses. A *special-purpose* computer, as the name implies, is designed to perform one specific task. The program of instructions is built into the machine. Specialization results in the given task being performed economically, quickly, and efficiently. A disadvantage, however, is that the machine lacks versatility; it is inflexible and cannot be used to perform other operations. Special-purpose computers designed for the sole purpose of solving complex navigational problems are installed aboard our atomic submarines, but they could not be used for other purposes unless their circuits were redesigned. In the future, inexpensive microcomputers will be found in a growing number of specialized applications—e.g., in the family car to control fuel, ignition, and other systems.

A *general-purpose* computer is one that has the ability to store *different* programs of instructions and thus to perform a variety of operations. In short, the stored program concept makes the machine a general-purpose device—one that has the versatility to make possible the processing of a payroll one minute and an inventory control application the next. New programs can be prepared, and old programs can be changed or dropped. Because it is designed to do a wide variety of jobs rather than perform a specific activity, the general-purpose machine typically compromises certain aspects of speed and efficiency—a small enough price to pay in many cases for the advantage of flexibility.

---

[1]Alas, later more accurate work showed that this computer had made an error in the 7,480th decimal place.

Scientific and Business Applications

A general-purpose central processor is used for both scientific and business applications. What is the difference between these types of applications? What a coincidence that you should ask. . . .

Scientific processing applications A research laboratory may wish to analyze and evaluate a product formula involving 3 variables and 15 terms (which results in 45 different values for each variable). The computer *input* would be the 15-term formula, the 135 values for the 3 variables, and the set of instructions to be followed in processing. The input is thus quite small. The *processing* involved, however, may well consist of hundreds of thousands of different computations—computations that might represent many months of labor if performed by other methods. The *output* necessary for a problem of this type may consist of a few typed lines giving a single evaluation or a few alternatives.

In short, the volume of I/O in scientific data processing is relatively small, and the speed with which these operations are performed is usually not too important. Computational speed, on the other hand, is a critical consideration since the bulk of the total processing job involves complex calculation. Storage capacity need only be sufficient to hold instructions, input data, and intermediate and final computational results.

Business processing applications In contrast to scientifically oriented applications, business tasks generally require faster input and output of data and larger storage capacity. An examination of a typical business application will usually show that the volume of data input and information output is quite large. For example, the billing operation associated with the credit card purchases of an oil company's products involves thousands of customers and hundreds of thousands of sales transactions each month. Each transaction represents input data, while each customer represents an output statement. The running time required by the computer to complete such a business application is usually determined by the I/O speeds obtainable.

Computational speed is less critical in business applications because (1) arithmetic operations performed on each input record represent a relatively small proportion of the total job and (2) the internal arithmetic speed of the slowest computer is frequently much greater than the speed of I/O devices.

To summarize (see Figure 3-1), scientific and business applications typically differ with respect to (1) I/O volume, (2) I/O speed

Processing Characteristics	Scientific Applications	Business Applications
Input/output volume	Low	Very high
Input/output speed	Relatively unimportant	Very important
Ratio of computations to input	Very high	Low
Computation speed	Very important	Relatively unimportant
Storage requirements	Modest	High

FIGURE 3-1

needed, (3) amount of computation, (4) importance of computational speed, and (5) storage requirements.

The stored program, digital, general-purpose computer used for business purposes (henceforth called *computer* for apparent reasons) possesses certain capabilities, which are summarized in the next section.

COMPUTER CAPABILITIES

As we saw in Chapter 1, many writers (and cartoonists) have tended to view the computer in several roles. Computer systems are pictured as having *human, superhuman,* and *extrahuman* characteristics. Such characteristics tend to exaggerate certain computer capabilities. Yet it is clear that the computer is a powerful *tool* for

" The principal wants to see you ! "

extending people's brainpower. Peter Drucker has pointed out that human beings have developed two types of tools: (1) those that add to their capabilities and enable them to do something that they otherwise could *not* do (e.g., the airplane) and (2) those that multiply their capacity to do that which they are *already capable* of doing (e.g., the hammer).

The computer falls into the latter category. It is an intelligence amplifier. Carl Hammer, Director of Computer Sciences for UNIVAC, notes that today's computers have built into our society a mind-amplifying factor of 2,000 to 1; i.e., behind every man, woman, and child in the United States there stands the power of 2,000 human data processors.[2] Computers can enlarge brainpower because of the properties presented below. These properties have led to the human, superhuman, and extrahuman images.[3]

1 *The ability to provide new time dimensions* The machine works one step at a time; it adds and subtracts numbers; it multiplies and divides numbers (in most cases merely a repetitive process of addition and subtraction); and it can be designed or programmed to perform other mathematical operations such as finding a square root. There is nothing profound in these operations—even the author can perform them! What is significant, as we know, is the speed with which the machine functions. Thus, people are freed from calculations to use their time more creatively. Their time dimension has been broadened; they can obtain new information that could not have been produced at all a few years ago or that could not have been produced in time to be of any value. Karl Gauss, a German mathematician, at a young age had ideas that might have reshaped the study of mathematics in his time. Twenty years of his life were spent, however, in calculating the orbits of various heavenly objects. Were Gauss alive today, he could duplicate his calculations on a computer in a few hours and then be free to follow more creative pursuits. Similarly, the 2 years spent by John Adams in the 1840s in laboriously calculating the position of the planet Neptune could now be duplicated (with greater accuracy) by a computer in a little over a minute. Finally, a more recent illustra-

---

[2]See "DPMA's 1973 Computer Sciences Man of the Year," *Data Management,* pp. 14–20, June 1973.

[3]Of course, the computer has also been characterized as being *inhuman,* e.g., the source of heartless decisions made without regard for human feelings, and *subhuman,* e.g., the moron responsible for stupid and infuriating errors in billing. In the next section we shall look at the computer limitations responsible for these illusions.

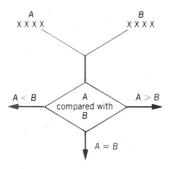

FIGURE 3-2

tion will serve to conclude this discussion of computer speed. John Kemeny of Dartmouth College has estimated that the calculations it took a year to complete working around the clock at the atomic laboratories at Los Alamos in 1945 could be done in one afternoon by an undergraduate student while sharing the computer's time with 30 others.

2 *The ability to perform certain logic operations* When two values, *A* and *B,* are *compared,* there are only three possible outcomes: (1) *A* is *equal to B* ($A = B$); (2) *A* is *greater than B* ($A > B$); or (3) *A* is *less than B* ($A < B$).[4] The computer is able to perform a simple comparison and then, depending on the result, follow one of three *predetermined branches,* or courses of action, in the completion of that portion of its work. (See Figure 3-2.) Thus, the computer has made a "decision" by choosing between alternative possible courses of action. Actually, however, it might be more appropriate to say that the computer has *followed* decisions made earlier by the programmer. But this simple ability to compare is an important computer property because more sophisticated questions can be answered by using combinations of comparison decisions. To illustrate, for more than a century mathematicians had been trying to prove the "four-color conjecture" that held that no more than four colors are needed to shade any map so that no adjoining nations are represented by the same color. Finally, two University of Illinois mathematicians examined, in mathematical terms, every imaginable map that could possibly be drawn. They then fed these possible map configurations into a computer to determine if all maps could indeed be drawn with only four colors. The computer "wrestled with the question for some 1,200 hours, during which it made some 10 billion separately logical decisions. Finally, the machine replied yes, and the four-color conjecture turned from theory into fact."[5]

3 *The ability to store and retrieve information* We know that the computer places in internal storage both facts and instructions. The ease with which instruction programs can be changed gives the computer great flexibility. The *access time* required for information to be recalled from internal storage and be available

---

[4]The possible outcomes form what logicians forbiddingly call the *law of trichotomy.* Computers also compare numbers to see whether they are positive, negative, or equal to zero.

[5]"Eureka!" *Time,* p. 88, Sept. 20, 1976. This example illustrates computer capabilities both in providing new time dimensions and in performing logic operations. It also shows some of the characteristics of scientific processing applications.

for use is measured in microseconds or more precise units. Few machines that we use have this stored program ability—the instructions generally reside in the human mind and thus are outside the machine. Instructions and data are in a coded form that the machine has been designed to accept. The machine is also designed to perform automatically and in sequence certain operations on the data (add, write, move, store, halt) called for by the instructions. The number of operations that can be performed varies among computer models. The stored program may, as we have just seen, allow the computer to select a branch of instructions to follow from several alternative sequences. The program may also allow the computer to *repeat* or *modify* instructions as required. Computers communicate with human operators by using input and output devices, and they communicate with other machines.

4 *The ability to control error* It is estimated that you or I would make one error in every 500 to 1,000 operations with a desk calculator. A computer, on the other hand, can perform hundreds of thousands of arithmetic operations every second and can run errorless for hours and days at a time. Computers also have the ability to check their own work. By a method known as *parity checking,* computers check on data when they enter storage, when they are moved internally, and when they leave in the form of output. Each character (e.g., number or letter) fed into the computer is represented in a coded form by several binary digits (0s and 1s) called *bits,* just as each number or letter in a punched card is represented by a code. The parity check performed by the computer involves the examination of each character's code to determine whether bits have been added or lost by mistake. More will be said about parity checking in a later chapter.

It should not be assumed, however, that computers have unlimited capabilities or that they are free of error. They do have their limitations, and they have been involved in some classic mistakes.

COMPUTER LIMITATIONS

Jack and Jill
Went up the hill
With great anticipating
Jack came down
And with a frown
Gave up computer dating
Edmund Conti

"I am very annoyed to find out that you have
branded my son illiterate. This is a dirty lie as I was
married a week before he was born."
"I am forwarding my marriage certificate and 5
children, one of which is a mistake as you can see."
"You have changed my little boy to a girl. Will this
make a difference?"
"My husband got his project cut off and I haven't
had any relief since. . . ."

*From letters to a computer-using Welfare
Department*

A publishing company customer received a computer-produced
invoice requesting that he pay his bill in the amount of "W-2.C." The
customer promptly forwarded his check for W-2.C as directed with a
note saying. "Out here in the sticks, we dig this crazy new currency
you folks have invented." Billing operations have produced other
computer goofs. For example, an insurance company kept sending a
policy holder a bill for $0.00 and demanding payment, and in Fort
Worth, Texas, a man was surprised a few months ago to receive a
brief, rather cool, letter from an oil company telling him that his
account was past due by $34.32. The man can be excused his
surprise because he had never received a credit card from any oil
company. Six weeks passed before the error was discovered, during
which time the man kept protesting and the form letters (getting less
and less cordial) kept coming in. Of course, it is not always the
individual who is victimized. In another case, an aircraft manufacturer sent a supplier a computer-prepared check for $3,000,000 to
settle a $3,000 bill. (The supplier could not resist then going to the
sales office of the manufacturer and offering to buy an expensive
airplane for cash!)

Or consider the case of the genteel New York City man who one
month received an unsolicited Playboy Club key and who for months
thereafter received bills for $7.50 from Playboy's computer. An
attorney's letter was required to get the rabbit off his back. These
victims, along with the Phoenix man who was treated for pneumonia
and charged for the use of the nursery and the delivery room,
perhaps felt as did another victim who said: "The computer is a
complete revolution in the ways of doing business, . . . and as in any
revolution some innocent people always get slaughtered."

That such stories are carried in newspapers is indication enough
that they occur only infrequently. Perhaps in most cases the errors
may be traced to humans who failed to give proper attention to the
following limitations:

"This is the bridge! Abort computerized firing! Abort computerized firing!"

© DATAMATION ®

1 *Application programs must always be prepared* The machine does what it is programmed to do and *nothing else.* It can only operate on data; i.e., it can accept data, process them, and communicate results, but it cannot directly perform physical activities such as bending metal. (The processed information may be used, however, to control metal-bending machines.) Furthermore, a program may *seem* to be flawless and operate satisfactorily for some months and then produce nonsense (a bill for $0.00, for instance) because some rare combination of events has presented the computer with a situation (1) for which there is no programmed course of action or (2) where the course of action provided by the programmer contains an error that is just being discovered. Of course, a truly flawless program, supplied with incorrect data, may also produce nonsense. And once incorrect facts are entered into a computer system, they are usually not as easy to purge as is the case when manual methods are used.

2 *Applications must be able to be quantified and dealt with logically* The computer will not be of much help to people in areas where *qualitative* considerations are important. It will not, for example, tell you how to "get rich quick" in the stock market; it will not improve much on random selection in arranging a date between Jack and Jill (they both have outrageous personalities, and they both have been less than candid in filling out computer input forms); and it will not signal a change in an economic trend until after the fact. Thus, it will not tell a manager whether or not a new product will be successful if marketed. The ultimate market decision is of a qualitative nature because it is involved with future social, political, technological, and economic events; and sales volume levels are thus impossible to predict with certainty. However, the computer will *by simulation* let a manager know how a new product will fare under *assumed* price, cost, and sales volume conditions. The computer, in short, is limited to those applications that may be expressed in the form of an *algorithm;* i.e., the application must consist of a finite number of steps leading to a precisely defined goal, and each step must be specifically and *clearly defined.* Thus, we might say that an algorithm operates on data to produce information. If the steps in the solution of the problem cannot be precisely written down, the application cannot be performed on today's commercial computers. And, as you know, each time the computer must make a choice the appropriate alternative steps must have been foreseen and provided for by the programmer.

3 *Applications must weigh resources* Merely because a computer can be programmed to do a job does not always mean that it *should.* Writing programs, although less tedious than in the past because of developments in software, is still a time-consuming and expensive human operation. Thus, nonrecurring tasks or jobs that are seldom processed are often not efficient areas for computer application at the present time. In business data processing, it is usually most economical to prepare programs for large-volume, repetitive operations that will be used many times and that promise fast returns on the time invested in program preparations.[6]

EXPERIMENTS IN ARTIFICIAL INTELLIGENCE Much has been written in the past few years pro and con about the question of whether computers can be programmed to "think" and "learn." Most of the controversy probably stems from (1) a lack of understanding about the processes involved in human thinking and learning and (2) the absence of acceptable definitions of such words as *think* and *learn.*

---

[6]In engineering and scientific computing, the importance of a nonrecurring task often warrants the necessary investment in programming time. An example might be the engineering planning and construction scheduling, by computer, of a single multimillion-dollar office building.

One test—a game—to determine whether a computer might be considered to possess intelligence and the ability to think was proposed by Alan Turing, a British mathematician. Participants in the game would be two respondents—a machine and a human—and a human interrogator who tries to determine which of the unseen respondents is the human. In answering questions posed by the interrogator (communications terminals are used), the machine tries to deceive while the human respondent tries to convince the interrogator of his or her true identity. Intelligence and the ability to think would, according to "Turing's Test," be demonstrated by the machine's success in fooling the interrogator. Using this test, Turing anticipated that machines with thinking ability would exist by the year 2000.[7]

Although the superhuman computers found in science fiction do not exist, science fiction has a way of becoming science fact. Research efforts and experiments are currently being conducted in the use of computers to solve relatively ill-structured problems These research efforts, which are sometimes classified under the heading of *artificial intelligence,* and which are combining concepts found in disciplines such as psychology, linguistics, and computer science, are aimed at learning how to prepare programs (or construct systems) that can do tasks that have never been done automat-

---

[7]Of course, many do not agree with this concept of thinking. As computer scientist Paul Armer has facetiously observed, computers cannot think because people keep redefining thinking to be a process that is just beyond whatever the current ability of the computer happens to be.

"CHECKMATE!"

ically before and that have usually been assumed to require human intelligence. For example, computers have been programmed to play checkers and chess and to modify their programs on the basis of success and failure with moves used in the past against human opponents. In one checkers-playing program, the computer has continually improved its game to the point where it regularly defeats the author of the program. Thus, the machine has "learned" what not to do through trial and error.

Computers have also been programmed to prove mathematical theorems and compose music, but thus far such research activities are limited and involve "thinking" on the part of the machine in a most limited sense.

Heuristic[8] is a word that means *serving to discover.* It is used to describe the judgmental, or *common sense,* part of problem solving. That is, it describes that part of problem solving which deals with the definition of the problem, the selection of reasonable strategies to be followed (which may or may not lead to optimum solutions), and the formulation of hypotheses and hunches. Human beings are *far superior* to the computer in the heuristic area of intellectual work. As people's thinking and learning processes become better understood, however, it may be possible to develop new programs and machines with improved heuristic abilities. Certainly, some very able researchers are working toward this end. The role of the computer will continue to be that of an intelligence amplifier in an alliance with humanity. The potential of such an alliance, although not unlimited, cannot be restricted in any way that we can now anticipate.

COMPUTER ORGANIZATION

The computer solves problems and produces information in much the same way that you do. Let us illustrate this fact by first making a most disagreeable assumption: that in the near future you will have to take a written examination on the material covered in the first few chapters of an accounting book. For the past few days you have been reading the text, trying to catch up on your homework problems, and listening to your professor's lectures. You have written several pages of notes and have memorized various facts, concepts, and procedures. Finally, the examination period arrives, and you begin to work the test problems. Transactions are noted, and proper (?) accounts receive debits and credits. Procedures are followed, you hope, in the correct order. As time runs out, you turn your paper

---

[8]Pronounced *hew-ris' tik.*

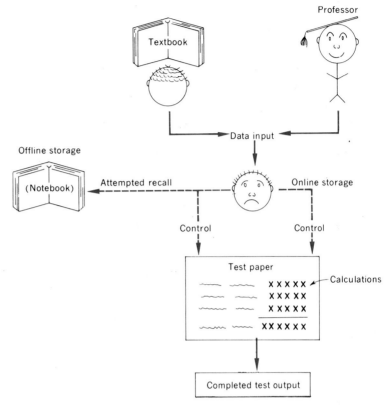

FIGURE 3-3

in to the professor and leave, resolving to pay somewhat closer attention to what she or he has to say in the future.

Five functions were performed in the above illustration (see Figure 3-3). These functions are:

1 *Input* The input function involves the receipt of facts that can be used. You received data from your accounting textbook and from your professor.
2 *Storage* Facts received must be stored until they are needed. Your notebook (offline storage) and your brain (online storage) were used to store accounting information and the procedures to use for solving problems.
3 *Calculation* On your test you performed the arithmetic operations of addition, subtraction, multiplication, and division, either manually or with the help of a calculator.
4 *Control* On the exam it was necessary to follow certain procedures in the proper order, or sequence; i.e., you could not total

an account until all transactions had been recorded, and you did not record the last transaction of the month first because it might have been based on transactions occurring earlier in the month. Control, then, simply means doing things in the correct sequence.

5   *Output* Your finished test was the output—the result of your data processing operations. It will provide your professor with part of the information needed to arrive at a decision about your 'inal grade.

All computer installations perform these five functions. Figure 3-4 illustrates the *functional* organization of a computer. Let us briefly examine each part of this diagram.

Input

Computers, obviously, must also receive facts to solve problems. Data and instructions must be put into the computer system in a form that it can use. There are a number of devices that will perform this input function, as we shall see in the following chapter. They may allow direct human/machine communication without the necessity of an input medium (e.g., the keyboard of a timesharing remote station), or they may present information that typically has been produced offline in batches on an input medium (e.g., punched cards). Regardless of the type of device used, they are all instruments of interpretation and communication between people and the machine.

FIGURE 3-4
Computer functional organization.

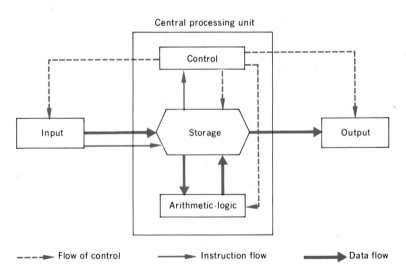

Storage

The heart of any computer installation is the central processing unit (CPU). Within CPUs of all sizes are generally located storage, control, and arithmetic-logic units (see Figure 3-5). It is this central processor that makes comparisons, performs calculations, and selects, interprets, and controls the execution of instructions.

The storage section of the central processor is used for *four purposes,* three of which relate to the data being processed. First, data are fed into the storage area where they are held until ready to be processed. Second, additional storage space is used to hold data being processed and the intermediate results of such processing. Third, the storage unit holds the finished product of the processing operations until it can be released in the form of output information. Fourth, in addition to these data-related purposes, the storage unit also holds the program instructions until they are needed.

Arithmetic-Logic

All calculations are performed and all comparisons (decisions) are made in the arithmetic-logic section of the central processor. Data flow between this section and the storage unit during processing operations; i.e., data are received from storage, manipulated, and returned to storage. No processing is performed in the storage section. The number of arithmetic and logic operations that can be performed is determined by the engineering design of the machine.

To briefly summarize, data are fed into the storage unit from the input devices. Once in storage, they are held and transferred as needed to the arithmetic-logic unit, where processing takes place. Data may move from storage to the arithmetic-logic unit and back again to storage many times before the processing is finished. Once completed, the information is released from the central processor to the output device.

Control

How does the input unit know when to feed data into storage? How does the arithmetic-logic unit obtain the needed data from storage, and how does it know what should be done with them once they are received? And how is the output unit able to obtain finished information instead of raw data from storage? It is by selecting, interpreting, and executing the program instructions that the control unit of the central processor is able to maintain order and direct the operation of the entire installation. It thus acts as a central nervous system for the component parts of the computer. Instructions are *selected* and

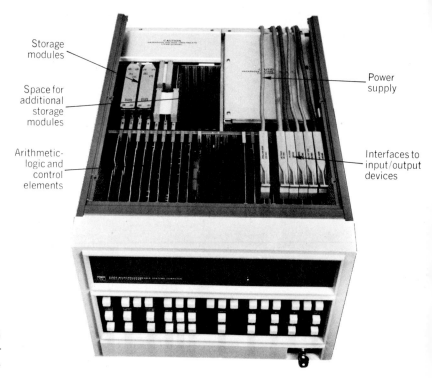

Storage modules

Space for additional storage modules

Arithmetic-logic and control elements

Power supply

Interfaces to input/output devices

FIGURE 3-5
Minisized CPU (courtesy Hewlett-Packard Company).

fed in sequence into the control unit from storage; there they are *interpreted;* and from there signals are sent to *other* machine units to *execute* program steps. The control unit itself does not perform actual processing operations on the data.

Output

Output devices, like input units, are instruments of interpretation and communication between people and machine. They take information in machine-coded form and convert it typically into a form that can be used (1) by humans (e.g., a printed report) or (2) as machine input in another processing operation (e.g., magnetic tape). In the following chapter we shall take a closer look at several output devices.

Extensive Variations Possible

All computer systems are similar in that they perform the basic functions just described. However, computers vary widely in their external configurations. Some computers are housed in three boxes, as implied in Figure 3-4; some are in a single cabinet; some have multiple units for the input and output functions; some *distribute* parts of the storage and control functions to equipment peripheral to the CPU; and some use a single cabinet to house both input and output functions. Figure 3-6 illustrates some of the possible machine combinations. (The I/O and other peripheral hardware and media shown will be surveyed in the next two chapters; a closer look at the CPU will be the subject of Chapter 6.) The boxes labeled "channels" in Figure 3-6 require a brief explanation here.

A *channel* consists of hardware that, along with other associated monitoring and connecting elements, controls and provides the path for the movement of data between relatively slow I/O devices, on the one hand, and high-speed central processor primary storage, on the other. Because of the differences in operating speeds, the CPU would be idle much of the time if it had to hold up processing during the periods that input was being received and output was being produced. Fortunately, most computers built since the mid-1960s have features that make it possible to *overlap* input, processing, and output operations in order to make more efficient use of computing resources. Once the channel has received appropriate instruction signals from the central processor, it can operate independently and without supervision while the CPU is engaged in performing computations. For example, at the same time that the CPU is processing one group of records, one channel can be receiving another group for subsequent processing while a second channel can be supplying processed information to the appropriate output device.

Before concluding this section, it might be appropriate to mention another type of variation that can exist in computer systems—the variation in the design and construction (or architecture) of the functional elements in the CPU. Figure 3-4 shows the *traditional* design. This design features *single* control, storage, and arithmetic-logic units in the CPU. But there are several ways this traditional design can be modified in order to achieve even greater computing speeds. Among the possible alternative designs used by the *larger* computer systems are the following:

1   *The multiprocessor design* By adding additional control and arithmetic-logic units [see Figure 3-7(a)], several instructions can be processed at the same instant in time. As we saw in the last chapter, multiprogramming involves executing a portion of one program, then a segment of another, etc., in brief *consecutive* time periods. Multiprocessor design, however, makes it possible for the system to *simultaneously* work on several program segments. Thus, this design represents, in effect, a system with two or more central processors.

2   *The concurrent (or pipeline) design* Computing speed can also be increased by separating the arithmetic-logic unit into func-

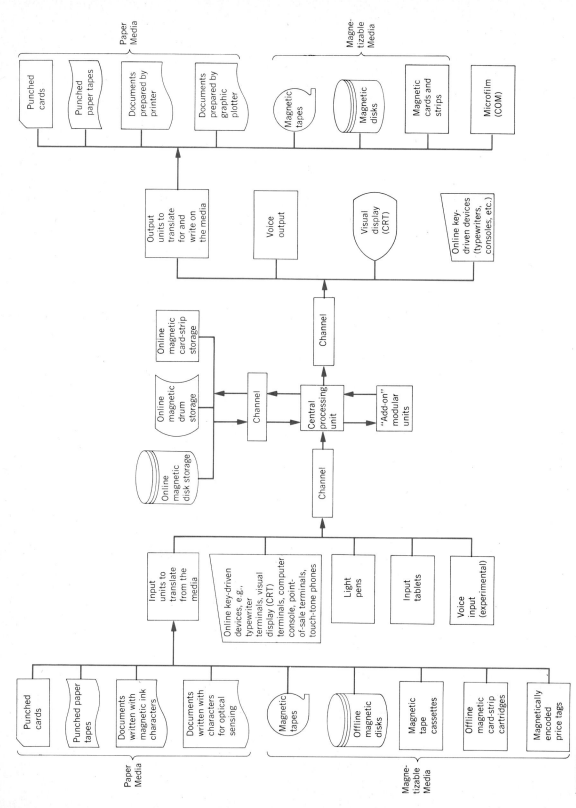

FIGURE 3-6
Input-output hardware and media.

tional subunits, each of which can operate independently under the direction of the control unit [see Figure 3-7(*b*)]. When, for example, consecutive and independent program instructions call for the use of separate subunits (e.g., addition, multiplication, and division), the control unit will signal the proper elements to proceed *concurrently* to process all these instructions. Lacking functionally independent subunits, a traditionally designed arithmetic-logic unit will take the first instruction in the sequence and execute it before moving to the next instruction.

FIGURE 3-7

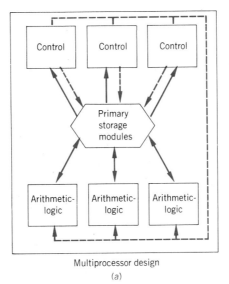

Multiprocessor design
(a)

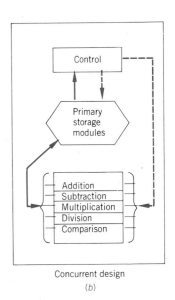

Concurrent design
(b)

3 *The parallel design* The ILLIAC IV is a massive "number-cruncher" with a control unit that directs the operations of 64 arithmetic-logic units. Each arithmetic-logic unit has its own storage unit.

These variations from traditional design result in faster computation speed and will be used in many future computer systems.

SUMMARY Electronic computers may be classified in a number of ways. In this book we are interested in digital machines that count sequentially and very accurately, and we are interested in general-purpose equipment that can do a variety of jobs.

Computers extend human brainpower; they are intelligence amplifiers that provide new dimensions in the time available for creative work. They are able to perform certain logic operations. Sophisticated questions can be answered by the combination of many simple machine "decisions." Computers can store and retrieve information rapidly and accurately.

But machines, like humans (especially like humans), are not infallible. They make errors, and they must be told exactly and precisely what to do. Although experiments are being conducted by extremely able researchers in the attempt to improve the machine's heuristic capabilities, they are restricted in practical use to applications that can be quantified and structured into a finite number of steps to achieve a specific goal.

Computers are organized to perform the functional activities of input, storage, arithmetic-logic, control, and output. A multitude of machine configurations and media are used in the performance of these functions. The composition of the CPU is subject to design variation; the most powerful computers generally depart in some way from the traditional design, which features single control, storage, and arithmetic-logic units in the CPU.

REVIEW AND DISCUSSION QUESTIONS

1 Disucss the various ways in which computers may be classified.

2 (**a**) What is an analog computer? (**b**) How does it differ from a digital computer?

3 How does a special-purpose computer differ from a general-purpose machine?

4 Compare and contrast the processing characteristics typically found in business and scientific applications.

5 Why is it possible to say that the computer is an intelligence amplifier?

6 Identify and discuss the limitations of computer usage.

7 Why does controversy surround the question of whether or not computers can be programmed to "think"?

8 Identify and discuss the five functions which are performed by computers.

9 "The storage section of the central processor is used for four purposes." What are these four purposes?

10 (**a**) What functions are performed in the arithmetic-logic section of the central processor? (**b**) In the control section?

11 What is the role of a data channel?

12 Differentiate between traditional CPU design and (**a**) multiprocessor design, (**b**) concurrent design; and (**c**) parallel design.

COMPUTER INPUT/OUTPUT: I

After studying this chapter and answering the discussion questions, you should be able to:

Explain how data are organized in business information systems.

Discuss the advantages and limitations of punched cards and explain the purposes cards serve.

Describe how data are represented on punched paper tape, and how paper tape compares with punched cards.

Explain the ways in which data are entered and coded on magnetic tape, and the advantages and limitations of this medium.

Describe some of the characteristics of direct-access devices that use magnetic drums and magnetic disks for I/O and online secondary storage.

CHAPTER OUTLINE

DATA ORGANIZATION CONCEPTS

PUNCHED CARDS

PUNCHED PAPER TAPE

MAGNETIC TAPE
Direct Data Entry on Magnetic Tape □ Magnetic Tape Coding □ Magnetic Tape Equipment □ Advantages and Limitations of Magnetic Tape

DIRECT-ACCESS DEVICES
Magnetic Drums □ Magnetic Disks □ Magnetic Cards and Strips

SUMMARY

Why have I/O media and devices? The answer to this question, of course, is that they make it possible for data processing to occur, i.e., they make it possible for people to place data into and receive information out of the central processor. The computer installation can perform the necessary processing steps and communicate with humans only through the I/O equipment. In this chapter we will study some of the ways in which communication is accomplished. But before moving on to specific media and machines, let us look briefly at a few *data organization concepts* that have an important bearing on I/O activities.

DATA ORGANIZATION CONCEPTS

To perform efficiently the data processing steps (classifying, sorting, etc.) mentioned in Chapter 1, data must first be organized in some logical arrangement. In business information systems, a data hierarchy consisting of files, records, and items (remember Figure 2-11?) generally exists, and business data processing involves operations on these records and files. Therefore, since our I/O activities will be concerned primarily with the maintenance of records and files, let us make sure we have a clear understanding of these data organization concepts.

A hypothetical accounts-receivable application in a manual accounting system will be used to illustrate data organization. The accounts-receivable file contains records for each customer showing such information as customer name, account number, address, amount owed, and credit limit. Each record is filed alphabetically, by customer name, in the *transaction file* drawer, as shown in Figure 4-1. Each record folder contains credit sales transaction tickets (items), which have been (1) *recorded* and *classified* by customer name, (2) *sorted* alphabetically, and (3) *stored* in the file drawer until the end of the month.

At the end of the month, the record folders are removed from the transaction file drawer, and the following processing steps are performed:

1 *Calculations* are made to determine the total amount purchased by each customer during the month.
2 The monthly transactions are used to revise and update the information contained in the *master file* in the bottom two drawers of the file cabinet.
3 The total amount owed is *communicated* to the customer in the form of a bill.

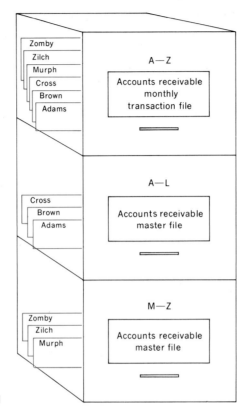

FIGURE 4-1

4 A report is prepared that *summarizes* for managers the pertinent
information contained in the files, e.g., the total credit sales for
the month, records that show slow payment, etc.

Processing is done sequentially (in alphabetical order) beginning
with Adams and ending with Zomby. Thus, the data processing
functions and the I/O activities take place within the organizational
framework of the accounts-receivable files. The master file has a
degree of permanency, while transaction file data are emptied each
month.

Computers replace manual methods, but files still must be maintained that continually receive and transmit information. Figure 4-2
charts the general flow of activites involved in file processing. Files
may be sequentially organized and stored offline on media such as
punched cards or magnetic tape. Or they may be randomly orga-

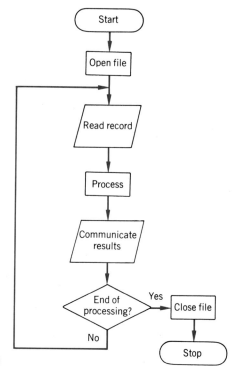

FIGURE 4-2

nized and stored on magnetizable devices found in directly accessible online storage units.

Records may be sequentially *processed* (batch processing), or they may be immediately accessed and updated by random-access *processing.* Since it is quite easy to become confused about the meaning of the terms *sequential* and *random* when they are used with the words *processing* and *organization,* let us pause to clarify this semantic entanglement.

When master files are stored offline, they are almost always sequentially *organized.* And when such files are updated, sequential *processing,* by means of appropriate I/O devices, is used. But when files are located in online storage, they may be organized sequentially *or* randomly. Thus, as Figure 4-3 conceptually shows, random-access *processing* is possible with files organized *both* sequentially and randomly.

Still confused? Perhaps a final example will help clarify matters. Let us assume that you have a sound tape player and a record player—devices that are being used to drive your neighbors to distraction. Your favorite tape has ten pieces of music arranged alphabetically by song title; your favorite record has seven pieces of music arranged in no discernible order. Suppose you only want to listen to the sixth song on the tape and the fourth song on the record. As you know, you cannot get to the sixth song on the tape unless you put it on the player and wind it past the first five until you get to the beginning of the selected music. Although your player may move the tape quickly past the first five pieces, it nevertheless *does* take several seconds. With the record player, on the other hand, you need only turn it on and move the pickup arm directly and quickly across the record to the groove where the fourth song begins. In summary, then, the songs on the tape are sequentially organized, accessed, and played (processed); the songs on the record can be organized

FIGURE 4-3
(*a*) Random-access processing with sequential file organization, (*b*) random-accessing processing with random file organization.

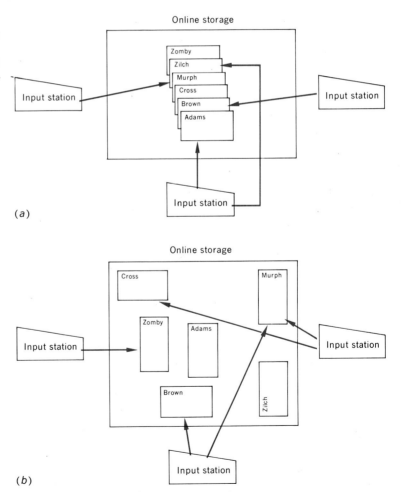

either in a random fashion or in some sequence, but random access and playing (processing) is possible in either case.

Because files vary in character, size, and location (online or offline), a number of I/O media and devices have been developed. In choosing from among the possible alternatives, managers must consider such factors as (1) the nature and volume of the data input, (2) the accessibility of stored data and the speed with which files must be updated, and (3) the costs of I/O alternatives. Not surprisingly, a compromise choice is often necessary.

In the following pages, we shall *first* examine paper and magnetizable media and related equipment employed for high-volume batch processing applications. We shall then devote the *remaining* pages of this chapter and much of the following chapter to I/O devices that are frequently found in random processing situations. Figure 4-4 summarizes some of the characteristics of the media and devices introduced in this chapter.

PUNCHED CARDS

The punched card is the most familiar I/O medium. It serves a *threefold purpose:* it is used to (1) provide data *input* into the CPU, (2) receive information *output* from the CPU, and (3) provide secondary offline *storage* of data and information. Details were presented in Chapter 1 on some card processing concepts and on card coding.

Manually operated keypunch machines are the primary means of preparing punched cards. Although this is a tedious and expensive operation, the use of keypunch equipment has through the years remained a popular data entry method.

Once the data are punched into the cards, they are fed into the central processor by means of a *card reader* (Figure 4-5). Cards are placed into a read hopper from where, on command from the program in the central processor, they are moved through the card feed unit past either brush-type or photoelectric-cell reading stations. These stations sense the presence or absence of holes in each card column and convert this information into electric pulses that the computer can accept. The speed with which a card reader can supply input data to a CPU is relatively slow when compared with most other methods (see Figure 4-4).

Cards may also serve as an output medium through the use of a *card punch* machine. Blank cards are placed in a hopper. Upon command from the program, they are moved, one at a time, to a punch station where processed information is received. The card punch function is frequently housed with the card reading activity in a machine called a *read punch*. In small card-oriented computer systems, a single *multifunction card machine* is used to perform input, output, sorting, and collating functions.

Medium	Input Device Used	Output Device Used	Typical I/O Speed Ranges (Characters per Second)		Typical Storage Uses		Typical Storage Capacity
			Input	Output	Online Secondary	Offline Secondary	
Punched card	Card reader	Card punch	150–2,667	80–650		X	Virtually unlimited (but bulky)
Paper tape	Tape reader	Tape punch	50–1,800	10–300		X	Virtually unlimited (but bulky and fragile)
Magnetic tape	Tape drive	Tape drive	15,000–350,000	15,000–350,000		X	Virtually unlimited (compact, with up to 20 million characters per tape)
Magnetic drum	Drum storage unit	Drum storage unit	230,000–1,500,000	230,000–1,500,000	X		From 1 to 4 million characters with high-speed drums; up to 200 million characters on slower drum units
Magnetic disk	Disk drive	Disk drive	100,000–1,000,000	100,000–1,000,000	X	X	Virtually unlimited off-line storage; from 2 to 100 million characters per online disk pack
Magnetic cards/strips	Card/strip storage unit	Card/strip storage unit	25,000–50,000	25,000–50,000	X	X	Virtually unlimited off-line storage; from 25 to 150 million characters per online card/strip cartridge

FIGURE 4-4
Summary of I/O media and devices—Chapter 4.

FIGURE 4-5

Card reader (courtesy IBM Corporation).

Card punches have proven useful in producing documents that are later reentered into processing operations. An example of such a *turnaround* application is the billing approach used by some public utilities. Bills sent to customers are in the form of cards prepared as computer output. Appropriate data are punched into this card. When a part or all of the card is returned by the customer with his or her payment, it may then be used as an input that requires no keypunching.

Many businesses use punched cards as an I/O medium because they were used with the firm's unit record equipment prior to the introduction of the computer. But *cards possess advantages* other than merely being an old, reliable, and available medium. For one thing, they are complete records of transactions and are thus easily understood. Particular records can be sorted, deleted, and replaced without disturbing other cards. It may be possible to add more data to the cards if necessary. Magnetic and paper tapes lack these advantages.

But *cards have certain inherent disadvantages* that may limit their use in or exclude them from use in a particular application. For example, the number of data characters that can be punched per card is quite low—much less than the number of characters that can be typed on the card with a typewriter. *Data density* is low even when all columns are punched. But in most applications *not* all the columns will be punched, and data density is thus further reduced. For example, if the dollar amount of credit sales transactions in an exclusive retail store may reach or exceed $10,000.00 then the purchase amount field on each card must provide seven columns of space even though most purchases will be for much less (e.g., three columns would be unused if a purchase were made for $75.00). Also, cards are fixed in length. If 100 characters are required, an additional card must be used. The size of the card deck is increased, as is the time required to process it. Because tapes are continuous in length, they do not have this drawback. In short, cards are relatively bulky and slow to process. Finally, cards may sometimes be misplaced from their proper deck, and, as you know, they cannot be folded, stapled, or mutiliated.

PUNCHED PAPER TAPE

Punched paper tape, like cards, is a triple-purpose medium that is suitable for input, output, and secondary offline storage. Perhaps its most popular business use is to capture data as byproducts of some other processing activity. Time and labor are thus saved. For example, paper tape attachments on many timesharing terminals permanently capture input data and output information on tape.

Data are recorded on the tape by punching round holes into it. Tape, like the punched card, is laid out in rows (*channels*) and

" I just wanted to see what would happen if
I folded, spindled or otherwise mutilated
my punch card. "

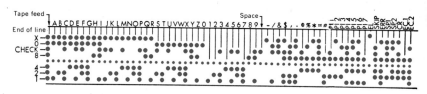

FIGURE 4-6

Eight-channel paper tape code.

columns (*frames*). A character of information is represented by a punch or combination of punches in a vertical column.

Figure 4-6 illustrates the method of representing data employed with the popular eight-channel tape. The bottom four channels are labeled to the left of the tape with the numerical values 1, 2, 4, and 8. (The holes between channels 4 and 8 are sprocket holes used to feed the tape through the machines and are not considered in the code.) Decimal digits 1 to 9 can be represented by a hole or a combination of holes in these bottom channels. For example, a single hole punched in channel 2 has a decimal value of 2, while holes punched in channels 4, 2, and 1 denote a decimal 7. The X and 0 channels serve the same purpose as zone punches in cards; i.e., they are used in combination with numerical punches to form alphabetic and special characters. Channel 0 used alone is the code for zero. The letter A is represented by zone punches in X and 0 plus numerical 1 hole. The letter B has the same zone punches plus numerical 2, etc. You can examine the remainder of the letters to see the code pattern.

The data coded on punched tape are fed into the CPU by means of a *paper tape reader.* Tape readers, like card readers, sense the presence or absence of holes and deliver this information to the processor. *Paper tape punches* record information received from the CPU by punching holes in blank tape. As you can see in Figure 4-4, the speed of paper tape input and output is very slow.

Punched paper tape provides certain advantages over punched cards. First, because it is a continuous-length medium, there is no upper-limit restriction on the length of records and no wasted space when records are short. Tape thus provides greater data density, which makes for easier handling and storage. Also, it is more economical than cards.

But *punched tapes have their faults.* It is more difficult to verify the accuracy of tape output than is the case with cards. Errors that are discovered cannot be corrected as easily as in the case of cards. And changes such as the addition to or deletion of records are more difficult with tape than with cards.

MAGNETIC TAPE   Because of its relatively fast *transfer rate*[1] (the speed at which data can be transferred from the input medium to CPU storage), magnetic tape is the most popular I/O medium being used today for high-speed, large-volume applications. In addition to providing rapid input and output, it is the most widely used secondary offline computer storage medium.

The tape itself may be in a large *reel* or a small *cartridge* or *cassette* and is quite similar to the kind used in a sound tape recorder. It is a plastic ribbon coated on one side with an iron-oxide material that can be magnetized. By electromagnetic pulses, data are recorded in the form of tiny invisible spots on the iron-oxide side of the tape, just as sound waves form magnetic patterns on the tape of a sound recorder. Both the data and the sound can be played back as many times as desired. And like the tape used on a recorder, computer tape can be erased and reused indefinitely. Data contained in a tape are automatically erased as new data are being recorded.

Direct Data Entry on Magnetic Tape

How is information recorded on magnetic tape? In some cases new input data are initially captured in punched card or paper tape form and are then transcribed on magnetic tape by a special offline *data converter*. In addition to this *indirect* approach to entering data on magnetic tape, however, there are several alternative data entry approaches in which the data are keyed from source documents *directly* into a magnetizable form. Among the popular direct data entry alternatives being used are:

1 *Single-station key-to-tape units* In this approach the single (or *stand-alone*) tape encoder system includes all components required to produce a prepared tape by keying the data found in a source document. The keyed data may be recorded on standard-size magnetic tape, or they may be recorded on the smaller-sized tape found in special *cartridges* or *cassettes* Data recorded on the smaller tape may need to be converted to standard-size tape prior to computer entry.

---

[1]The transfer rate for magnetic tape depends on such factors as (1) the data density of the magnetized marks (which varies) and (2) the speed with which the tape moves (usually about 100 inches per second). Did you care to know that? Don't tell me your answer, it might depress me.

2 *Multistation key-to-tape configurations* In this approach there are several keyboard consoles connected to one or more magnetic tape units by a central controlling device. The controller consolidates the data from the keyboards on the appropriate tape units.

3 *Single-station key-to-diskette units* Data are recorded on a small, flexible, magnetizable diskette—a "floppy" disk that looks like a thin 45 rpm sound record. Recorded data may then be transferred to magnetic tape for processing.

4 *Multistation key-to-disk configurations* In this type of data entry system, a minicomputer controls the input from a number of key stations. Data keyed in by a station operator are displayed, edited, and checked for errors, then stored on a magnetic disk resembling a large LP sound record. Periodically, the data stored on the disk are transferred to magnetic tape (Figure 4-7).

Magnetic Tape Coding

The approach used to represent data on magnetic tape is similar to that used with punched paper tape. Magnetic tape is divided horizontally into rows (called *channels,* or *tracks*) and vertically into columns or frames. The most commonly used tape codes employ seven and nine channels. Figure 4-8 illustrates the *seven-channel* tape format. You will note that channel designations are quite similar to those used in punched tape. Data are represented in a coded form.[2] Each vertical frame represents one data character, and the tape-recording density may be from 200 to 1,600 frames per inch depending on the computer system used.

The numerical values are determined by one or a combination of the bottom four channels, while the A and B zone tracks are used in conjunction with the numeric channels to represent letters and special characters. For example, the decimal 7 is represented by an "on" condition in channels 4, 2, and 1. You can test your understanding by observing the coding pattern used for the other alphanumeric characters.

You may have noticed that there are "check" channels in both Figures 4-6 and 4-8. These channels perform a special *parity checking* function. In Figure 4-8, for example, you will notice that there are

---

[2]The code used here is called *binary coded decimal* (BCD). In Chapter 6 we will become better acquainted with BCD. We will also examine an extended version of BCD at that time.

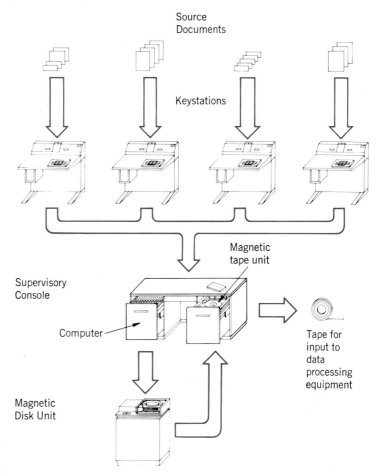

Source
Documents

Keystations

Magnetic
tape unit

Supervisory
Console

Computer

Tape for
input to
data
processing
equipment

Magnetic
Disk Unit

FIGURE 4-7

Key-to-disk data entry.

an even number of marks in each frame. When the basic code—e.g., for the digit 1—requires an odd number of marks, there is an additional mark in the check channel. Thus, all valid characters are formed with an even number of marks, and this becomes the basis for a system check of the accuracy of the tape. Both even- and odd-parity codes are used in computer systems.

An *extended* version of the seven-channel tape format is also provided by most computer manufacturers. As with seven-track tape, this *nine-channel* format employs four numeric tracks and a parity check channel. However, *four* (rather than two) zone positions are available. The additional zone tracks make it possible to extend the code to include lowercase alphabetical and other special charac-

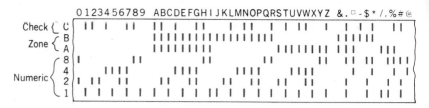

FIGURE 4-8

Seven-channel magnetic tape code.

ters. Figure 4-9 shows a few characters coded in the nine-channel format. The most frequently used tracks are grouped near the center of the tape so as to reduce the chances of losing data owing to the physical deterioration of the outer edges of the tape. This arrangement gives the code format a peculiar appearance. The equivalent seven-channel tape code positions are shown in Figure 4-9 to aid in interpretation. For example, the numeral 7 is represented here by an "on" condition in the four zone positions and in the channels equivalent to 4, 2, and 1.

Magnetic tape, like paper tape, is a continuous-length, sequential file medium. How then can the computer distinguish between different records on the tape? The answer is that the records are separated by blank spaces in the tape called *interrecord gaps*. Figure 4-10 shows an accounts-receivable file organized on magnetic tape. Customer records may be of varying lengths. They may also be combined into tape *blocks* of several records (Figure 4-11). Interrecord gaps are automatically created by the computer system after the last character in a record (or block of records) has been recorded.

FIGURE 4-9

Nine-channel extended magnetic tape code.

Track number	Equivalent 7-channel tape code position			
		0123456789	ABCMNOXYZ	&$*,/'%
9	8			
8	2			
7	Added zone			
6	Added zone			
5	B			
4	Check*			
3	A			
2	1			
1	4			

*The check position here produces odd parity.

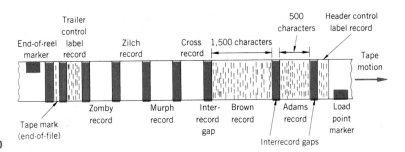

FIGURE 4-10

The first several feet of tape are unrecorded to allow for threading on the equipment. A reflective marker known as the *load point* indicates to the equipment the beginning of usable tape, while a similar *end-of-reel* marker signals the end of usable tape. The markers are placed on opposite edges of the tape for machine identification purposes. Between the load-point marker and the first data record is a *header control label,* which identifies the tape contents, gives the number of the program to be used when the tape is processed, and supplies other control information that helps to prevent an important tape from accidentally being erased. Following the last data record in a file is a *trailer control label,* which contains a count of the number of blocks in a file. A comparison between the number of blocks processed and the number in the file may be made to determine that all have been accounted for. The end of a file may be signaled by a special one-character record. This special character is called a *tape mark.*

FIGURE 4-11
Fewer interrecord gaps save tape and speed data input. This is important when record lengths are short. The program of instructions separates the records within a block for processing.

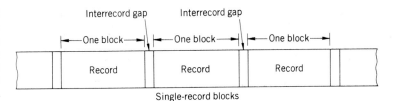

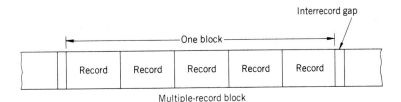

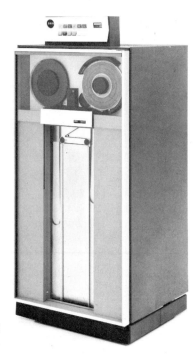

FIGURE 4-12

Magnetic tape unit (courtesy IBM
Corporation).

Magnetic Tape Equipment

The magnetic tape unit shown in Figure 4-12 is used for both data
input (*reading*) and output (recording or *writing*). Called by such
names as *tape drives* and *tape transports,* these machines read and
write data on the tape by the use of *read-write heads* (Figure 4-13).
There is one read-write head for each tape channel. Each head is a
small electromagnet with minute gaps between the poles. In the
writing operation, the tape moves over the gaps while electric pulses
from the CPU flow through the write coils of the appropriate heads
causing the iron-oxide coating of the tape to be magnetized in the
proper pattern. When the tape is being read, the magnetized patterns induce pulses of current in the read coils that feed the data into
the CPU.

The tape is loaded onto the tape drive in much the same way that
a movie projector is threaded (Figure 4-14). The tape movement
during processing is from the supply reel past the read-write heads
to the take-up reel.

There are usually several tape drives used in an installation. In
most applications, a tape is either read or written in a single pass.
Therefore, if we wish to update our master accounts-receivable file,

FIGURE 4-13

Two-gap read-write head.

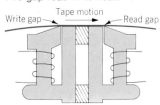

Write gap — Tape motion — Read gap

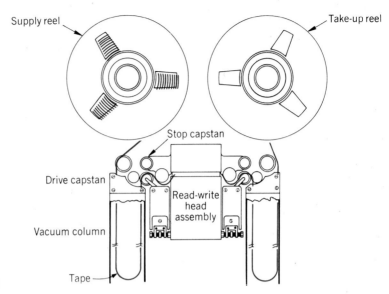

Supply reel

Take-up reel

Stop capstan

Drive capstan

Read-write head assembly

Vacuum column

Tape

FIGURE 4-14

we may have one unit reading in the old master file, another feeding in recent transactions, a third introducing the processing instructions, and a fourth writing the updated master file.

Advantages and Limitations of Magnetic Tape

One *advantage* of magnetic tape is that the data density is far greater than that of cards and paper tape. (One standard reel of magnetic tape is capable of storing as much information as 250,000 punched cards.) In addition, a tape costs less than the hundreds of thousands of cards that it can replace, storage space is reduced, and the tape can be reused many times. Neither cards nor punched tape can compare with magnetic tape in I/O speed.

Unfortunately, however, magnetic tape has several *limitations*. It is not generally suitable for jobs that require rapid and random access to particular records. Tape file processing is also not efficient when the job being processed calls for the use of only a small proportion of the total tape records. In either situation, too much time is wasted in reading records that will not be used. Furthermore, the magnetized spots are invisible and cannot be read directly by humans, but specks of dust on a tape may be read as data characters or may cause an improper reading. Finally, careful control procedures must be followed to prevent an important file from being erased by mistake. (Instead of losing a card or two, the entire file might be lost—a revolting development!)

Many organizations make use of the I/O media and devices we have now examined to perform much of their batch processing work. But many concerns also utilize different types of direct-access devices in their processing operations.

DIRECT-ACCESS DEVICES

In the remainder of this chapter we shall look at different types of popular direct-access devices used for I/O and online secondary storage. It is interesting to note that some of these devices are *flexible* in the sense that the storage instruments associated with their use may be either online or offline. Magnetic disk packs, for example, can be used indefinitely for online purposes. But the disks (and the data contained) can be removed and stored offline just like tapes and cards. It is also interesting to note that *selection among direct-access devices involves compromise*. As Figure 4-4 shows, there is frequently an inverse relationship between I/O speed on the one hand and storage capacity on the other. That is, as online storage capacity increases, the I/O speeds decline. Also, as online storage capacity increases, the cost per character stored tends to decrease.

Magnetic Drums

Magnetic drums were an early means of primary storage. Now, however, they are generally used as online secondary storage when fast response is of greater importance than large capacity. For example, they may be used to store mathematical tables, data, or program modifications that are frequently referred to during processing operations.

A magnetic drum is a cylinder that has an outer surface plated with a metallic magnetizable film. A motor rotates the drum on its axis at a constant and rapid rate. Data are *recorded on* the rotating drum and *read from* the drum by *read-write heads,* which are positioned a fraction of an inch from the drum surface. The recording and reading operations are similar to those used with magnetic tape. The writing of new data on the drum erases data previously stored at the location. The magnetic spots written on the drum surface remain indefinitely until they, too, are erased at a future time. Reading of data recorded on the drum is accomplished as the magnetized spots pass under the read heads and induce electric pulses in the read coils.

The stored data are arranged in *bands* or *tracks* around the circumference of the drum. A *fixed* read-write head may be employed for *each* band, or horizontally movable heads (each of which serve a *number* of adjacent bands) may be used.

The computer is able to access stored records directly because each drum has a specific number of addressable locations. A band may be divided into sections, and each section may be given an identifying number. The *direct-access time*—i.e., the elapsed time between the instant when a data transfer from (or to) a storage device is called for and the instant when the transfer is completed—is basically determined by the delay time required for an addressed location to be positioned under a read-write head.[3] If there is a read-write head for each band on the drum, then the speed of rotation will determine the *rotational delay* and thus the access time; if there is only one read-write head for a number of bands, then there will be a further *positional delay* while the head is moved and positioned over the proper band.

Magnetic Disks

Magnetic disks are the most popular direct-access I/O and online storage medium. They are typically made of thin metal plates coated on both sides with a magnetizable recording material. Although disks in some units remain permanently in their cabinets, a more popular approach is for several disks (the number varies) to be permanently mounted in *disk pack* form on a vertical shaft which rotates at a high, constant speed. A space is left between the spinning disks to allow access arms with small read-write heads to move to any storage location. Data are organized into a number of concentric circles or *tracks,* each of which has a designated location number. There are typically 200 or more tracks on the disk surface (Figure 4-15).

Reading and writing operations are similar to those for drums. Data are recorded in specific locations as magnetized spots. Figure 4-16 shows one type of read-write head arrangement. Arms move horizontally among the individual disks. The two heads mounted on each arm service *two* surfaces—the top and the underside of a disk.

---

[3]Technically speaking, most online devices, including drums, have *direct* but not *random* access to records. *Random access* refers to a storage device in which the access time is independent of the physical location of the data. Since the drum access time varies with the physical location of stored data, it is more technically correct to say that drums provide direct access. The distinction is often not observed, however, and the online units presented here are often described as random-access equipment.

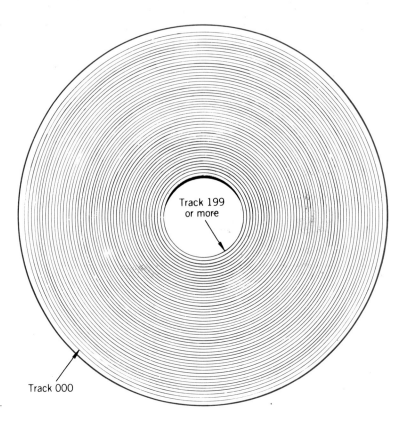

FIGURE 4-15

Tracks on disk surface.

Track 000

Track 199
or more

FIGURE 4-16

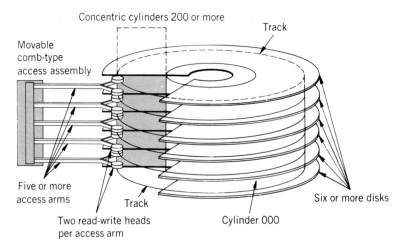

Concentric cylinders 200 or more

Track

Movable
comb-type
access assembly

Five or more
access arms

Track

Two read-write heads
per access arm

Cylinder 000

Six or more disks

On command from the CPU, the proper head moves to the specified disk surface and track, and the desired data are read as soon as their location spins under the head. Since the heads for *all* disks move in and out *together,* a number of related records extending vertically through the disk pack may be quickly accessible. For example, if the access arm that serves the top recording surface is positioned at the twentieth track, each of the other access arms would be *similarly positioned.* Thus, *each* of the read-write heads could operate on data in the twentieth track. All the twentieth tracks together make up the twentieth *cylinder* of the disk pack. Just as there are 200 or more tracks on a single surface, so, too, are there 200 or more cylinders in a disk pack (see Figure 4-16).

Other reading-writing arrangements are possible. Some devices have multiple read-write heads on a single access arm (each head serves a number of adjacent tracks), and some devices have a separate head for *each* track. What advantages over the arrangement shown in Figure 4-16 do you think there might be to these alternatives?

Interchangeable disk packs come in various sizes and storage capacities. The pack held by the operator in Figure 4-17, for exam-

FIGURE 4-17
Disk storage facility (courtesy IBM
Corporation).

ple, contains 12 disks and 20 recording surfaces (the top and bottom disks of the pack are used to protect the data surfaces). Storage capacity of the pack is 100 million characters. It may be housed in the unit shown in Figure 4-17 with seven others to provide a total of 800 million characters of storage. Interchangeable single "floppy" disks are also used in minicomputer systems. The flexible disk is stored in a paper or plastic covering, as shown in Figure 4-18, and is not removed from this protective envelope. Rather, the envelope is inserted into the disk drive, the disk rotates inside the envelope, and the read-write head accesses the disk surface through a slot in the covering.

The access time required for data to be transferred from a disk to primary storage (and vice versa) is determined by such factors as: (1) the number of access arms (if only a single arm is used, there is a *vertical* positional delay); (2) the amount of *horizontal movement* (or *seek time*) required for the arm to position a head over the proper track (to answer the question you were asked a few sentences earlier, multiple heads on each arm reduce the average length of movement and thus decrease the access time, but they are more expensive); and (3) the *rotational delay* (or *search time*) encountered, i.e., the time required to move the needed data under the read-write head.

Advantages and limitations of magnetic disks When compared with magnetic tape, disks have the *advantage* of providing quick and direct access to records without the need to sort transactions into a specific order. Also, a single input transaction into a data

FIGURE 4-18
Dual diskette drive (courtesy Data
General Corporation).

"Oh, I'm sorry . . . . . I thought this was a laundromat."

© DATAMATION ®

base may be used to quickly update records in several related files stored on different disks.

But disks also have *limitations* when compared with magnetic tape. Disks are more expensive than the tape required to provide the same storage capacity; sequential batch processing using disks may be slower and less efficient than when tapes are used; and it may not be feasible (as it is with tape) to keep old disk master files unchanged for backup purposes when disk-stored records are updated.

Magnetic Cards and Strips

Wouldn't it be nice to combine the magnetic tape advantages of low cost and high storage capacity with the advantages of rapid and direct record accessibility? This is essentially the objective of devices that utilize magnetic cards and tape strips for mass online storage. A magnetic card may be considered to be a length of flexible plastic material upon which short strips of magnetic tape have been mounted. A number of cards may be placed in a cartridge which, like disk packs, may be removed and stored offline. One device (the IBM Data Cell) uses a card cartridge that resembles a snare drum, and another (the IBM 3850 Mass Storage System or MSS) arranges tube-shaped cartridges in honeycomb storage compartments (Figure 4-19).

Card and strip equipment has high storage capacity (the MSS, for example, can store online the contents of over 100,000 books of the

FIGURE 4-19
(Courtesy IBM Corporation).

size you are reading), and the cost per character stored is very low. Data are erasable, but access speed is slow when compared with drums and disks.

SUMMARY   The information needed by managers is the output obtained by processing files. These files may be organized either sequentially or randomly. Batch processing is possible with files organized in either way. A wide variety of I/O media and devices is available, and many factors must be considered in their selection.

Punched cards are a familiar medium. They are easily understood, and they possess advantages because of their fixed length and unit record nature. However, their data density is low, they are bulky, and they represent a slow means of input and output. Punched paper tape provides greater data density than cards, but, like cards, paper tape is a relatively slow I/O medium.

Magnetic tape is much faster. Its transfer rate is significantly improved by its high data density. It can be erased and reused many times and is thus very economical. Data may be recorded on some other medium and then transferred to magnetic tape by a conversion process, or several alternative data entry approaches may be used to key data from source documents directly onto magnetic tape. Data are usually represented by either a seven- or nine-channel code, and parity checking is used to reduce the chance of error. However, the coded magnetized spots are invisible, and thus a printing operation is required to check or verify tape data. Tape records lack random accessibility.

When direct access to records is required, several types of devices may be used for I/O and online secondary storage. Selection from among these devices typically involves compromise: There is frequently an inverse relationship between the speed of data transfer on the one hand and storage capacity on the other. Magnetic drum units, for example, tend to provide faster data transfer than magnetic disk devices, but disks tend to provide greater storage capacity. Magnetic disks are currently the most popular direct-access medium.

REVIEW AND DISCUSSION QUESTIONS

1 How are data organized in business information systems, i.e., what organizational hierarchy is employed?

2 Discuss the factors to be considered in selecting the alternative I/O media and devices.

3 Compare and contrast the characteristics of sound tapes and phonograph records with those of magnetic tapes and magnetic disks.

4 A punched card is a triple-purpose medium. (**a**) What is the meaning of triple purpose? (**b**) What other media are triple purpose?

5 Define the following terms: (**a**) Turnaround document, (**b**) Read punch, (**c**) Data density, (**d**) Channels, (**e**) Frame, (**f**) Parity checking, (**g**) Transfer rate, (**h**) Tape-recording density, (**i**) Interrecord gaps, (**j**) Load-point marker, (**k**) Header label, (**l**) Trailer label, (**m**) Record, (**n**) Item, (**o**) Direct-access time, (**p**) Disk pack, (**q**) Seek time, (**r**) Search time.

6 Discuss the advantages and limitations of punched cards.

7 Discuss the advantages and limitations of punched paper tape.

8 Explain how data are read from and written on magnetic tape.

9 Discuss the advantages and limitations of magnetic tape.

10 Explain the approaches used to provide direct data entry on magnetic tape.

11 "With direct-access devices there is frequently an inverse relationship between speed and cost per character stored, on the one hand, and storage capacity on the other." Explain and give examples, using Figure 4-4.

12 (**a**) What factors determine the direct-access time of magnetic drums? (**b**) What factors determine the direct-access time of magnetic disks?

13 A manufacturer makes a disk drive that has permanently mounted disks, and each disk has a read-write head for each track. What might be the advantages and limitations of this approach?

14 When compared with magnetic tape, what are the advantages and limitations of magnetic disks?

COMPUTER INPUT/OUTPUT: II

LEARNING OBJECTIVES

After studying this chapter and answering the discussion questions, you should be able to:

Summarize the uses, advantages, and limitations of direct-input devices utilizing MICR and OCR character-reading techniques.

Discuss the approaches used to produce high-speed printed and microfilmed output from computers.

Describe the use of online terminals in multiunit data stations, visual display applications, and distributed processing systems.

Identify and discuss the most commonly used services for transmitting data from one location to another.

Distinguish between serial and overlapped processing.

A s we saw in the last chapter, data are often taken from printed documents and recorded in machine-acceptable form by a manual keying operation. Several devices, however, have been designed to eliminate manual keying by reading the characters printed on the source documents and converting the data *directly* into computer-usable *input.* In the first pages of this chapter we shall look at these *character readers,* which are generally used in high-volume, batch processing applications. *High-speed printing* and *microfilming output* devices are then considered. Finally, some I/O devices that are frequently found in *online, random-access processing situations* along with some *complimentary tools and concepts that facilitate I/O operations* are discussed. Figure 5-1 presents a summary of some of the equipment included in this chapter.

MAGNETIC INK CHARACTER RECOGNITION

The magnetic ink character recognition (MICR) concept is widely used by banking and financial institutions as a means of processing the tremendous volume of checks being written. Figure 5-2 shows a sample check coded with a special ink which contains tiny iron-oxide magnetizable particles. The code number of the bank to which the check will be written and the depositor's account number are precoded on the checks. The first bank to receive the check after it has been written encodes the amount in the lower right corner. The check at this point may then be handled automatically through regular bank collection channels—e.g., from (1) the initial bank receiving the check to, perhaps, (2) the Federal Reserve bank to (3) the depositor's bank to (4) the depositor's account.

FIGURE 5-1

Summary of I/O media and devices—Chapter 5.

Medium	Input Device Used	Output Device Used	I/O Speed Range, Characters/Second	
			Input	Output
Magnetic ink	MICR reader		700–3,200	
Paper documents	OCR reader		100–3,600	
	Keyboard	Character printer	5–120	5–120
		Line printer		440–39,000
Microfilm		Recorder		25,000–300,000
None		CRT visual display		250–50,000

YOUR NAME   No. *84*   53-105
                                                        113

                                    August 12 ___ 19 ___

PAY TO THE   *A.B.C. Distributing Company* $ *150 96*
ORDER OF
        One Hundred Fifty and 96/100 ————————— DOLLARS

Valley Bank   S A M P L E   O N L Y
AND TRUST COMPANY
SPRINGFIELD · MASSACHUSETTS
                            1738-323 4

   ⑆0113⑈0105⑆   ⑆738⑈323 4⑈   ⑈00000 ⑈5096⑈

Combined			Check	Amount of item
Routing symbol	Transit number	Account number	digit	

FIGURE 5-2

(Courtesy NCR).   Numbers at bottom of check are printed in approved E-13B character shape

Magnetic ink character *reader-sorter* units (Figure 5-3) interpret the encoded checks and make the resulting data available to the CPU. They also sort the checks by account number, bank number, etc., into pockets. As checks enter the reading unit, they pass through a strong magnetic field which causes the iron-oxide particles in the ink to become magnetized. The read heads in the unit are then able to produce recognizable electronic signals as the magnetized characters pass beneath them.

There are several *advantages* associated with the use of MICR. First, checks may be roughly handled, folded, smeared, and stamped, yet this does not prevent recognition with a high degree of accuracy. Second, processing is speeded because checks can be fed directly into the input device. And third, the type font used is easily recognized and read, if necessary, by clerical personnel. The

FIGURE 5-3

MICR   reader-sorter   (courtesy
Burroughs Corporation).

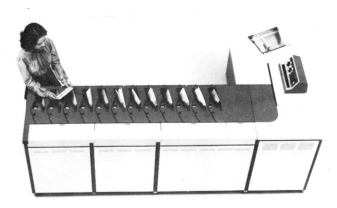

primary *limitation* of MICR is that only a *small number of characters* are used. Since it was designed by and for the banking industry, MICR uses only the 14 characters needed for bank processing. No alphabetic characters are available.

OPTICAL CHARACTER RECOGNITION

Unlike MICR, optical character recognition (OCR) techniques make possible the reading of *any* printed character (not just 14), and no special ink is required. Thus, the flexibility of OCR may make it possible for organizations to eliminate or reduce the input keying bottleneck.

Although machines are available that will read hand-printed characters, the automatic reading of handwritten script is still some years in the future. (While your penmanship is undoubtedly beautiful, the author's presents a formidable challenge to the equipment designers.) Most OCR devices being used in business are designed to read *machine-printed* characters, bar codes, and simple handmade marks.

One popular use of OCR is in credit card billing. When a credit sale is made at a gasoline station, for example, the attendant uses an inexpensive imprinter to record the data from the customer's credit card and the amount of the transaction onto a form that is then forwarded to a central processing point. There the document is read automatically by an optical instrument prior to computer processing. Figure 5-4 traces pictorially the approach used by one optical reading system.

In another growing application of optical scanning, light and dark bars are used to code products sold in retail stores. This Universal Product Code (UPC) is printed on the product by the manufacturer. The next time you spring (?) out of bed at 6 A.M. to have a hearty breakfast before your 8 o'clock class, you might find (champion that you are) that your cereal box has a code similar to the one shown in Figure 5-5. When UPC-marked items are received at a merchant's automated checkout stand (Figure 5-6), they are pulled across a scanning window and placed in bags. As items are scanned, the UPC symbol is decoded and the data are transmitted to a computer that looks up the price, possibly updates inventory and sales records, and forwards price and description information back to the check stand.

The primary *advantage* of OCR is that it eliminates some of the duplication of human effort required to get data into the computer. This reduction in human effort (1) can *improve the quality (accuracy)* of input data and (2) can *improve the timeliness of information processed.* However, *difficulties* in using OCR equipment may be

Data are then recorded on magnetic tape and/or line printer

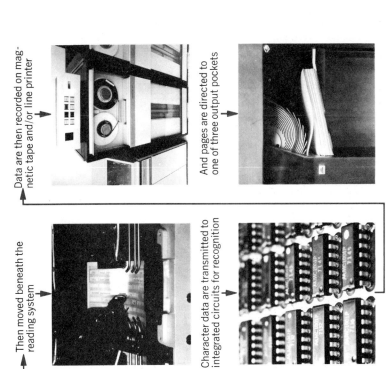

Then moved beneath the reading system

And pages are directed to one of three output pockets

Character data are transmitted to integrated circuits for recognition

Programmed controller directs input operation

Pages are automatically fed from the input hopper

Pages containing many possible character patterns are placed in the input hopper

```
O P Q R S T U V
M N V 4 5 6 7 8
t u v 4 5 6 7 8
a a A 4 5 6 7 8
K W A 4 5 6 7 8
M C B 4 5 6 7 8
/ 2 3 4 5 6 7 8
N O P 4 5 6 7 8
```

FIGURE 5-4
(Courtesy Recognition Equipment, Inc.).

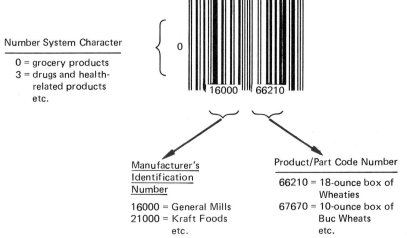

Number System Character

0 = grocery products
3 = drugs and health-
related products
etc.

16000 66210

Manufacturer's
Identification
Number

16000 = General Mills
21000 = Kraft Foods
etc.

Product/Part Code Number

66210 = 18-ounce box of
Wheaties
67670 = 10-ounce box of
Buc Wheats
etc.

FIGURE 5-5
Universal Product Code for box of
Wheaties.

encountered when documents to be read are poorly typed or have
strikeovers, erasures, etc. Also, form design and ink specifications
become more critical and must be more standardized than is the
case when keypunch source documents are prepared. Finally, many
optical readers are not economically feasible unless the daily volume of transactions is relatively high.

FIGURE 5-6
Optical scanning checkout
(courtesy IBM Corporation).

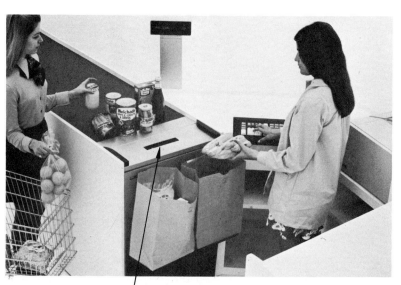

Optical scanning window

FIGURE 5-7

High-speed impact line printer (courtesy Sperry UNIVAC Division, Sperry Rand Corporation).

PRINTED AND MICROFILMED OUTPUT

High-Speed Printers

High-speed printers (Figure 5-7) provide information *output* from the CPU in the form of permanently printed characters which have meaning to humans. They are the primary output device when the information is to be used by people rather than by machine.

Significant improvements have been made in printers in the past few years. Many of the earliest printers were merely souped-up, one-character-at-a-time versions of electric typewriters. But these inadequate units soon gave way to *line-at-a-time impact printers* that are many times faster.

Impact printing is performed by the familiar method of pressing a typeface against paper and inked ribbon. There are, however, *nonimpact* printers available that are much faster in their operation than the impact type.[1] Since the vast majority of high-speed printers in use today are of the impact type, however, we shall limit our study to these machines.

Line printers do not have movable carriages. Rather, they use rapidly moving chains (or trains) of printing slugs or some form of a print *cylinder* to print lines of information on paper moving past the printing station. Figure 5-8 illustrates the *print chain* concept. The links in the chain are engraved character-printing slugs. The chain is capable of producing a number of different characters (in Figure 5-8, there are 48), and there are several sections of the character set in

---

[1]Impact printers will print up to two thousand 132-character lines per minute; nonimpact devices may utilize laser, electrical, and chemical technologies to produce reports at speeds of up to 18,000 lines per minute.

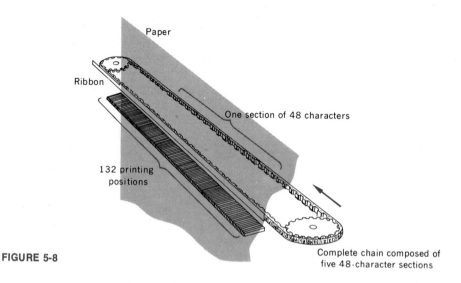

Paper

Ribbon

One section of 48 characters

132 printing
positions

FIGURE 5-8

Complete chain composed of
five 48-character sections

the length of the chain. The chain moves at a constant and rapid speed past the printing positions. Magnetically controlled hammers behind the paper are timed to force the paper against the proper print slugs. The ribbon between the paper and the character leaves an imprint on the paper as a result of the impact.

The *drum printer* uses a solid cylinder. Raised characters extend the length of the drum (Figure 5-9). There are as many circular *bands* of type as there are printing positions. Each band contains all the possible characters. The drum turns at a constant speed, with one revolution being required to print each line. A fast-acting hammer opposite each band picks out the proper character and strikes the paper against that character. Thus, in one rotation, hammers of

FIGURE 5-9

A print drum.

The number of bands corresponds
to the number of printing positions

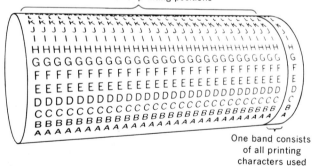

One band consists
of all printing
characters used

"Not only is it a fake, but it's been done with an on-line plotter!"

several printing positions may "fire" when the A row appears; several others may strike to imprint D's, etc. At the end of the rotation, all necessary positions on the paper are printed. The paper then moves to the next line.

In addition to printing computer output in the form of characters, some devices are also capable of producing graphical output under computer control. For example, a computer-controlled *plotter* can produce engineering drawings, maps, and other pictorial output in a very short time.

The COM Approach

In spite of printer progress, there is still a substantial mismatch between output by printing and output by the use of other media such as magnetic tape.[2] Even when multiple printers are used (see Figure 1-15, page 32), only a small portion of the time of the CPU may be needed to drive these units. Thus, in some cases it is more efficient and economical to reduce the role of the printer by replacing paper output documents with *microfilm.*

The computer-output-to-microfilm (COM) approach is shown in Figure 5-10. Output information may be read onto magnetic tape and then, in an offline operation, recorded on microfilm. Or, the *microfilm recorder* may receive the information directly from the CPU. Most

---

[2]Magnetic tape drives, you may recall, can write characters at the rate of over 300,000 per *second;* the fastest impact printer cannot write that many characters in a minute.

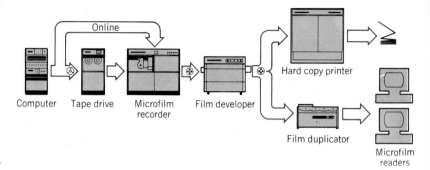

FIGURE 5-10

Computer output to microfilm.

microfilm recorders project the characters of output information onto the screen of a *cathode ray tube* (CRT), which is similar to a television picture tube. A high-speed microfilm camera then films the displayed information at speeds much faster than are possible with printers. After being developed, the film can be viewed directly through special readers by the users of the information; when necessary, paper documents can be produced from the film by a special printer.

Much of the tremendous volume of data and information that enters and leaves business computers each year is processed by the I/O media and machines that have now been introduced. However, other means of communication between people and machine are possible. In the following pages we shall examine some I/O devices that may have the ability to (1) produce direct I/O of information without data-recording media being *required,* (2) create an online relationship between user and machine, and (3) handle economically a lower and/or more irregular volume of input data.

ONLINE TERMINALS

Yon Console
It twinkles as the starry night.
O, what a beauty is in thee!
Through eons, neons shining bright,
For an admiring world to see.
And should there be a program plight
'Twill guide us to the glitch with glee.
Jackson Granholm

One type of online terminal is located near the *console control panel* of the central processor (see Figure 5-11). The control panel is used, among other things, to display the contents of a number of special CPU storage locations during program execution, determine the

Console typewriter

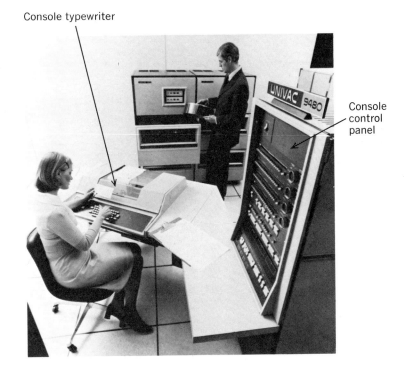

Console control panel

FIGURE 5-11

Computer console (courtesy Sperry UNIVAC Division, Sperry Rand Corporation).

causes of certain equipment malfunctions, and reset the computer after malfunctions have been corrected. And the console keyboard enables the computer operator to enter data directly into and receive information directly from the storage unit of the central processor. When the keys are depressed, the code designation of the keyed characters is entered into storage. A visual record is also typed or displayed. In addition, the console keyboard may be used to (1) modify a portion of the program instructions, (2) test the program, (3) inquire about the contents of certain storage areas, and (4) determine intermediate computing results.

Online terminals may be classified as (1) *typewriterlike machines,* (2) *multiunit data stations,* (3) *visual display units,* or (4) *intelligent devices.*

Typewriter Terminals

Typewriter terminals may be quite similar to console typewriters, but they are located away from the computer room. They may be in the next office, in a nearby building, or in the next state. And they may be connected to the CPU by a short cable or by a complex data communications system. Users transmit input data via the keyboard and receive output information from the character-at-a-time typewriter.

Multiunit Data Stations

The term *multiunit data stations* may be used in several ways to describe the equipment used in particular types of applications. Let us look at some of the possibilities.

1 *Remote job-entry stations* Data may be read into a distant CPU by multiple station units. Card and tape readers and/or a manual keyboard may be used for *input,* and *output* information may be either visually displayed or printed at the station. A wide variety of I/O options is available.

2 *Data collection stations* These stations (and the transaction recording stations discussed below) typically perform limited operations. They have been developed to get data from remote points into the computer as quickly as possible. For example, data collection stations are often used in factories to control the inventory of parts and materials used in production. Let us assume that an employee needs a dozen hinges to complete a job. The hinges may be obtained from a supply point. A data collection terminal may then be used to transmit the type and number of hinges taken along with the job number to the computer. After an accuracy check is made, the data are accepted and used to update inventory and job cost records.

3 *Transaction recording stations* Savings institutions are among the leading users of online transaction recording devices (Figure 5-12). Let us assume that a deposit is to be made by a customer. The customer presents his or her bankbook and the amount of the deposit to the teller, who inserts the book into a recorder and keys in the transaction data. The data are then sent to the computer, which adjusts the customer's savings balance. The updated information is relayed back to the remote station where it is entered in the customer's bankbook. The entire transaction is accounted for in a matter of seconds. And in addition to teller-operated terminals, unattended *automated teller machines* may be located on or off the financial institution's premises to receive and dispense cash and to handle routine financial transactions. For example, you might use a plastic "currency" or "debit" card (which incorporates, perhaps, a magnetically encoded strip of material to supply the computer

FIGURE 5-12

(Courtesy Burroughs Corporation)

with your account number and credit limit) to make a deposit to your account, to withdraw cash, or to achieve an *electronic transfer of funds* from your account to the account of one of your creditors.

4 *Point-of-sale stations* As you saw in Figure 5-6, point-of-sale (POS) terminals with automated scanning features are replacing cash registers in supermarkets because they can do everything a cash register does plus many other things. And other POS terminals in department stores can be used to (*a*) make direct inquiry about the credit status of the customer, (*b*) improve inventory control, and (*c*) produce faster and more accurate sales information. Such a POS terminal may be equipped with a handheld "wand" that can be used to speed up the sales transaction. By passing the wand across a special tag attached to the merchandise, the clerk reads the item description and price into the terminal. (Credit card numbers can also be read in this way.) The terminal may then automatically display the price, compute the total amount of the purchase including taxes, and print a sales receipt. Finally, electronic funds transfer system (EFTS) terminals connected to bank computers may be located at the checkout counters of retail stores, hospitals, hotels, etc. (Figure 5-13) to (*a*) transfer funds between accounts—e.g., from the shopper's to the merchant's account; (*b*) identify customers, authorize credit, and/or authorize debit or credit card cash advances; and (*c*) guarantee the availability of funds to cover customer checks.

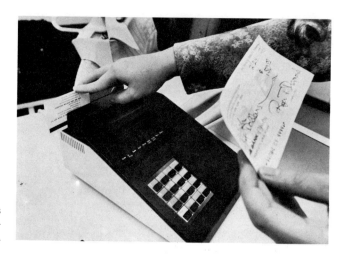

FIGURE 5-13

POS station for electronic funds transfer (courtesy IBM Corporation).

Visual Display Terminals

Considerable emphasis is now being placed on visual display terminals, which look like small television sets equipped with a manual keyboard. Although input by means of the keyboard may be no faster than with typing, output is silent and very fast—the screen of the terminal's CRT can be instantly covered with hundreds of characters of displayed information.

There are two basic classes of CRT display terminals. In the *first* category are lower-cost units, which display *only alphanumeric* information. In the *second* class are expensive units, which are capable of projecting graphs, charts, and designs as well as alphanumeric characters. The first category might be considered a clever "paperless electronic typewriter"; the second class of display units possesses graphic art capabilities not available with typewriter devices. Let us briefly look at some of the ways in which these display units are currently being used.

Alphanumeric display applications Terminals that display only alphanumeric information are well suited for the following purposes:

1 *Obtaining quick response to inquiries* The visual display unit provides a window into the computer's data base. Status of a customer's credit, prices quoted on stock exchanges, current inventory levels, availability of airline seats, locations of truck shipments and railroad freight cars, locations of unsold seats in

a theater or stadium, location and telephone number of students and employees of a university—information such as this is being kept current by various organizations in online files so that it is instantly available for display upon inquiry.

2 *Providing convenient human/machine interaction* We saw in Chapter 2 that data management software would enable a manager to probe and query files in order to obtain information relevant to some unique problem. The combination of an easy-to-use inquiry language and a visual display unit facilitates this process. The manager may carry on a "conversation" with the computer system by supplying data and key phrases, while the system responds with displayed end results, intermediate results, or questions. The questions may be in a multiple-choice format so that the manager need only key in the response number.

Graphical display applications When a designer first gets a new-product thought, he or she may make some preliminary sketches to get the idea down on paper so that it may be more thoroughly analyzed. As the design is modified, additional drawings may be required; when the idea is approved, further detailed production drawings are prepared. Thus, the preparation of drawings may occupy a substantial portion of the designer's time.

Large input tablet

CRT
graphical
display
unit

Small input tablet

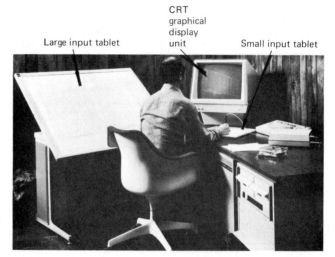

FIGURE 5-14
Interactive graphic design
(courtesy Tektronix, Inc.).

In recent years, visual *input* instruments such as *input tablets*[3] and *electronic light pens*[4] have been developed which make it possible for the computer to receive human sketching directly. As the designer draws (Figure 5-14), the computer may display the developing sketch on the CRT. Changes and modifications in the drawing can be quickly made; e.g., a line can be "erased" from (or shifted on) the display unit with a movement of a special pen. Once the initial sketching is finished and displayed on the CRT to the satisfaction of the designer, the computer may then be instructed to analyze the design and report on certain characteristics. For example, the computer might be asked to work out the acoustical charac-

---

[3]An input tablet may be made of glass or plastic and may come in different sizes as shown in Figure 5-14. The tablet typically contains hundreds of copper lines, which form a fine grid that is connected with the computer. Each copper line receives electric impulses. A special pen or stylus attached to the tablet is sensitive to these impulses and is used to form the sketches. However, the pen does not mark directly on the tablet. To communicate with the machine, the designer merely draws on a piece of paper placed on the glass or plastic. The tablet grid then senses the exact position of the stylus as it is moved and transmits this information to the computer.

[4]The electronic light pen is a photocell placed in a small tube. When the pen is moved by the user over the screen, it is able to detect the light coming from a limited field of view. The light from the CRT causes the photocell to respond when the pen is pointed directly at a lighted area. These electronic responses are transmitted to the computer which is able to determine that part of the displayed information that is triggering the photocell response.

teristics of a theater that the designer has sketched. The sketch may then be modified by the designer on the basis of the computer analysis, or the machine may be instructed to display a theater with more desirable acoustics. Such direct human/machine graphical communication enables the designer to (1) learn what effect certain changes have on the project and (2) save valuable time for more creative work. Graphical display techniques are currently being used in the design of ships, highways, aircraft, electronic circuits, and buildings.

Intelligent Terminals

By combining programmable microcomputers or minicomputers with terminal hardware, designers have built terminal systems (Figure 5-15) that are similar to some smaller computer installations. In fact, the distinction between the small stand-alone computers in a computing network and these *intelligent terminals* is becoming blurred.

A growing number of organizations are using intelligent terminals as an integral part of a *distributed processing system.* On the local level, small jobs are processed using the terminal's user-program-

FIGURE 5-15
Intelligent terminal with self-standing computing capability using COBOL, RPG, and BASIC high-level programming languages (courtesy Datapoint Corporation).

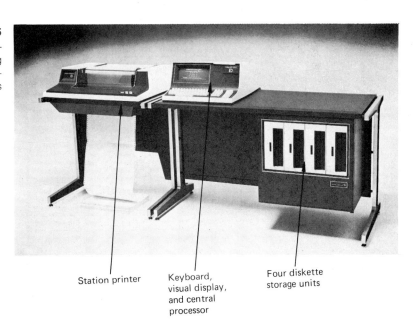

Station printer   Keyboard, visual display, and central processor   Four diskette storage units

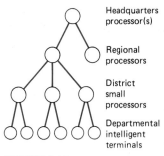

FIGURE 5-16
Hierarchical distributed processing system.

mable microcomputer or minicomputer and assorted peripheral and secondary storage devices without any interaction with a higher-level computer. But the terminals are also used to make programmed error-detection checks to determine the validity of locally produced data and to classify and order these facts in a specified way prior to forwarding them to the computer(s) at a higher level in the organization for storage or further processing. The higher-level computer(s) in the organization may be used to manage large data bases and to serve the lower-level processors by executing jobs that require extensive computations. In short, intelligent terminals may be low-level satellite processors in a distributed processing *hierarchy* that may have several levels (see Figure 5-16).

VOICE COMMUNICATION

Input units, basically, do nothing more than convert human language into machine language. Why, then, doesn't someone invent a machine that will enable a person to talk to the computer in English? As a matter of fact, a few manufacturers have done just that. Although the vocabulary is quite small, sound waves have been converted into machine language. Speech recognition, however, is not a widely used input technique at this time.

When we look at the *output* side of verbal communication, however, we find that computers are now being used to give English responses in reply to human inquiries transmitted to a central computer over regular telephone lines. All the spoken words needed to process the possible inquiries are generally prerecorded on a magnetic or photographic film drum. Each word is given a code. When inquiries are received, the processor composes a reply message in a coded form. This coded message is then transmitted to an *audio-response* device, which assembles the words in the proper sequence and transmits the audio message back to the station requesting the information.

Audio-response techniques, combined with briefcase-sized keyboard devices, turn every standard telephone into a potential computer terminal. An equipment sales representative, for example, can use any available phone to check on product availability prior to contacting an important customer. An inquiry may be keyed directly into the home-office computer system. A computer-compiled audio response could then give the sales representative the necessary inventory information. If the sales efforts lead to success, another phone may later be used to enter an order directly into the information system.

DATA COMMUNICATIONS

Data communication refers to the means and methods of transferring data between processing locations. It is certainly not a new activity. Human runners and messengers have been used since the beginning of recorded history. The Greek runner carrying the message of victory on the plains of Marathon has inspired a present-day athletic event. And the Pony Express won the admiration of a nation in the brief period of time before it was replaced by telegraph service.

Data Transmission Services

Data transmission services are available from telephone, telegraph, and other companies. Figure 5-17 shows the most commonly used transmission *channels* for carrying data from one location to another. Since many of the data transmission channels now in use are telephone facilities that were designed primarily for voice communications, you will notice in Figure 5-17 that between the computing

FIGURE 5-17

Data transmission services.

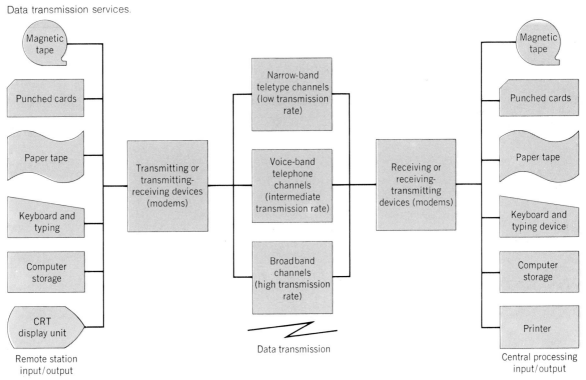

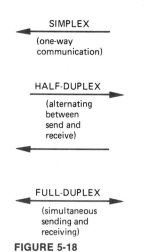

FIGURE 5-18

Data transmission circuits.

equipment and the transmission channels are located devices called *modems* which convert the computing equipment digital signals into signals that can be used by voice-oriented transmission systems.[5] You will also notice in Figure 5-18 that three types of circuits are used for data transmission purposes. The *simplex circuit* permits data to flow in *only* one direction. A terminal connected to such a circuit would be either a *send-only* or *receive-only* device. But a terminal connected to a *half-duplex* line could *alternately* send data to and then receive information from a CPU. Half-duplex circuits are widely used. When two-way *simultaneous* transmission is needed between a terminal and a CPU, a *full-duplex* connection must be used.

Teletype channels transmit data at slow speeds (from about 5 to 30 characters per second), but this is quite adequate for input by means of manual keying. Standard *telephone* lines permit more rapid transmission. The actual maximum rate depends on the type of telephone service used; e.g., private (leased) lines may be somewhat faster than public lines. Telephone circuits are used to communicate large amounts of data originating in the form of punched cards, punched tape, and magnetic tape.

Broadband channels use very high frequency electric signals to carry the data message at maximum speeds of around 100,000 characters per second. These broadband circuits may be groups of voice-grade wire channels, or they may be microwave radio circuits. Such transmission facilities are expensive and are now required by only the largest companies. Broadband facilities are used for transmitting data between magnetic tape units or from one computer storage unit to another.

Coordination of Data Communications

The data communications environment has changed significantly in recent years. A typical online system in the mid-1960s is shown in Figure 5-19(*a*). A number of terminals were linked by transmission facilities to a central computer. But some of today's large distributed computing/communications networks are quite different, and the coordination required for efficient network use is quite complex. These systems must link together hundreds of terminals at dozens of

---

[5]You will be thrilled to know that modem stands for <u>mod</u>ulator-<u>dem</u>odulator. Modems are not necessary when newer transmission facilities designed specifically to transmit data are used.

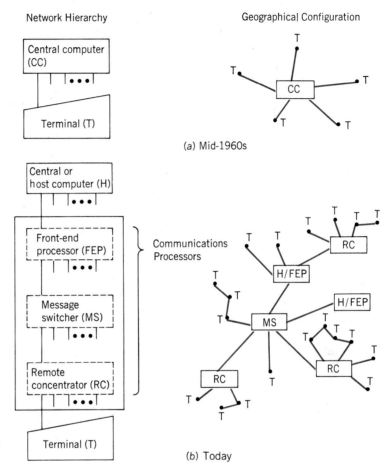

FIGURE 5-19
Data communications environ-
ments.

dispersed locations [Figure 5-19(*b*)]. Thus, *communications processors* (typically programmable minicomputers) are used to (1)
concentrate messages at remote locations for more economical
transmission, (2) *switch messages* between points in the network,
and (3) *relieve the main computers*—i.e., the *host* computers—of
"front-end" *communications work.*

OVERLAPPED PROCESSING

You will recall from Chapter 3 that computer systems may use
specialized hardware called channels to overlap input, processing,
and output operations in order to make more efficient use of computing resources. In addition to channels, high-speed storage elements
called *buffers* also play an important role in overlapped processing.

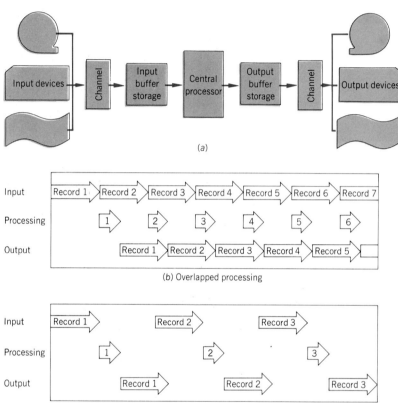

(a)

(b) Overlapped processing

(c) Serial processing

FIGURE 5-20

As shown in Figure 5-20(a), data from input equipment are fed under channel control into input buffer storage (which may be located in peripheral devices or may be a reserved section of the CPU primary storage). This input buffer has an important characteristic: It can accept data at slow input speeds and release them at electronic speeds. (The reverse is true of the output buffer.) The first input record is entered into the buffer and then transferred, under program control, to the main storage unit where processing begins immediately. While the first record is being processed, the input unit is automatically reading a second record into buffer storage [Figure 5-20(b)]. The processed information for the first record is transferred under program control to the output buffer and then, under channel control, to an output device where the writing operation begins. As soon as the first record is released, the program instructs the buffer to transmit the second record for processing. Thus, at this time in a synchronized system,[6] record 3 is being fed into the input buffer, record 2 is being processed, and record 1 is being written by an output device. The procedure continues until the task is finished. Compared with nonoverlapped or *serial processing* [Figure 5-20(*c*)], overlapped processing is much more efficient.

Data may be fed simultaneously into the buffers of the communications processors discussed in the last section from a number of stations. Computer and communications networks, of course, require sophisticated buffering techniques.

SUMMARY Character readers reduce the manual effort involved in data input operations. Financial institutions have supported the development of MICR as a means of handling billions of transactions each year. Unfortunately for organizations outside the banking community, there are no alphabetic characters available in MICR. Optical character readers, however, have alphabetic as well as numeric capability and perform efficiently in a number of applications.

A high-speed printer is the primary output device when the information is to be used by people rather than by machine. Such printers have been improved significantly in the last decade. Character-at-a-time printers have been replaced by machines that print hundreds of lines each minute. In some cases printed output has been replaced with microfilm output.

Typewriter terminals, multiunit data stations, visual display terminals, intelligent terminals—all these online instruments may enable a person to communicate directly and randomly with any record stored in direct-access devices. Audio communication from computer to people has proved practical. And a wide range of data transmission services and network communications approaches is available to relay information between remote points.

REVIEW AND DISCUSSION QUESTIONS

1 Obtain a canceled check and explain the magnetic ink coding along the bottom of the check.
2 (**a**) What are some advantages and limitations of MICR? (**b**) Of OCR?
3 Give some examples of how OCR might be used.
4 Define the following terms: (**a**) Line printer, (**b**) Impact printer,

---

[6]Although a *perfectly* synchronized system is rare, the use of buffering permits a much closer balance.

(**c**) Universal Product Code, (**d**) Cathode ray tube, (**e**) Light pen, (**f**) Microfilm recorder, (**g**) Console control panel, (**h**) Electronic funds transfer, (**i**) Data communication, (**j**) Multiunit data station, (**k**) Modem, (**l**) Buffer storage, (**m**) Remote job-entry station, (**n**) Intelligent terminal, (**o**) Distributed processing system, (**p**) Half-duplex circuit, (**q**) Automated teller machine.

5 (**a**) What is the purpose of a data collection station? (**b**) Of transaction recording stations? (**c**) Of POS stations? (**d**) Of intelligent terminals?

6 (**a**) What two basic classes of CRT display terminals are available? (**b**) How may each category be used?

7 How may audio-response units be used? Give examples.

8 Identify and discuss the most commonly used transmission channels for carrying data from one location to another.

9 Assume that you are a manager faced with deciding what type of data communications service to use. Discuss how you would evaluate the alternatives in light of such factors as (**a**) the number and location of I/O stations, (**b**) the volume of data to be communicated, (**c**) the timing of messages, and (**d**) the speed requirements.

10 (**a**) What is serial processing? (**b**) What is overlapped processing?

11 "The use of overlapped processing permits the processing system to work at greater efficiency." Discuss this statement.

THE
CENTRAL
PROCESSOR

It is now time to take a closer look at the central processor. As you will remember, the typical CPU contains the storage unit, the arithmetic-logic unit, and the control unit. Therefore, we shall be concerned first with the *storage unit* and related topics. More specifically, we shall examine (1) the *conceptual areas* of the storage unit, (2) the *locations* in the storage unit, (3) the *capacity* of storage locations, (4) the *numbering systems* associated with computers, (5) the methods of *data representation* used, and (6) the *types of primary storage devices*. Following these sections, we shall then turn our attention to the *arithmetic-logic* and *control* units.

CONCEPTUAL STORAGE AREAS

We know that the storage unit contains the data to be processed and the program of instructions. As a general rule, any storage location in the central processor has the ability to store *either* data or instructions; i.e., a specific physical space may be used to store data for one operation and instructions for another. The programmer (or the software prepared by the programmer) determines how the location will be used for each program.[1]

For each program, there will be, typically, four areas assigned to group-related types of information. These conceptual areas are shown in Figure 6-1. Three of the four areas (input, working, and output) are used for *data-storage* purposes. The *input storage* area, as the name indicates, receives the data coming from the input media and devices. The *working storage* space corresponds to a blackboard or a sheet of scratch paper; it is space used by the program to hold data being processed as well as the intermediate results of such processing. The *output storage* section contains processed information that is awaiting a writing (or *read-out*) operation. The *program storage* area, of course, contains the processing instructions.

A typical *data-flow* pattern is indicated in Figure 6-1. Data remain in the input area until needed. Since the actual processing occurs in the arithmetic-logic unit, data are delivered to this unit from input storage and processed, and the final results move through the output storage area to the user. Intermediate figures, generated in the arithmetic-logic unit, are temporarily placed in a designated working storage area until needed at a later time. Data may move back and forth between working storage and the arithmetic-logic unit a number of times before the processing is completed.

---

[1]There are exceptions to this statement. Some "read-only" storage elements, for example, have predetermined functions and are not available to the programmer.

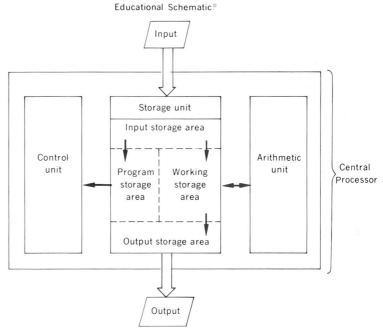

Educational Schematic*

FIGURE 6-1

Conceptual storage areas
(courtesy Sperry UNIVAC Division,
Sperry Rand Corporation).

* The specific areas of storage used for a particular purpose (input storage, program storage, etc.) *are not fixed but rather vary from program to program.* The programmer defines the limits of these reserved areas for each program. Therefore, broken lines (rather than solid ones) are used in the diagram to indicate this flexibility of area boundaries.

Instructions move from the program storage area to the control unit. The first program instruction is sent to the control unit to begin the step-by-step processing procedure. Other instructions move into the control unit at the proper time until the job is completed.

STORAGE LOCATIONS AND THEIR USE

There are storage locations in the computer that may be compared to a post office box. These locations are identified by a specific number and are capable of holding both data and instructions. Such "boxes" are referred to as *addresses*. Like a post office box number, the address number remains the same and is independent of the contents. But unlike a post office box, which can hold several different messages at the same time, an address stores only one datum or instruction item at a time.

The addresses in a storage unit containing 4,096 locations would be numbered from 0000 to 4095. Thus, one unique address will be designated 1776. It is necessary to emphasize that *there is an important distinction between the address number and the contents of the address.* Why is this distinction important? It is important because one of the principles of programming is that basic machine language instructions deal directly with address numbers rather than with the contents of the address. For example, suppose that $315 is stored in address 1776. If the programmer wants that amount printed, she will not instruct the computer to print $315. Rather, she will order the machine to print 1776, and the computer will interpret this instruction to mean that it should *print the contents of address 1776.* Just as you can locate friends in a strange city if you know that their home address is 4009 Sarita Drive, so, too, can the computer locate the desired information if it knows the location number.

Perhaps an example illustrating some of the concepts that have been introduced would be appropriate at this time. In our example let us consider "a atlas aardvark." What is "a atlas aardvark"? Well, A. Atlas Aardvark is not a "what," he is a "who"—he is the Zoology Editor for Imprint Publishing Company. He is also the first person paid each week (Atlas has gone through life being first in line). Let's look at how his paycheck might be processed by Imprint's PAC (Peculiar Automatic Computer).

The payroll *data* are prepared on punched cards each week for each employee. Last week the following data were punched into Atlas's card: (1) he worked 40 hours; (2) he receives $10 an hour; (3) he has 20 percent of his total income taken out for taxes; and (4) he has hospitalization insurance, which costs him $5 each week.

Instructions have been prepared by Imprint's programmer to direct the computer in the payroll operation. The following steps must be performed:

1 The machine must be started.
2 An employee's payroll data must be read into storage for processing.
3 Hours worked must be multiplied by the hourly rate to find the *total earnings.*
4 Total earnings must be multiplied by the withholding percentage figure to find the amount of tax deduction.
5 To the tax withheld must be added the hospitalization insurance deduction to arrive at the *total deduction* figure.
6 The total deduction must be subtracted from the total earnings to find the take-home earnings.
7 A check must be printed for the amount of the take-home earnings, and it must be payable to the correct employee.
8 The machine must be stopped at the end of the processing operation.

Program instructions are also presented to the PAC in the form of punched cards.

Figure 6-2 shows the PAC storage locations. Although the programmer may assign the instructions to *any section* of the storage unit, she has chosen to read them into addresses 06 to 18. These locations thus become the *program storage* area. The first instruction (in address 06) identifies the locations for the payroll data (00, 01, 02, 03, and 04). The data could just as well have been placed in addresses 19 to 23, and so this is also an arbitrary decision.[2]

---

[2]Obviously, the data could not go into addresses 06 to 18 since these locations are now occupied by instructions. If a payroll item were mistakenly entered into a program section location, it would "erase" the instruction properly located in the address. At some later time the item would enter the control unit where it would be interpreted as an instruction. If such an error should occur, the result would be quite unpredictable but invariably disastrous.

FIGURE 6-2

PAC storage.

00	01	02	03	04	05
06 Read payroll data card into addresses 00, 01, 02, 03, and 04.	07 Write contents of address 01 into arithmetic unit.	08 Multiply contents of arithmetic unit by contents of address 02.	09 Duplicate preceding answer in address 05.	10 Multiply contents of address 03 by preceding answer in arithmetic unit.	11 Add contents of address 04 to preceding answer in arithmetic unit.
12 Subtract preceding answer in arithmetic unit from contents of address 05.	13 Move preceding answer to address 23.	14 Write check for amount in address 23.	15 Make check payable to contents of address 00.	16 If last card, then go to address 18.	17 Go to address 06.
18 Stop processing.	19	20	21	22	23

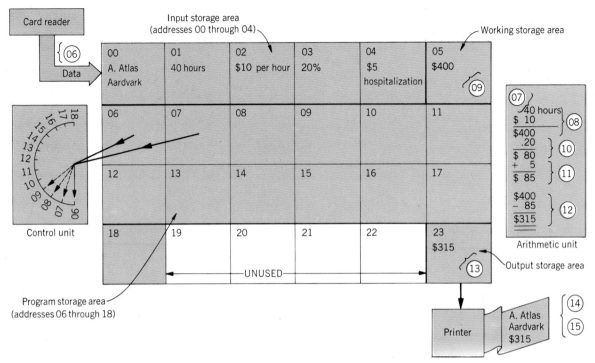

FIGURE 6-3

Let us use Figure 6-3 to follow through the process that is required to prepare Atlas's paycheck. (The circled address numbers represent each step in the process.) After the computer operator has loaded the instructions into storage, the payroll data cards are placed into the card reader, the PAC controls are set at address 06, and the processing begins. This initial control setting feeds the first instruction into the control unit where it is interpreted. Signals are sent to the card reader, which carries out the command. Atlas's card is read, and the data are transferred to *input storage*. The control unit will execute the instructions automatically *in sequence* after the initial control setting until it is directed by a specific instruction to do otherwise. Therefore, as soon as the instruction in address 06 has been complied with, the control unit automatically begins interpreting the contents of address 07.

The next command instructs the control unit to copy the contents of address 01 into the arithmetic-logic unit. The control unit is not interested that the contents of 01 are 40 hours (the next employee's time may differ). It is merely concerned with carrying out orders, and so 40 hours is placed in the arithmetic unit. And, in sequence, the processing continues: The 40-hour figure is multiplied by $10 per hour to find total earnings (instruction in address 08); this total earnings figure is duplicated (instruction, 09) in address 05, which is the *working storage* area; the tax deduction is found to be $80 (instruction, 10); the total deduction figure is $85 (instruction, 11); and Atlas's take-home pay is $315 (instruction, 12). The $315 is transferred to address 23 by the next order in the sequence. (It could just as easily have been placed in any of the unused locations.) From this *output storage* area, the information is sent to the printer, which, under program control, prints the paycheck. If Atlas's card had been the last one in the deck, the instructions in addresses 16 and 18 would have halted the process. Since other cards follow, however, the control unit receives the next order in the sequence. This instruction tells the control unit to reset itself to address 06. And so the process automatically begins again.

To summarize, several important concepts have been demonstrated in this example:

1   Input, working, output, and program storage areas are required, but they are not fixed in the PAC. Rather, they are determined by Imprint's programmer.
2   The PAC is able to obey several *commands,* e.g., READ, WRITE, ADD, SUBTRACT, MOVE. This ability to execute specific orders is *designed and built into* the machine. Every computer has a particular set, or *repertoire,* of commands that it is able to obey.
3   Computers execute one instruction at a time. They follow sequentially the series of directions until explicitly told to do otherwise. Figure 6-4 is a diagram, or *flowchart,* of the payroll procedure. The computer moves through the instructions in sequence until it comes to a *branchpoint* and is required to answer a question: Have data from the last card been fed into storage? The answer to the question determines which path or branch the computer will follow. If the answer is no, then the procedure is automatically repeated by the use of the technique known as *looping;* if the answer is yes, the processing stops. Instructions that result in the transfer of program control to an instruction stored at some arbitrary location rather than to the next location in storage may be *conditional* or *unconditional* transfer commands. If the change in sequence is based on the outcome of some test, then it is a conditional transfer; if not, it is an unconditional branch. Can you identify the conditional and unconditional transfer instructions in Figure 6-4?

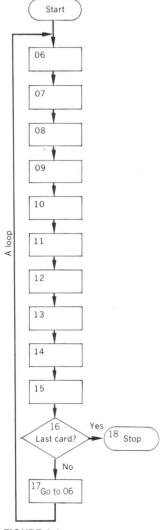

FIGURE 6-4

CAPACITY OF STORAGE LOCATIONS

Man does not live by words alone despite the fact
that sometimes he has to eat them.
Adlai Stevenson

He uses short, easy words, like 'What about Lunch?'
The House at Pooh Corner

Computer storage locations must be used in such a way that
sequences of characters (e.g., AARDVARK, $315, ADD) can be
stored and manipulated to produce output information. A sequence
of characters stored in a computer and treated as a single entity is
called a *computer word*. There are several approaches used to
organize characters into words in storage.

In some machines, *each* numbered address contains *only a
single character* (A, 3, $). Such processors are said to be *character-
addressable.* Thus, a sequence of characters such as AARDVARK
would require eight storage addresses while $315 would require
four addresses. The character-addressable approach, then, permits
the use of *variable-length words* [Figure 6-5(*a*)]. A second storage
approach is to design the computer to store a *fixed number of
characters* in each numbered address location. The machine then
treats the contents of each address as a *fixed-length word*.[3] When

---

[3]The number of characters found in a fixed-length word varies depending on the
make and model of computer.

FIGURE 6-5

(*a*) Variable word-length storage;
(*b*) Fixed word-length storage.

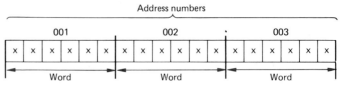

(*b*)

this storage organization approach is used, the computer is said to be *word-addressable* [Figure 6-5(*b*)].

Each of these approaches to organizing the storage unit has advantages and drawbacks.[4] Recognizing this fact, the ingenious Peculiar Company designers of the PAC (and, incidentally, the designers of larger modern computers) developed a *flexible machine* that could use program control to organize the computer to operate on *either* single characters *or* fixed-length words. How is this possible? You ask such perceptive questions.

Each alphanumeric character placed in storage is represented by a code consisting of 8 binary digits (bits);[5] and *each* of these coded characters, or *bytes,* is identified in storage by a *specific address number.* Thus, by using an appropriate set of instructions, the programmer can manipulate these characters into words of varying lengths as needed.

But bytes can also be *grouped together and operated on as a unit.* Programmers can elect to use, for example, other available instructions that will cause the computer to automatically retrieve, manipulate, and store as a single unit a fixed word of *4* bytes.[6] Or, they may choose to group 8 bytes into a *double word* and have the machine function in this fixed-word format. Figure 6-6 illustrates the word formats possible with many currently used computers. (How-

---

[4]For example, variable word-length processors generally make more efficient use of the available storage space (unused capacity may exist when a number of fixed words consist of only a few characters), but they have slower calculating capabilities (a computer with a fixed-length word of six characters can manipulate and add two 6-digit numbers in a single step while six steps would be needed by a character-addressable processor). Although it is beyond the scope of this book to go into these matters in more detail, you can find a more thorough presentation in Donald H. Sanders, *Computers in Business,* 3d ed., McGraw-Hill Book Company, New York, 1975, pp. 251–257.

[5]We will discuss bits in some detail in a few pages.

[6]The gospel according to some designers was: "In the beginning there was The Word, and The Word was four bytes long."

FIGURE 6-6

Address formats.

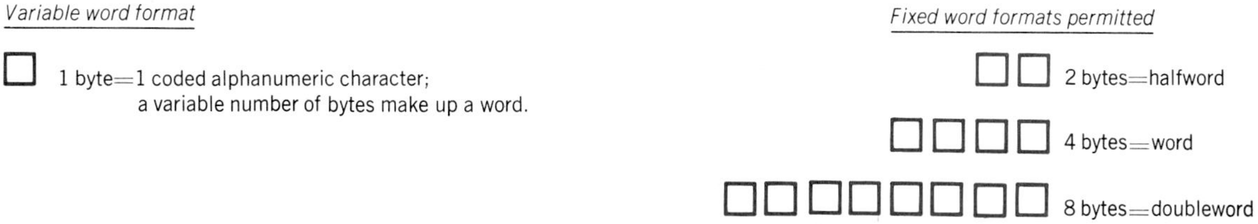

Variable word format

☐ 1 byte=1 coded alphanumeric character;
      a variable number of bytes make up a word.

Fixed word formats permitted

☐☐ 2 bytes=halfword

☐☐☐☐ 4 bytes=word

☐☐☐☐☐☐☐☐ 8 bytes=doubleword

ever, minicomputers generally lack this flexibility, and many use
only a single fixed-word format of 2 bytes.)

Regardless of the capacity of the available storage locations,
however, the numbers, letters, and special characters contained in
storage must be in a coded form that the computer can use.

**COMPUTER
NUMBERING
SYSTEMS**

Anthropologists have reported on the primitive
number systems of some aboriginal tribes. The
Yancos in the Brazilian Amazon stop counting at
three. Since their word for "three" is
"poettarrarorincoaroac," this is understandable.
Albert Sukoff

Computers represent data in a code that is related to a binary
numbering system. It is thus desirable to understand numbering
systems.

Decimal Numbers

The first numbering systems were of an *additive* nature. That is, they
consisted of symbols such as | for one, || for two, ||| for three, etc.
Each symbol represented the *same value* regardless of the position
it occupied in the number. Unfortunately, calculations are difficult
when such systems are used. In fact, you can calculate answers to
problems that would have baffled wise people of earlier centuries. A
big reason for your advantage has been the development of *positional* numbering systems. In such systems there are only a limited
number of symbols, and the symbols represent different values
according to the position they occupy in the number (5 = the Roman
numeral V, but 51 does not equal VI because the meaning of 5 has
changed with the change in its position). The number of symbols
used depends on the *base* or *radix* of the particular system. The
decimal system, of course, has a base of 10 and has 10 symbols (0
to 9).[7] The *highest* numerical symbol will always have a value of one
less than the base.

---

[7]There is nothing particularly sacred about a base of 10. Probably the only reason it
was originally developed and is now in widespread use is that people happen to have
10 fingers. Other systems have been created. For example, the Babylonians had a
base of 60 (of course, they also did their writing on mud pies); the Mayas of Yucatán
used a base of 20 (a warm climate and a group of barefooted mathematicians?); and a
base of five is still used by natives in New Hebrides.

By the arrangement of the numerical symbols[8] in various positions, any number may be represented. We know that in the decimal system the successive positions to the left of the decimal point represent units, tens, hundreds, thousands, ten thousands, etc. We sometimes fail to remember, however, that what this means is that each position represents a particular *power* of the base. Thus, the number 15,236 represents the sum of[9]

$$(\underline{1} \times 10^4) + (\underline{5} \times 10^3) + (\underline{2} \times 10^2) + (\underline{3} \times 10^1) + (\underline{6} \times 10^0)$$

In *any* positional numbering system, the *value of each position represents a specific power of the base.* To test your understanding of the concepts that have now been introduced, let us look at the following problems:

1 What is the decimal equivalent of 463_8? (The subscript 8 following the number 463 indicates that this is an *octal* base number.) Since the *base* is *now eight* rather than 10, the possible symbols are 0 to 7 (the symbols 8 and 9 do not exist in this case). Each position in the number 463_8 represents a power of its base. Therefore,

$$(\underline{4} \times 8^2) + (\underline{6} \times 8^1) + (\underline{3} \times 8^0). \leftarrow \text{Octal point}$$
or $(4 \times 64) + (6 \times 8) + (3 \times 1).$
or $(256) + (48) + (3). = 307_{10}$ The decimal equivalent

2 What is the decimal equivalent of 1001_2? (We are now using a base of two.) With a base of two, the only possible symbols are 0 and 1. Again, each position in the number 1001_2 represents a power of its base. Therefore,

$$(\underline{1} \times 2^3) + (\underline{0} \times 2^2) + (\underline{0} \times 2^1) + (\underline{1} \times 2^0). \leftarrow \text{Binary point}$$
or $(1 \times 8) + (0 \times 4) + (0 \times 2) + (1 \times 1).$
or $(8) + (0) + (0) + (1). = 9_{10}$ The decimal equivalent

---

[8]There is also nothing sacred about the shape of the symbols we use to represent quantities. We know that the symbol 2 has a certain meaning, but any number of other marks could be defined to serve the same purpose. A version of the Arabic numerals we use is thought to have originated in India around 200 B.C.
[9]Students occasionally forget their algebra and have to be reminded that n^0 is, by definition, 1; i.e., any number raised to the zero power equals 1.

These problems have demonstrated that (1) the lower the numbering base, the fewer the possible symbols that must be remembered, and (2) the smaller the base, the more positions there must be to represent a given quantity. Four digits (1001) are required in base two to equal a single decimal digit (9). You may also have observed that the decimal point becomes the *octal point* in a base-eight system and the *binary point* in base two. It would thus appear that we have sneaked up on the *binary* or *base-two* numbering system used by digital computers.

Binary Numbers in Computers

It was pointed out in Chapter 1 that John von Neumann suggested that binary numbering systems be incorporated in computers. Although the suggestion came too late to prevent the very first machines from using the decimal system, von Neumann's suggestions were quickly adopted in subsequent designs.

Why the rush to binary? There are several very good reasons:

1 It is necessary that circuitry be designed only to handle 2 binary digits (bits) rather than 10. Design is simplified, cost is reduced, and reliability is improved.

2 Electronic components, by their very nature, operate in a binary mode. A switch is either open (0 state) or closed (1 state); and a transistor either is not conducting (0) or is (1).

3 Everything that can be done with a base of 10 can be done with the binary system.

COMPUTER DATA REPRESENTATION

Up to this point we have been discussing "pure" binary numbers, but most modern computers use some *coded,* or *modified,* version of pure binary to represent decimal numbers. Numerous data representation formats have been developed. The most popular for business purposes, however, are the *binary coded decimal* (BCD) codes.[10]

Binary Coded Decimal System

With BCD it is possible to convert *each* decimal digit into its binary equivalent rather than convert the entire decimal number into a pure binary form. The BCD equivalent of each possible decimal digit is shown in Figure 6-7. Because the digits 8 and 9 require 4 bits, *all* decimal digits are represented by 4 bits. Converting 405_{10} into BCD would yield the following result:

$$405_{10} \text{ in BCD} = 0100/0000/0101 \text{ or } 010000000101$$
$$\phantom{405_{10} \text{ in BCD} = } 4 \qquad 0 \qquad 5$$

With 4 bits there are 16 different possible configurations (2^4). The first 10 of these configurations are, of course, used to represent decimal digits. The other six arrangements (1010, 1011, 1100, 1101, 1110, and 1111) have decimal values from 10 to 15. These six arrangements are *not used* in BCD coding; i.e., 1111 *does not* represent 15_{10} in BCD. Rather, the proper BCD code for 15_{10} is 0001/0101. The "extra" six configurations are used by programmers for other purposes, which we need not dwell on here.

We have seen that BCD is a convenient and fast way to convert numbers from decimal to binary. But it is hardly sufficient for business purposes to have only 16 characters available. The following section explains how additional characters are represented in the central processor.

FIGURE 6-7

Binary coded decimal numeric bit configurations.

Decimal Digit	Place Value			
	8	4	2	1
0	0	0	0	0
1	0	0	0	1
2	0	0	1	0
3	0	0	1	1
4	0	1	0	0
5	0	1	0	1
6	0	1	1	0
7	0	1	1	1
8	1	0	0	0
9	1	0	0	1

---

[10]Many modern computers use both BCD and pure binary forms of data representation. For example, input data are received and stored in the CPU in a BCD format. Prior to computations, those numbers that are to be used in arithmetic operations *may* be converted to a pure binary form by the computer. Following binary arithmetic operations, the results are converted back to a BCD format before being written out.

"I'm sorry, Miss Conley, but last week I explained to you in great detail binary coded decimal notation at the Malgren's cocktail party."

‹ DATAMATION ›

Six-Bit Alphanumeric Code

Instead of using 4 bits with only 16 possible characters, equipment designers commonly use 6 or 8 bits to represent characters in *alphanumeric versions* of BCD. Two *zone* positions are added to the four BCD positions in the 6-bit code. With 6 bits it is thus possible to represent 64 different characters (2^6). A seventh parity checking position is commonly added (Figure 6-8). We have already seen examples of 6-bit alphanumeric BCD code being used to represent data in paper tape and seven-channel magnetic tape. It was pointed out in the discussion of magnetic tape coding that the decimal 7 is represented by an "on" condition in the numeric channels marked 4, 2, and 1. It is now apparent that being "on" means that a 1 bit is represented in these positions, i.e., that 7 = 0111 in BCD.

FIGURE 6-8

Check bit	Zone bits		Numeric bits			
C	B	A	8	4	2	1

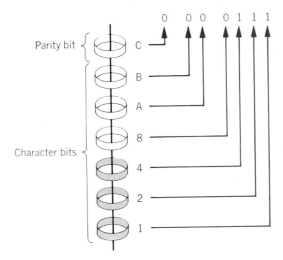

Parity bit

Character bits

FIGURE 6-9

Alphanumeric BCD character location.

Data are often stored internally by the use of tiny doughnut-shaped "cores," which may be magnetized in either of two directions. These cores are thus capable of representing a 1 or a 0. Seven cores stacked in a vertical column are used in some computers to represent a number, letter, or special character. Figure 6-9 shows how the decimal 7 is represented. An imaginary line passes through the cores. The shaded cores are magnetized in a direction that corresponds to a 1 bit. Like a switch, they may be considered in an "on" state. The unshaded cores are in an "off" state and represent a 0 bit. The A and B cores are the zone cores. A combination of zone (A and B) and numeric (8, 4, 2, and 1) cores may be used to represent alphabetic and special characters just as they do in tape coding. The parity check core is also shown in the "off" state, indicating that odd parity is used in this particular code.

The 6 bits permit 64 different coding arrangements. This number is sufficient to code the decimal digits (10), capital letters (26), and a number of punctuation marks and machine control characters. Six bits are *not sufficient,* however, to provide lowercase letters, capital letters, and a greatly expanded number of special and control characters.

Eight-Bit Alphanumeric Codes

To permit greater flexibility in data representation, equipment designers have *extended* the 6-bit alphanumeric BCD code to 8 bits. With 8-bit coding, it is possible to provide 256 different arrangements (2^8). Each 8-bit unit of information, you will remember, is called a *byte*.

Character	Hollerith Card Code	Standard BCD Interchange Code	Extended BCD Interchange Code (EBCDIC)	ASCII-8
0	0	00 1010	1111 0000	0101 0000
1	1	00 0001	1111 0001	0101 0001
2	2	00 0010	1111 0010	0101 0010
3	3	00 0011	1111 0011	0101 0011
4	4	00 0100	1111 0100	0101 0100
5	5	00 0101	1111 0101	0101 0101
6	6	00 0110	1111 0110	0101 0110
7	7	00 0111	1111 0111	0101 0111
A	12-1	11 0001	1100 0001	1010 0001
B	12-2	11 0010	1100 0010	1010 0010
C	12-3	11 0011	1100 0011	1010 0011
D	12-4	11 0100	1100 0100	1010 0100
E	12-5	11 0101	1100 0101	1010 0101

FIGURE 6-10

Common data representation codes.

The nine-channel magnetic tape format discussed in Chapter 4 utilizes an 8-bit extended version of BCD. There are *four* (rather than two) *zone bit positions* available in an 8-bit code. Eight data cores plus a check bit core are again stacked in a column and used internally in many CPUs to represent a coded character.

Selected characters are presented in Figure 6-10 in the four codes most commonly encountered in data processing. In addition to Hollerith and 6-bit alphanumeric codes, there are two 8-bit codes in current use—the Extended Binary Coded Decimal Interchange Code (EBCDIC) developed by IBM, and the American Standard Code for Information Interchange (ASCII) developed by the American National Standards Institute.

PRIMARY STORAGE DEVICES

Primary storage is the built-in storage section of the CPU; it is a vital element in the storage hierarchy found in computer-based information systems. Although generally lacking the storage capacity of direct-access drums and disks, the primary storage section is capable of storing and retrieving data at much faster speeds than is possible with those supplementary online devices.

The ENIAC used a vacuum-tube primary storage section. Each tube represented a single bit, and storage capacity was minuscule. A popular computer of the mid-1950s (the IBM 650) used a magnetic drum as the internal storage instrument. But during the 1950s magnetic core storage appeared, and since that time cores have been used in many computers.

Magnetic Core Storage

If a wire carrying a sufficiently strong electric current passes through a core, the core will be magnetized by the magnetic field created around the wire. Perhaps you have wrapped a wire around a nail and connected the ends of the wire to a battery to make an electromagnet. You might have been surprised when you disconnected the battery to find that the nail still had the ability to act as a magnet. The core, like the nail, remains magnetized after the current stops.

In Figure 6-11, the current flow from left to right has magnetized the core in a counterclockwise (0-bit) direction. But when the current flows in the opposite direction, the core becomes magnetized in a clockwise (1-bit) fashion. A core can be quickly changed from an "off" or 0-bit condition to an "on" or 1-bit state simply by reversing the current flow passing through the core.

A large number of cores are strung on a screen of wires to form a *core plane.* These planes, resembling small square tennis rackets, are then arranged vertically to represent data, as indicated in Figure 6-9. (Nine planes are needed to code 8-bit bytes and provide for a parity check.)

With hundreds of thousands of cores in a CPU, how is it possible to select and properly magnetize a few in such a way that the desired character is *read into* storage? Let us use an imaginary plane to see how 1 bit in a character is selected (Figure 6-12). The other bits making up the character are similarly chosen in the other planes. To make selection possible, two wires must pass through each core at right angles. By sending only *half* the necessary current through each of two wires, only the core at the intersection of the wires is affected. All other cores in the plane either receive no current at all or receive only half the amount needed to magnetize.

With a character now read into core storage, how does the computer *retrieve* it? For retrieval a third *sense* wire may be threaded diagonally through each core in a plane. The computer tests, or reads out, the magnetic state of a core by again sending electric current pulses through the two wires used in the read-in operation. The direction of this current is such that it causes a 0 to be written at that core position. If the core is magnetized in an "on" or 1 state, the

FIGURE 6-11

Current is applied   Core is magnetized   Current is reversed;
the core reverses
its magnetic state

1/2 current

1/2 current ⟶

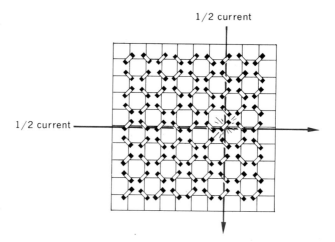

FIGURE 6-12
Core selection.

writing of a 0 will abruptly *flip* the magnetic condition of the core and the changing magnetic field will induce a current into the sense wire. The reaction picked up by the sense wire tells the computer that the core contained a 1 bit. If *no reaction* is sensed, the computer will know that the core is already magnetized in the 0 state.

But wait a minute! If all cores storing a character have been changed from a 1 to a 0 state as a result of the reading, haven't we destroyed the character in its original location? The answer to this is usually yes, but only momentarily. Fortunately, by means of a fourth *inhibit* wire the cores containing 1 bits are restored to their original state. Simply stated, the processor now tries to write back 1s in every core read an instant earlier. If the core in the plane was originally a 1, it will be restored; if it was originally a 0, it will remain that way, and a pulse of current will be sent through the inhibit wire in the plane to cancel out the attempt to write a 1 (Figure 6-13).

Magnetic cores have been popular for primary storage because they are durable, safe, reasonably fast, relatively inexpensive, and compact. However, the cost of core-plane fabrication and the circuitry necessarily associated with cores have made them less desirable in recent years.

FIGURE 6-13

Current wires

Sense wire

Inhibit wire

Code represents 0

Current wires

Sense wire

Inhibit wire

Core remains 0

Thin-Film Storage

In the early 1950s, it was found that a tiny film of magnetic material could be deposited on a flat plane of insulating glass or plastic so that film spots could be magnetized in either of two stable preferred directions. However, the promise offered by planar technology was not achieved rapidly enough, and so the emphasis in the development of new storage techniques shifted to other approaches.

Of course, thin-film storage cells do not have to be in the form of flat spots. Instead, they may be in a plated-wire form. Manufacturing cost per bit of storage capacity is low because of the automatic production techniques employed. Plated-wire primary storage is currently used in some UNIVAC and NCR computers.

Semiconductor Storage

Semiconductor storage elements are tiny integrated circuit chips[11] that contain many fast microscopic switches. For our purposes, these switches can be considered the electronic equivalents of mechanical toggle switches. Like a toggle switch, each electronic switch can be in an "on" or "off" condition and can thus be used to represent a binary 1 or 0.

Semiconductor memory chips have found their way into the newer models of most manufacturers for several very good reasons: (1) they require only about half the space needed by core storage of similar capacity, (2) they are capable of faster performance than core or thin-film memories, and (3) their cost per bit of storage capacity has recently dropped below the cost required with core and film technologies. Thus, these memories will likely occupy a dominant position during the late 1970s and early 1980s. Of course, other promising primary storage technologies are currently being studied and may eventually replace semiconductors.

THE ARITHMETIC-LOGIC UNIT

The arithmetic-logic unit is where the actual data processing occurs. All calculations are performed and all logical comparisons are made in this unit. Earlier, we traced through a simplified program to process Editor Aardvark's weekly paycheck. Some of the program instructions used then are reproduced in Figure 6-14.

The instruction in address 07 calls for the computer to write the contents of address 01 into the arithmetic unit. Implicit in this instruction is the requirement that the arithmetic-logic unit have storage capability. It must be able to store temporarily the data contained in address 01. Such a special-purpose storage location is called a *register*. Several registers will be discussed in the following paragraphs because they are basic to the functioning of the arithmetic-

---

[11]Figure 1-12, page 30, shows a microcomputer with semiconductor primary storage elements.

07	08	09	10	11
Write contents of address 01 into arithmetic unit	Multiply contents of arithmetic unit by contents of address 02	Duplicate preceding answer in address 05	Multiply contents of address 03 by preceding answer in arithmetic unit	Add contents of address 04 to preceding answer in arithmetic unit

FIGURE 6-14
(*Source:* Figure 6-2).

logic and control units. The number of registers varies among computers, as does the data-flow pattern. Before briefly examining some variations, let us trace the instructions in Figure 6-14 through the PAC computer.

Up to this point we have written the instructions in addresses 07 to 11 so that we would understand them. Figure 6-15 shows how these same instructions may be coded and stored for PAC's convenience. The first processing instruction, CLA 01, tells PAC to CLear the contents of the arithmetic-logic unit of all data and to Add (store) the contents of address 01 to a register known as the *accumulator*. Thus, 40 hours—the contents of address 01—are now held in both address 01 and the accumulator [Figure 6-16(a)].

The second instruction in address 08 is MUL 02. The computer interprets this instruction to mean that the contents of address 02 ($10) are to be MULtiplied by the contents in the accumulator (40 hours) to get Aardvark's gross pay. Execution of this instruction may take the following form [Figure 6-16(b)]:

1 The contents of address 02 are read into a storage register in the arithmetic-logic unit.
2 The contents of the accumulator and the contents of the storage register are given to the *adder*. The *adder* (and its associated circuits) is the primary arithmetic element because it also performs subtraction, multiplication, and division on binary digits.
3 The product of the multiplication *is stored in the accumulator*. The 40 hours previously there has been erased by the arithmetic operation.

The third instruction in the processing sequence is STO 05. The contents in the accumulator are STOred in address 05. The read-in to

FIGURE 6-15

07	08	09	10	11
CLA 01	MUL 02	STO 05	MUL 03	ADD 04

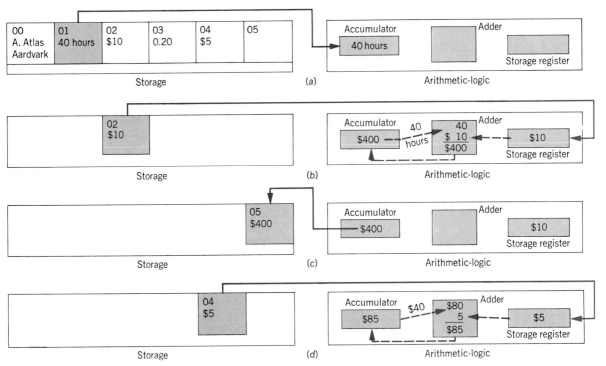

FIGURE 6-16

address 05 is destructive to any information that might be there. The read-out from the accumulator is nondestructive [Figure 6-16(c)]. The fourth instruction, MUL 03, is handled exactly like the second instruction, so we need not repeat the execution.

The fifth instruction in the sequence, ADD 04, simply tells the computer to ADD the contents of address 04 to the contents of the accumulator. The hospitalization insurance deduction of $5 is the contents of 04; the tax deduction of $80 is now the contents of the accumulator. Why? Because when the fourth instruction is carried out, the $400 in the accumulator is multiplied by 20 percent (the contents of 03) to get a product, which is then stored in the accumulator. As Figure 6-16(d) shows, the contents of 04 are read into the storage register (thus erasing the previous contents); the adder totals the contents of the accumulator and the storage register; and the sum is stored in the accumulator.

It is apparent that every arithmetic operation requires two numbers and some result. Subtraction, for example, requires a minuend and a subtrahend to find a difference. Although obviously two numbers and a result are handled by every computer arithmetic-logic unit, different processing and storage approaches have been developed to manage the two data words and the result.

Logic operations usually consist of comparisons. The arithmetic-logic unit may compare two numbers by subtracting one from the other. The sign (negative or positive) and the value of the difference tell the processor that the first number is equal to, less than, or greater than the second number.

THE CONTROL UNIT

The control unit of the processor *selects, interprets, and executes* the program instructions. The arithmetic-logic unit responds to commands coming from the control unit. There are at least two parts to any instruction: the *operation*, or *command*, that is to be followed (for example, ADD, SUB, MUL, and GO TO) and the *address*, which locates the data or instructions to be manipulated. The basic components contained in the PAC control unit are the *instruction register, sequence register, address register,* and *decoder.*

Let us trace an instruction through the PAC control unit to see how it is handled. We shall again use Aardvark's pay data along with the payroll program shown in Figure 6-15. Let us assume that the instruction in address 07 has just been executed and that 40 hours is the contents of the accumulator. The following steps are performed in the next *operating cycle* (the circled numbers in Figure 6-17 correspond to these steps):

1 The instruction in address 08 (MUL 02) is *selected* by the *sequence register* and read into the *instruction register* in the control unit. (The sequence register does not store the instruction. We shall have more to say about the sequence register in step 5 below.)

2 The operation part of the instruction (MUL) and the address part (02) are *separated*. The operation is sent to the decoder where it is *interpreted*. The computer is built to respond to a limited number of commands, and it now knows that it is to multiply.

3 The address part of the instruction is sent to the *address register.*

4 The signal to move the contents of address 02 into the arithmetic-logic unit is sent; the command to multiply goes to the arithmetic-logic unit where the instruction is *executed*.

5 As the multiplication is being executed, the sequence register in the control unit is increased by one to indicate the location of the next instruction address. When the program was started, the sequence register was set to the address of the first instruction by the programmer. By the time the first program instruction was

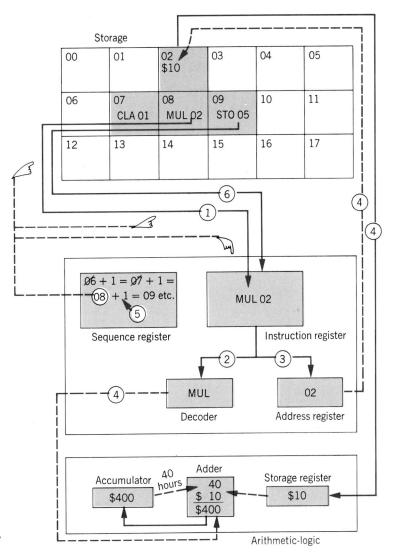

FIGURE 6-17

finished, the contents of the sequence register had automatically been advanced to the next instruction address number. In other words, the first address in the payroll program was 06 (read data in), and the sequence register was set to 06. As that instruction was being executed, the sequence register automatically moved to 07 and then to 08, and now it is again automatically moved to 09. It keeps this up until instructed to do otherwise. You will recall that when the sequence register gets to address 17, it

encounters an instruction that reads GO TO 06. This command
alters the normal stepping of the sequence register and resets it
at address 06.

6   The instruction at address 09 moves into the instruction register,
and the above steps are repeated.

We may identify separate processor phases, or cycles, in the
above procedure. Step 4 is the *execution cycle.* The other steps
comprise the *instruction cycle.* Thus, there are two phases in the
performance of each instruction. Computers are generally *synchronous;* i.e., the various operations are synchronized by an electronic
clock, which emits millions of regularly spaced electronic pulses
each second. Commands are interpreted and executed at proper
intervals, and the intervals are timed by a specified number of these
pulses.

SUMMARY   Storage locations may contain either data or instructions. For each
program, data are typically stored in three conceptual areas—the
input storage area, the working storage area, and the output storage
area. Instructions are held in a program storage area.

Locations in storage are identified by address numbers. The
programmer (or software prepared by programmers) keeps track of
address contents because when instructions are written to manipulate these contents, they must indicate in some way the address
locations. The programmer has a fixed number of instruction commands at his disposal. These commands are built into the particular
machine being used. When a program is run, the machine is set at
the first instruction and it then follows sequentially the series of
directions until told to do otherwise.

Each address may contain either a single character or a word
consisting of a fixed number of characters. Most larger computers
produced in the last decade are flexible processors that may be
operated as either variable or fixed word-length machines.

Binary numbers are used to simplify computer design and take
advantage of the two states that electronic components may be in.
Computers typically use a binary-related code to designate numbers, letters, and special characters. Six- and eight-bit codes are
used to represent alphanumeric data.

The fastest storage units are found internally in the CPU. Primary
storage is usually provided by planes of magnetic cores, plated-wire
units, or semiconductor devices.

The arithmetic-logic unit does the actual processing under program control. During the execution cycle, data stored in primary

storage or in registers are moved to the arithmetic-logic unit. There they are manipulated by adder circuits to yield a result that may be stored in a register (e.g., the accumulator) or transferred to some other storage location. The control unit selects, interprets, and sees to the execution of instructions in their proper sequence. Several basic registers are required to perform the control function.

REVIEW AND DISCUSSION QUESTIONS

1 (**a**) Identify and discuss the four conceptual storage areas. (**b**) What is the typical data-flow pattern in the storage unit?

2 Define the following terms: (**a**) Address, (**b**) Command repertoire, (**c**) Branchpoint, (**d**) Looping, (**e**) Conditional transfer, (**f**) Unconditional transfer, (**g**) Byte, (**h**) Register, (**i**) Synchronous computer.

3 Explain the distinction between the address number and the contents of the address.

4 (**a**) Distinguish between word-addressable and character-addressable computers. (**b**) Compare fixed and variable word-length storage systems.

5 "Many modern computers can be operated as either variable word-length or fixed word-length machines." Discuss this comment.

6 Why have computers been designed to use the binary numbering system?

7 Why has the 6-bit Standard BCD code been extended to 8 bits?

8 Identify and discuss the types of primary storage devices used in modern computers.

9 (**a**) What is the accumulator? (**b**) What is the adder?

10 Define and explain the function of (**a**) the instruction register, (**b**) The sequence register, (**c**) the address register, and (**d**) the decoder.

SOLVING PROBLEMS: THE SYSTEM DEVELOPMENT/ PROGRAMMING PROCESS

The purpose of the chapters in this Part is to outline and then consider in some detail seven basic problem-solving steps that make it possible for the computer hardware to produce the information needed by decision makers. The first three steps, dealing with problem analysis and system development, are included in Chapter 7; two programming steps required to create a system solution are considered in Chapters 8 and 9; and the final two programming steps necessary to the implementation of the system solution are discussed in Chapter 10.

SYSTEM DEVELOPMENT CONCEPTS

After studying this chapter and answering the discussion questions, you should be able to:

Outline the process that is followed in using computers to solve business problems.

Explain what a system is and why it is needed.

Identify the steps in the system development approach.

Describe a system flowchart and explain how it is used.

Discuss the objectives of the study team duing the data-gathering, data-analysis, and system-design stages.

Suggest approaches to be used to evaluate and acquire new computing equipment.

CHAPTER OUTLINE

SOLVING PROBLEMS USING COMPUTERS

NEED FOR A SYSTEM DEVELOPMENT STUDY
Reducing Economic Risk □ Avoiding Common Pitfalls

SYSTEM DEVELOPMENT APPROACH
System Development Prerequisites □ The Data-gathering Phase □ Data Analysis and System Design □ Decision Making: Study Team □ Study-Team Recommendations □ Top-Management Decisions

SUMMARY

On Tuesday when it hails and snows
The feeling in me grows and grows
That hardly anybody knows
If those are these and these are those.
                               Winnie-the-Pooh

This quote could describe the feelings of managers with important decisions to make. Fortunately, computers can supply decision makers with necessary information. But computer hardware, by itself, does not solve a single business problem. As Figure 7-1 indicates, there are usually many activities that lie between the realization of a need for information and the use of computer hardware to satisfy the need on a regular basis. Until the processor is given a detailed set of problem-solving instructions, it is merely an expensive and space-consuming curiosity. In fact, as far as most users of information are concerned, the solution of problems is what is important, and the use of computer hardware in the solution process may be only incidental.

SOLVING PROBLEMS USING COMPUTERS

The process to be followed in using computers to solve problems involves several steps:

1   *Definition of the problem and the objectives* The particular problem to be solved, or the tasks to be accomplished, must be clearly identified; the objectives of managers in having the tasks performed must be known.

FIGURE 7-1

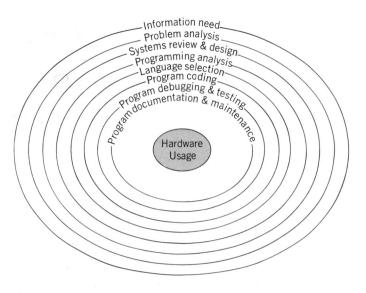

2 *Problem analysis* Data pertaining to the problem must be gathered, organized, and interpreted. From this analysis may come a recognition of computer potential, i.e., a recognition that the computer could be used to achieve a problem solution.

3 *System review and design* The present procedures should be reviewed to determine what improvements are possible. These procedures should be redesigned to meet current needs. New system designs should consider the scope of the problem, the form and type of input data to be used, and the form and type of output required.

4 *Programming analysis* The new system specifications must be broken down into the specific arithmetic and logic operations required to solve the problem.

5 *Program preparation* The specific steps must next be translated or coded into a language and form acceptable to the processor.[1]

---

[1]As used here, programming is defined as the process of converting broad system specifications into usable machine instructions. It is *not* merely program preparation or *coding;* rather, programming consists of steps 4 through 7 and is a time-consuming and error-prone process that does not begin and end with the writing of lines of code on a sheet of paper. In some organizations the system specifications are prepared by system analysts and the later steps are generally handled by programmers and computer operators. Close cooperation is, of course, required. In other organizations, combination analyst/programmers are used to develop information system projects.

6 *Program debugging and testing* The coded program must be checked for errors and tested prior to being used on a routine basis to ensure that the correct problem is being solved and that correct results are being produced.

7 *Program documentation and maintenance* Conversion to the new approach must be made; the program must be properly stored when not in use; it must be described in writing (and supporting written documents must be developed and kept on file); and it must be revised and maintained as needs change.

The purpose of this chapter and the three that follow is to survey these seven steps that comprise the system development/programming process. The *first three steps* are included in the *system development phase,* which is the subject of this chapter. The *programming steps* required to create a system solution (steps 4 and 5) are considered in Chapters 8 and 9, and the final two programming steps necessary to the *implementation* of the system solution are studied in Chapter 10. Figure 7-2 summarizes (1) the steps involved in using computers to solve business problems and (2) the organizational outline of the text in discussing these steps.

NEED FOR A SYSTEM DEVELOPMENT STUDY

A *system study* is the investigation made in an organization to determine and develop needed informational improvements in *specified* areas. Such a study is needed to (1) *reduce the risk of financial loss* and (2) *steer clear of* some of the *pitfalls associated with inadequate information system planning.*

FIGURE 7-2
Procedure for solving problems with computers.

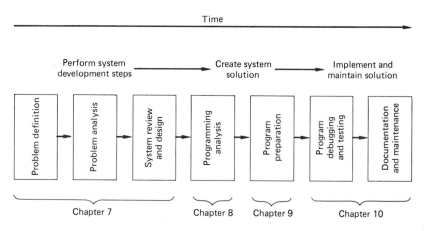

"The top item on the agenda today is the problem of how best to inform our stock-holders that we poured another 11 million dollars down the rat hole in the first half of '75."

© DATAMATION ●

Reducing Economic Risk

Computer usage is justified when the investment in the system is offset by tangible or intangible economic benefits. Yet there are numerous examples of businesses that have not achieved economic gains from their computers. In one case, a utility company estimated that a customer information system would cost $2.5 million to develop and would achieve economic benefits sufficient to pay for this investment over a 4-year period. The project was abandoned, however, after $7 million in development costs had been incurred and it was then estimated that an additional $8 million would be required to complete the system. Such gloomy examples show that system development can be risky. A properly conducted system study will not eliminate economic risk, but it can substantially reduce it.

Avoiding Common Pitfalls

Common mistakes that have contributed to financial loss in the past may be avoided with a good system study. Included among these past mistakes are: (1) the failure of top executives to provide the needed leadership, (2) the failure to specify system objectives, (3) the lack of participation in the study of those who will be expected to use the new system, and (4) the attempt to install a system on an unrealistic "crash program" basis.

SYSTEM DEVELOPMENT APPROACH

A system study is conducted to provide answers to such questions as: (1) What data processing improvements are needed? (2) Should new information systems be designed? and (3) Should a computer be used to achieve data processing objectives? In answering these and other questions, the team[2] making the study should follow a step-by-step system development approach to (1) *accomplish planning prerequisites and identify the objectives,* (2) *gather data on current operations,* (3) *analyze current operations and determine feasible solutions,* and (4) *decide on the most appropriate solution.*[3] (In addition to these steps, as we will see in the next chapters, it will also be necessary to program and then *implement* the solution.)

System Development Prerequisites

The account of an early well-managed survey is found in the Bible in chapter 13 of the Book of Numbers. A team of 12 "analysts" was sent by Moses to spy out the Promised Land and report back their findings. *Three important prerequisite principles* were observed in this survey:

1 *The survey had support at the highest levels.* God told Moses: "Send men to spy out the land of Canaan . . . from each tribe of their fathers shall you send a man, every one a leader among them." Such top-level support is a prerequisite.

2 *The survey team consisted of highly respected individu-*

---

[2]In broader system studies involving extensive redesign of existing procedures, a team approach is generally followed; in less complicated system projects the "team" may shrink to one analyst.

[3]A more detailed treatment of these steps may be found in Donald H. Sanders, *Computers in Business,* 3d ed., McGraw-Hill Book Company, New York, 1975, pp. 440–463. See also Theodore C. Willoughby, "Origins of Systems Projects," *Journal of Systems Management,* pp. 18–26, October 1975.

als. Only tribal leaders were sent on the mission. System study members are often selected for the offsetting talents they can bring to the job. At least one team member should represent the interests of the *end-users* of a new system and should have a knowledge of the information needs of the business, while another (e.g., a *chief programmer*) should be familiar with systems and the technical side of data processing.

3 *The scope and objectives of the survey were clearly stated.* Moses specifically told the 12 to investigate the richness of the land, the physical and numerical strength of the occupants, and the defensibility of their cities. In a system study, the nature of the operation(s) that is (are) to be investigated, and the objectives that are to be pursued, should also be specifically stated at the outset.

The biblical survey team returned to Moses after 40 days. There was agreement on the richness of the land (and this report was "documented" with examples of the fruit that it produced). There was lack of agreement, however, on the strength of the people occupying the Promised Land. Sessions were held during which the differing viewpoints were presented.

It is usually desirable for the team members to hold preliminary sessions with the managers of all departments that the study will affect. Such *design sessions* allow the managers to participate in setting or revising specific systems goals. This participation is logical; it enables those most familiar with existing methods and procedures to make suggestions for improvement. Furthermore, these managers are the ones whose performance is affected by any changes, and they are the ones whose cooperation is needed if the study is to yield satisfactory results. When it appears that tentative approval has been reached on objectives, the study leader should put these goals *in writing* and send them to all concerned for approval. If differences remain, they should be resolved in additional design sessions.

The Data-gathering Phase

Go placidly amid the noise and waste and remember
what comfort there may be in owning a piece
thereof. Avoid quiet and passive persons unless you
are in need of sleep. Rotate your tires. Speak
glowingly of those greater than yourself and heed
well their advice even though they be turkeys.
                              Anonymous in Deteriorata

The study-team members must first gather data on current operations before they can design suitable alternatives to achieve specified goals. In identifying objectives, it is likely that preliminary data were gathered. But more details are now needed to determine the strengths and weaknesses of current procedures. The data gathered must be accurate, up to date, and sufficiently complete, for they will become the input to the design stage. Although these data will vary from one study to another, answers to the questions found in Figure 7-3 are generally needed. Among the tools and techniques that may be useful in gathering data are *system flowcharts, questionnaire forms,* and *personal interviews.*

FIGURE 7-3

Data-gathering questions.

What source information is used?

What source documents are received?
What source documents are used?
Where do they originate?
What is the frequency of input—daily, weekly, or monthly?

What work is done?

What records and files are being kept to support the operation?
How frequently—daily, weekly, or monthly—is the operation being performed?
What is the volume or magnitude of work in each phase of the operation? What is the flow of work?

What business resources are used?

What departments are involved in the operation? What place in the organization do they occupy? What is the primary function of these departments?
How many people are involved? What are their skill levels?
How many labor-hours are needed?
What equipment, materials, and supplies are being used?

What results are achieved?

What output reports are prepared?
What is their purpose?
Who uses the reports?

System flowcharts A *flowchart* is a graphic tool or model that provides a means of recording, analyzing, and communicating problem information. The *system flowchart* provides a broad overview of the processing operations that are being accomplished (and/or that should be performed). Primary emphasis is placed on data flow among machines, i.e., on input documents and output reports. The amount of detail furnished about *how* a machine is to convert the data on input documents into the desired output is limited. In the design of all flowcharts it is necessary that standard *symbols* be used to record and communicate problem information clearly. Symbols representing input, output, and general processing (Figure 7-4) are frequently used in system flowcharts. The same basic I/O symbol may be used to show any type of media or data. Frequently, the basic I/O symbol is replaced in system flowcharts by other I/O symbols whose shape suggests the type of media or device being employed (Figure 7-5). These symbols are familiar to us since they have been used in earlier chapters. Additional commonly used system flowchart symbols are shown and described in Figure 7-6. Preparing flowcharts is helpful in gathering data on current operations. Beginning with source-document inputs, each operation step is charted, using the proper symbols. Files and equipment being used are identified, the processing sequence is shown, the departments involved are located, and the output results are indicated.

Questionnaire forms These forms are often keyed to steps in a flowchart. They give the details of processing frequencies, input and output volumes, workers performing each activity, time required to complete each step, and materials and supplies used.

FIGURE 7-4
Basic system charting symbols.

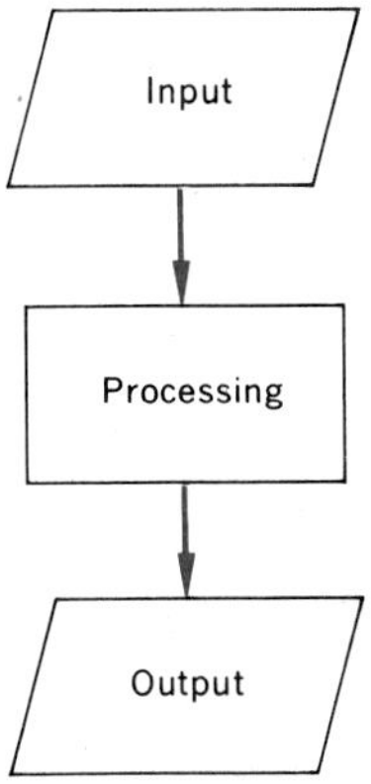

Personal interviews Interviews are needed to gather the information, prepare the flowchart, and fill in the questionnaire forms. Interviews also serve as a check on the reliability of procedures manuals and other existing system documentation. To verify the accuracy and completeness of interviews, an analyst may take an input document and "walk it through" the processing procedure. A walk-through also presents an opportunity for the analyst to obtain suggestions from employees about ways in which procedures might be improved. Interviews must be conducted with skill and tact.

Data Analysis and System Design
During the fact-finding stage, emphasis was placed on *what* was being done; now the team is interested in (1) learning *why* these activities are being performed and (2) designing the alternative ways

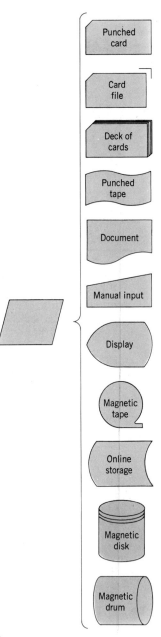

FIGURE 7-5
I/O (and storage) specialized
symbols.

in which these operations can be improved. Perhaps the first alternative that should be considered is a *modified and improved* version of present methods. An updating of current procedures may prevent useless forms and reports from being preserved in a conversion to an alternative.

During this analysis and design phase, the team is seeking to develop a set of specifications for the new or updated information system. Figure 7-7 lists some of the possible questions that should be answered during this review and design stage. However, the variety of different processing systems, the difficulty of describing these systems, the wide range of mechanical and electronic equipment that can be used, the speed with which equipment changes, the lack of static testing conditions caused by a rapidly changing environment—all these factors prevent the formulation of exact rules to follow in system analysis and design. Such factors also limit the number of alternative designs that can be manually evaluated. The questions in Figure 7-7 may be presented as a *guide.* But the success of the project is dependent upon the ingenuity of the team in arriving at answers that satisfy information needs.

It is assumed at this point that the study team has analyzed the current operations, prepared a detailed set of written (documented) system specifications to achieve the study goals, and settled on the alternatives that it feels will best achieve those goals. The prepared specifications should include:

1 *The input requirements* Included in the input specifications should be the source documents to be used, the means of preparing and transmitting those documents, the frequency of preparation, and the volume figures expected.
2 *The processing specifications* The new procedures must be defined. How the inputs will be used to prepare the desired outputs should be clearly indicated. All files and records to be used and maintained should be identified.
3 *The output requirements* The output specifications should include the form, content, and frequency of reports.
4 *Control provisions* The steps to be taken to provide the necessary system control should be specified.
5 *Cost estimates* Preliminary estimates of (a) set-up costs and (b) annual operating costs using the new system approach should be made.

Decision Making: Study Team

There are many system alternatives that may be used to solve information processing problems. In some situations, *noncomputer*

Symbols		Meaning of Symbols	Symbols		Meaning of Symbols
	Auxiliary operation	An operation which supplements the main processing function but which is performed by a machine that is not directly under the control of the CPU.		Merge	Used to indicate the combining of two or more sets of items into one set.
	Offline storage	A symbol representing data stored in external offline storage. Storage media may be cards, paper tapes, magnetic tapes, paper documents, etc.		Extract	Used to indicate the removal of one or more specific sets of items from a file or other set of items.
	Manual operation	Any offline process geared to the speed of a human being is represented by this symbol.		Collate	Combining merging with extracting. Two or more files or sets of items are combined and then two or more files or sets of items are extracted.
	Communications link	Automatic data transmission from one location to another.		Sort	Used to indicate the arranging of a file or other set of items into a sequence.
	Annotation flag	This "flag" is connected by the dashed line to a flow line to provide additional explanatory notes. The dashed line may be drawn on either the left or right. The vertical line may also be drawn on the right or left.			

FIGURE 7-6
Additional   system   flowchart
symbols.

"It's a bureaucratic hangover—everything in
triplicate. . . ."

Procedural considerations

1   Are documents being produced relevant to the needs of the business? When were they originated? Who originated them? For what purpose?

2   Is faster reporting desired? Is faster reporting necessary? Can the processing sequence be improved? What would happen if the document were delayed? If it were eliminated?

3   Is greater accuracy needed? Could less accuracy be tolerated, i.e., is the expense involved in error checking greater than the cost of committing the error? Is adequate control maintained over document preparation?

4   Does an output document cause action when it is sent to a manager? If not, why is it sent? If it does, what decisions are made?

5   Can documents be combined? Is the same information duplicated on other reports? In other departments? If so, can procedures be integrated?

6   Is there any part of the document which is ignored? Are unnecessary facts recorded? Are additional facts needed? Are the correct number of copies prepared?

Personnel and organizational considerations

7   Are documents being prepared in the proper departments? By the right people? Could departments be combined? Could any work units be eliminated? What effects would organizational change have on personnel?

8   What effect will procedural change have on personnel? Are personnel agreeable to such change? What has been done to reduce resistance to change? What will be done with workers whose jobs are eliminated or changed? If new jobs are created, has proper consideration been given to selecting and training workers to staff these vacancies?

Economic considerations

9   What will be the cost of processing data with revised current procedures? What will it cost to satisfy company needs by other alternatives? If the cost of using the computer is greater, are intangible benefits available which are worth the extra expense?

FIGURE 7-7
Questions for analysis and design.

options may be preferable. For other applications, the result of a study may indicate that the use of a *computer service center* or a *timesharing service* would be the best solution. In still other cases, problem-solving applications may be proposed to utilize the computer *hardware already installed* in an organization. And in some situations *new in-house computing* equipment may be required to achieve the study goals.

If new hardware is needed, the team must evaluate the ability of various machines to process the detailed set of written specifications that have been prepared. Among the *approaches that might be used* by the team *to evaluate and select hardware are:*

1 *Competitive-bidding approach* System specifications are given to equipment manufacturers with a request that they prepare bids. The vendors select what they believe to be the most appropriate hardware/software packages from their lines and submit proposals. Problems with this approach are that (*a*) the bids received are sometimes difficult to compare, and (*b*) processing times may be underestimated in the bids.
2 *Consultant-evaluation approach* Qualified independent data processing consultants may be used by the team to help with evaluation and selection.
3 *Electronic evaluation approach* Some consulting organizations have prepared computer programs that will project how different equipment models perform and respond to given system specifications. In other words, one computer can be used to give cost/performance estimates for other computer alternatives.

Regardless of the approach used, the team must compare such quantitative and qualitative factors as costs, hardware/software performance and reliability, maintenance terms and dependability, and the reputation of the vendor before making a hardware decision.

Once an equipment decision has been made, the team must then consider *acquisition methods*—i.e., the team must decide whether the equipment should be rented, purchased, or leased. *Renting* from the vendor is a flexible approach that does not require a large initial investment, but it may be the most expensive approach if the machine(s) are used for 4 or 5 years or longer. *Purchasing* may be the least-expensive method when the hardware is kept for several years, but a large capital outlay is required and there is the risk of being "locked-in" to a system that does not continue to meet changing company needs. Under a typical *leasing* arrangement, the user tells a leasing organization what equipment is desired. The leasing firm then arranges for the purchase of the equipment and leases it to the user for a period of from 3 to 5 years. This method has some of the advantages (and disadvantages) of both renting and purchasing.

Study-Team Recommendations

I go . . . the bell invites me,
. . . for it is a Knell
That summons thee to Heaven or to Hell.
William Shakespeare

Guided by a written charter, which defined the scope and direction of their efforts, the study team has analyzed the relevant facts; from this analysis has come a detailed set of system specifications designed to achieve the study goals. After careful consideration of alternatives, the team may have concluded that computer usage is justified. A particular hardware/software package may have been chosen, and the best acquisition method for the company has been agreed upon. The team has made many decisions. But the *final* decisions are made by top-level managers. It is the job of the team to recommend; it is the responsibility of the top executives to decide.

The report of the system-study team should cover the following points:

1 A restatement of study scope and objectives
2 The procedures and operations that will be changed
3 The anticipated effects of such changes on organizational structure, physical facilities, and company information
4 The anticipated effects on personnel and the personnel resources available to implement the change
5 The hardware/software package chosen, the reasons for the choice, and the alternatives considered
6 The economic effects of the change, including cost comparisons
7 A summary of the problems anticipated in the changeover
8 A summary of the benefits to be obtained from the change

Top-Management Decisions

I have two nights watched
with you, but can perceive
no truth in your report.
William Shakespeare

Top executives must evaluate the recommendations made by the team to detect any evidence of bias and decide whether the benefits outweigh the disadvantages. Suspicion of bias or of an inadequate effort may be justified if the points outlined above are not included in the recommendation. For example, suspicion is probably warranted if little or no mention is made of the personnel or organizational aspects of the change, if the alternatives considered are really just "straw men" which are obviously inadequate, or if feasibility depends solely on vaguely defined and suspicious intangible benefits.

If the decision is to accept the recommendations of the team, top executives should then establish subsequent project performance controls. Personnel must be assigned to create the system solution, an implementation schedule should be drawn up, and periodic reports on progress should be required. In the following chapters we shall look at these programming and system implementation steps shown earlier in Figure 7-2.

SUMMARY

Computers can supply decision makers with necessary information. But a multistep process must usually be followed before a computer can be used to provide this information.

A system study is often conducted prior to the development of computer applications. Such a study may help to reduce the risk of economic loss and to avoid the pitfalls often associated with inadequate information system planning. The steps in the system-study approach are to (1) identify the scope of the problem and the objectives to be gained, (2) gather the facts on current operations, (3) analyze current operations and determine suitable solutions, and (4) decide on the most appropriate solution. These four steps may be considered the system development phase, and they have been discussed in this chapter. In addition to these steps, however, it will also be necessary to (5) create the computer programs to implement the solution, and (6) follow up on the decisions made. These later steps are the subjects of the next chapters.

REVIEW AND DISCUSSION QUESTIONS

1 Identify and discuss the steps in the process to be followed in using computers to solve business information processing problems.

2 (a) What is a system study? (b) Why is it essential? (c) Identify and explain the steps in the system development approach.

3 What are the prerequisite principles that should be observed in making a system study?

4 What tools and techniques are useful during the data-gathering phase?
5 (**a**) What is a system flowchart? (**b**) How is it used?
6 What symbols are used in system flowcharts to represent input and output?
7 (**a**) What approaches could be used by the study team to evaluate and select new computing equipment? (**b**) How might such equipment be acquired?
8 At the conclusion of the initial system development phase, what topics should be covered by the study team in their recommendations to top executives?
9 Discuss the objectives of the system study team during the data-analysis and system-design stage.

PROGRAMMING ANALYSIS

Once the initial system development steps discussed in the last chapter have been employed by analysts to determine the broad system specifications, the programming process may begin. Breaking down the new system specifications into the detailed arithmetic and logic operations required to solve the problem is the purpose of programming analysis. Two common tools used for analysis purposes are the *program flowchart* and the *decision table*.

PROGRAM FLOWCHARTS

Flowcharts have existed for years and have been used for many purposes. As noted earlier, the system flowchart provides a broad overview of the processing operations that are to be accomplished, but it does not go into detail about how input data are to be used to produce output information. A *program flowchart,* on the other hand, does present a detailed graphical representation of how steps are to be performed *within* the machine to produce the needed output. Thus, the program flowchart evolves from the system chart.

FIGURE 8-1

Grade preparation system.

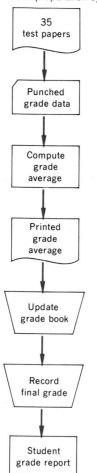

An Elementary Example

Professor Shirley A. Meany, an accounting professor, wishes to compute an average (arithmetic mean) grade for a beginning accounting student based on the 35 tests she has given during the semester. (Professor Meany teaches a rigorous course!) In Figure 8-1 we see that the system followed is one in which the grade data for the student are punched into cards that are then fed into a computer for processing. The computed average is printed, and Professor Meany manually updates her grade book and then prepares her final grade report on the student. We shall be concerned with only one student, but, of course, any number of student grade averages could easily be automatically processed by the computer.

In Figure 8-1 we can also see several flowcharting conventions. The arrows connecting the shapes indicate the direction of data flow. The main flow is generally charted from top to bottom and from left to right. The *shape* of the symbol and *not its size* identifies the meaning. For example, the rectangular processing box may vary in size, but the shape still designates that processing is being performed. Notation within the charting symbol further explains what is being done.

In Shirley's grade preparation diagram, a single processing box is labeled "compute grade average." Unfortunately, such an instruction is not sufficient for the computer. Thus, as a part of the programming process the programmer must specify each step needed to compute the average grade. In short, the *single* processing box labeled "compute grade average" becomes the basis for a detailed *program* flowchart.

Only a few symbols, when properly arranged, are needed in program charting to define the necessary steps. These symbols are illustrated in Figure 8-2 and are described below.

Input/output   The basic I/O symbol is also used in program flow-charting to represent any I/O function. The specific symbols designating cards, tapes, etc., are generally not used with program diagrams. Figure 8-3 presents a portion of a program chart (the total chart shows the steps required to compute the average grade by Professor Meany). The I/O symbol here means that a punched card containing a student grade is to be read into the computer. The same symbol, of course, could be used to represent any output form.

Processing   Again, the rectangle represents processing operations. But now the processing described is a *small segment* of the major processing step called for in the system chart. Arithmetic and data movement instructions are generally placed in these boxes.

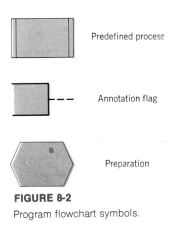

Symbol	Name
	Input/output
	Processing
	Terminal
	Decision
	Connector
	Predefined process
	Annotation flag
	Preparation

FIGURE 8-2
Program flowchart symbols.

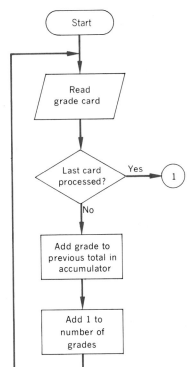

FIGURE 8-3
Partial flowchart of grade-averaging example. (This chart shows a loop with a counter and a test for last record.)

Two processing symbols are shown in Figure 8-3. The upper box provides for the accumulation of the total number of points in the CPU arithmetic-logic unit. Thus, when the last grade card has been read, the total of all the test scores will be stored in the accumulator. The lower processing box is a *counter* that is incremented (or stepped up by one) each time the *loop* in Figure 8-3 is executed. So when the last card has been processed, the counter will indicate the number of tests taken. To get an average grade, as you know, the total number of points must be divided by the number of tests taken. Therefore, the lower processing box gives the denominator, the upper box the numerator.

Termination   The terminal symbol, as the name suggests, represents the beginning and the end of a program. It may also be used to signal a program interruption point when information may enter or leave. For example, to detect certain errors in input data the programmer may provide a special program branch ending in a terminal symbol labeled "HALT."

Decision   The I/O and processing symbols, typically, have two flow lines (one entry and one exit), while the terminal has a single entrance or exit line. The diamond-shaped decision symbol, on the other hand, has one entrance line and *at least* two exit paths or

"SHE LOVES ME—SHE LOVES ME NOT"

branches.[1] As Figure 8-3 shows, exit paths may be determined by a yes or no answer to some stated condition or *test*—in this case, the condition to be determined is whether or not the last grade card has been processed. If the answer is yes, then the total of all exam scores is contained in the accumulator and the program can branch away from the loop that it has been following by reading cards and totaling scores successively. If the answer to the test is no, the program continues to process the grade cards until they are all accounted for. Other examples of the use of the decision symbols are shown in Figure 8-4.

Connector The *circular connector* symbol is used when additional flow lines might cause confusion and reduce understanding. Two connectors with identical labels serve the same function as a long flow line; i.e., they show an entry from another part of the chart, or they indicate an exit to some other chart section. How is it possible to determine if a connector is used as an entry point or an exit point? It is very simple: If an arrow *enters but does not leave a connector,* it is an exit point and program flow is transferred to that identically labeled connector that *does* have an outlet.

Figure 8-5 completes the chart begun in Figure 8-3 and shows the program steps that must be performed by Professor Meany to compute the average grade. This chart also illustrates the use of connec-

---

[1]Don R. Cartlidge writes that "to accurately represent all the weird and wonderful choices of data processing, several more arrows are needed. One should exit left and be labeled 'Maybe,' one to the top should say 'Maybe Not,' and one should point into the paper and say 'Who Knows?' Perhaps there should be one more that points out of the paper, aimed right between the reader's eyes, that says 'Who Cares?'" See "Go and Sin No More," *Computer Decisions,* p. 41, March 1976.

FIGURE 8-4

Decision symbol examples.

The number X is shown being tested to determine whether it is equal to zero, greater than (>) zero, or less than (<) zero, i.e., a negative value.

In this case, the two variables Y and Z are compared ("$Y:Z$" means to "compare Y to Z").

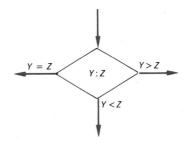

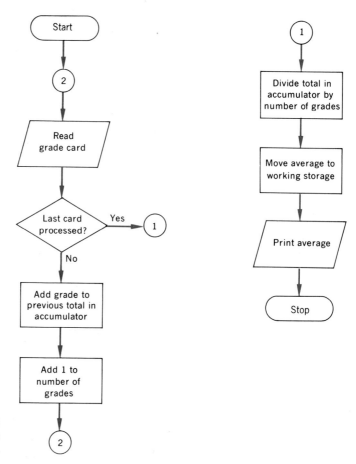

FIGURE 8-5
Program flowchart to average
grades.

tor symbols. As we have seen, when the last card is processed, the
computer is ready to figure the average grade. This step is performed by the first processing instruction below the upper connector
labeled "1." The remaining steps in the chart are self-explanatory.

Predefined process Programmers frequently find that certain
kinds of processing operations are repeated in one or more of the
programs used by their organization. For example, a department
store programmer may find that the steps needed to compute cash
discounts are being repeated several times in some programs and
used in a number of different programs. Instead of rewriting this
small subordinate routine each time it is needed, the programmer
can prepare it once and then integrate it into the program or programs as required. *Libraries* of these predefined processes, or

subroutines, are often maintained to reduce the cost and time of programming. Thus, a single predefined process symbol replaces a number of operations that are not detailed at that particular point in the chart. In short, the subroutine receives input from the primary program, performs its limited task, and then returns the output to the primary program.

Annotation flag The comments made in Figure 7-6 also apply to program flowcharts.

Preparation The preparation symbol indicates a program modification or change. It would be the appropriate symbol to use, for example, to indicate a switch setting.

A Simple Business Example

The flowchart in Figure 8-6 shows how an unsympathetic department store might handle the billing of *overdue* accounts. A late payment penalty is charged to accounts 30 or more days overdue.[2] The amount of the penalty is based on the unpaid balance in the account: If the balance is over $200, i.e., if the balance is *not* equal to or less than ($\leqslant$) $200, the penalty is 3 percent; otherwise a 2 percent charge is levied. The amount of the penalty must be added to the next bill sent to the customer. If the account is 60 days or more overdue ($\geqslant$ 60), a warning message is printed on the bill. Accounts which are *less than* 30 days overdue ($<$ 30) are not included in this procedure. But in the event that such an account is entered by mistake, provision is made to prevent it from being processed (see the left side of Figure 8-6). The store's credit manager, Fuller ("Hammer") Nastee, handles, on an individual basis, those accounts that remain unpaid after a certain time. To test your understanding of Figure 8-6, determine what actions would be taken if a particular account with a balance of $300 were 60 days or more overdue. (The answer is given a few pages later in this chapter.)

Benefits and
Limitations of Flowcharts

The following *benefits* may be obtained through the use of flowcharts:

---

[2]In Figure 8-6, the symbol $\geqslant$ means *equal to or greater than.* Therefore $\geqslant$ 30 refers to accounts equal to or greater than 30 days overdue. Similarly, $\leqslant$ means *equal to or less than.*

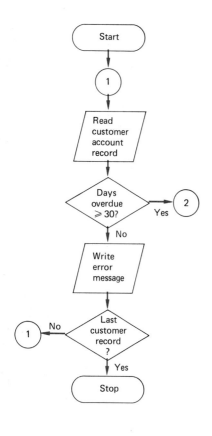

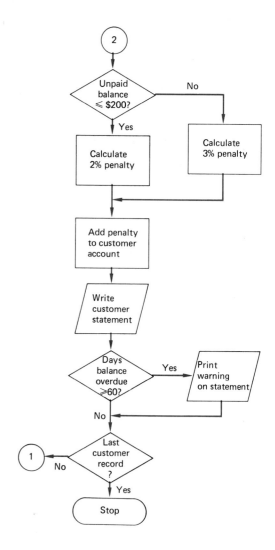

FIGURE 8-6
Program flowchart showing an accounts-receivable penalty procedure.

1 *Quicker grasp of relationships* Before any problem can be solved, it must be understood. The relationships that exist among problem elements must be identified. Current and proposed procedures may be understood more rapidly through the use of charts.

2 *Effective analysis* The flowchart becomes a model of a program or system that can be broken down into detailed parts for study.

3 *Effective synthesis* Synthesis is the opposite of analysis; it is the combination of the various parts into a whole entity. Flowcharts may be used as working models in the design of new programs and systems.

4 *Communication* Flowcharts aid in communicating the facts of a business problem to those whose skills are needed in the solution. The old adage that "a picture is worth a thousand words" contains an element of truth when the pictures happen to be flowchart symbols.

5 *Proper program documentation*–Program *documentation* involves collecting, organizing, storing, and otherwise maintaining a complete historical record of programs and the other documents associated with the organization's data processing systems. Proper program documentation is needed for the following reasons: (*a*) Documented knowledge belongs to an organization and does not disappear with the departure of a programmer. (*b*) If projects are postponed, proper documentation will indicate the problem definition, task objective, extent of prior work, etc., so that the work done will not have to be duplicated. (*c*) If programs are modified in the future, the programmer will have a more understandable record of what was originally done. (*d*) When staff changes occur, proper documentation serves a training function by helping new employees understand existing programs. (*e*) Proper documentation will aid greatly in future program conversion when new hardware/software packages are acquired. (*f*) Poor documentation represents a fundamental weakness in internal control and is an indication of poor management. From what we have seen of the nature of flowcharts, it is obvious that they provide valuable documentation support for all but the simplest of programs.

6 *Efficient coding* The program flowchart acts as a guide or blueprint during the program preparation phase. Instructions coded in a programming language may be checked against the flowchart to make sure that no steps are omitted.

7 *Orderly checkout of programs* If the program fails to run to completion and produce correct output when submitted to the computer, the flowchart may help in detecting and removing mistakes.

In spite of their many advantages, flowcharts have a few *limitations*. The *first* is that complex and detailed charts are sometimes

laborious to plan and draw, especially when a large number of
decision paths are involved.[3] A *second* limitation in such a situation
is that although branches from a *single* decision symbol are easy to
follow, the actions to be taken given certain specified conditions
would be difficult to follow if there were *several* paths. For example,
the answer to the question asked earlier about what action should be
taken with the $300 account that was 60 days overdue was probably
not immediately obvious even though Figure 8-6 outlines a relatively
simple procedure. But with more complex problems the appropriate
actions become much more obscure when flowcharts are used.
Under such circumstances, flowcharts may be replaced or supple-
mented by decision tables.

DECISION TABLES

A *decision table* can be a powerful tool for defining complex program logic. Figure 8-7 shows the basic table format. The table is
divided by the bottom horizontal colored line into two main parts: the
upper part, which contains the *conditions and questions* that are to
be considered in reaching a decision; and the lower part, which
contains the prescribed *action* to be taken when a given set of
conditions is present.

A Simple
Business Example—Again

The conditions and questions are written in the *condition stub* to the
left of the colored vertical line. The contents of the condition stub

---

[3]During the program preparation stage, sections of original charts may be added
to, deleted, patched, and otherwise marked up to the point where they become nearly
illegible. Since considerable time and effort could be required to manually redraw
complex charts, special automatic flowcharting programs have been developed,
which use a high-speed printer to produce the charts in good form.

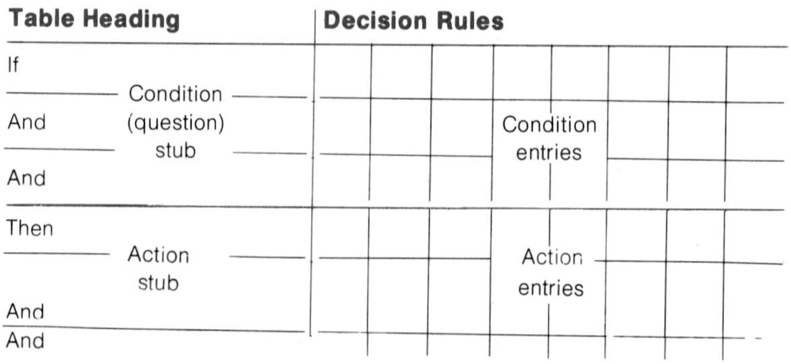

FIGURE 8-7
Decision table format.

correspond to the statements and questions contained in the *decision symbols* of the flowchart; the *condition entries* to the right of the colored vertical line in the figure correspond to the branches or *paths* going out from decision symbols in a flowchart. Thus a condition entry may be a simple yes (Y) or no (N); it may be a symbol which shows relationship between variables ($>$, $<$, $=$, $\geq$, etc.); or it may be the outcome of certain tests (code 1, code 2, etc.). The *action statements,* which correspond to the action statements located in nondecision symbols of a flowchart, are written in the *action stub.* The conditions may be listed in any convenient order; the actions are listed in the order in which they are normally executed. To briefly summarize, the upper (condition) parts of a decision table are generally concerned with "IF" statements (which are made or implied) and with the responses to those IF statements, while the lower (action) quadrants deal with "THEN" statements and responses to the specified conditions. In short, IF certain conditions exist, THEN specified actions should be taken.

A maze of possible flow paths may exist between START and STOP in a program. Each of the columns in the table *body* is the equivalent of *one* path through the flowchart and is called a *rule.* When a table is completed, each rule column which is used contains one or more condition entries. An example should help clarify matters.

Figure 8-8 shows the decision table for the accounts-receivable penalty procedure charted in Figure 8-6. You will notice that the statements in the condition stub correspond to the questions being asked in the flowchart decision symbols. You will also note that the action statements correspond to the directions given or implied by the other flowchart symbols. A few paragraphs earlier this question was asked: What actions would be taken if an account with a balance of $300 were 60 days or more overdue? Let us now look at column 6 (which follows that particular path through the flowchart) to check the answer. The first entry in the column shows that the account is 60 days or more overdue. The second condition is irrelevant in this case, and so the space in rule 6 is left blank. The second entry tells us that the unpaid balance is not equal to or less than $200, and so therefore it must be greater than that figure. The third entry merely shows that the last record has not yet been processed. Thus, the set of conditions in rule 6 has defined our problem! (The other condition sets have defined all the other feasible paths or situations.)

Now what about the *answer* (finally!) to the problem? An x has been placed in column 6 opposite each appropriate action that helps satisfy the given set of conditions. You can compare your

Accounts-Receivable Penalty Procedure		Decision Rule Number						
		1	2	3	4	5	6	7
Condition	Number days balance overdue	<30	<30	≥30	≥30	≥60	≥60	
	Number days balance overdue			<60	<60			
	Unpaid balance ≤ $200?			Y	N	Y	N	
	Last customer account record?	N	Y	N	N	N	N	Y
Action	Calculate 2% penalty			x		x		
	Calculate 3% penalty				x		x	
	Add penalty to customer account			x	x	x	x	
	Write customer statement			x	x	x	x	
	Print warning on statement					x	x	
	Write error	x	x					
	Go to next account record	x		x	x	x	x	
	Stop		x					x

FIGURE 8-8

Decision table for accounts-
receivable penalty procedure
(*Source:* Figure 8-6).

answer with the one indicated in Figure 8-8. You may also want to trace through the table and the flowchart to see what actions are taken when other possible conditions occur.

In our simple business example we have compared a decision table with the flowchart of the problem. But in actual practice, tables are not necessarily compared with charts. Why? Simply because there may be no flowchart. As noted earlier, tables may be used as chart substitutes. A number of small interconnected tables may be quickly constructed to express the logic required to solve complex problems.

Benefits and Limitations of Decision Tables

The following *benefits* may be obtained from the use of decision tables:

1 *Less danger of omitting a logical possibility* Tables force the analyst to think the problem through. For example, if there are

three conditions to be considered, each of which can be answered yes or no, then there are 2^3 or 8 possible paths or rules.[4] Some of these conceivable paths may not, of course, be pertinent to the problem. But by knowing the total number of paths, the analyst lessens the danger of forgetting one.

2 *Better communication between interested parties* Tables can perform a valuable communication function. An analyst may design a new system and present it in the form of a table or tables to other analysts, programmers, and managers. Tables appear to be easier for many managers to follow than flowcharts. Operating managers can quickly trace and verify those paths in the procedure that are of greatest interest to them.

3 *Easier construction and adaptability* Tables are easier to draw up than comparable flowcharts. They are also easier to change since it is a relatively simple matter to add conditions, rules, and actions to a table.

4 *More compact program documentation* Several pages of flow-charting may be condensed into one small table. And, of course, it is easier to follow a particular flow path down one column than it is to follow the same path through several flowchart pages.

5 *Direct conversion into computer programs* It is possible for the contents of a decision table to be coded directly into a language that the computer understands.

Although decision tables appear to have an edge over flowcharts in expressing complex decision logic, they do have *limitations* and are not as widely used as flowcharts because (1) many problems are simple, have few branches, and lend themselves to charting; (2) charts are able to express the *total sequence* of events better; and (3) charts are familiar to, and preferred by, many programmers who resist changing to the use of tables.

SUMMARY Once broad system specifications have been determined, the programming process may begin. The first step in programming is to break the specifications down into specific arithmetic and logic operations. The remaining steps are to (1) prepare programs in a form that the processor can accept, (2) test the new programs, and (3) implement and maintain them as needed. These remaining steps will be considered in the next chapters.

---

[4]These rules contain the following entries:

(1)	(2)	(3)	(4)	(5)	(6)	(7)	(8)
Y	Y	Y	N	Y	N	N	N
Y	Y	N	Y	N	Y	N	N
Y	N	Y	Y	N	N	Y	N

The basic tools of programming analysis are flowcharts and decision tables. System flowcharts provide the broad overview required for programming analysis to begin. Program flowcharts evolve from the system charts. A set of standardized charting symbols is presented in Figure 8-2. Compared with pages of written notes, flowcharts help the programmer obtain a quicker grasp of relationships. Charts also aid in communication, provide valuable documentation support, and contribute to more efficient coding and program maintenance.

A decision table is an excellent means of defining complex program logic. In this respect it has an edge over flowcharts. A table is easy to construct and change. It is more compact, provides excellent program documentation, and is an aid in communication.

REVIEW AND DISCUSSION QUESTIONS

1 (**a**) What is the purpose of a program flowchart? (**b**) How does it differ from a system flowchart?

2 (**a**) What symbols are used in a program flowchart to represent input and output, processing, decision, terminal, and connector? (**b**) Construct a flowchart on a problem of your choice using these symbols.

3 What is a subroutine?

4 Discuss the benefits and limitations of flowcharts.

5 Why is proper documentation required?

6 (**a**) What is a decision table? (**b**) Explain the basic parts of the decision table. (**c**) What is a rule?

7 What benefits may be obtained from the use of decision tables?

PREPARING COMPUTER PROGRAMS

LEARNING OBJECTIVES

After studying this chapter and answering the discussion questions, you should be able to:

Summarize the steps in the programming process.

Identify the types of commands that may be executed by a computer.

Explain the differences between machine, symbolic, and high-level programming languages.

Discuss the factors that should be considered in the selection of a programming language.

Outline some of the characteristics and some of the strengths and weaknesses of FORTRAN, COBOL, PL/I, BASIC, and RPG.

We have seen that the programming process begins with the broad system specifications. The programmer analyzes these specifications in terms of (1) the *output solution* needed, (2) the *operations and procedures* required to achieve the necessary output, and (3) the *input data* that are necessary to produce the output. In connection with this analysis, the programmer develops a programming plan and prepares program flowcharts and/or decision tables which detail the procedures for converting input data into output information. Once the analysis phase is completed, the next step is to prepare the written instructions that will control the computer during the processing. These instructions are generally coded in a higher-level translatable language according to a specific set of rules. And as we saw in Chapter 2, higher-level source program statements must then be converted into the machine language object program that the computer can accept. If this conversion is successful, the object program must still be tested before it is used on a routine basis; if the conversion is not successful, or if difficulties arise during program testing, the program must be debugged to correct mistakes and errors. Finally, all supporting documents pertaining to the problem and the program solution must be assembled and put in good order, and the program must be maintained as required. Figure 9-1 summarizes this brief review of the programming process.

The purpose of this chapter is to give you an idea of what a programming language is and what is involved in expressing problems in a language that is acceptable to a computer. Therefore, in the following pages we shall look at (1) *computer instructions,* (2) *languages for computers,* and (3) *program coding with popular languages.* The subject of program debugging, testing, documentation, maintenance, and other topics necessary to the implementation of programs and systems are considered in the next chapter.

COMPUTER INSTRUCTIONS

A program, we know, is a complete set of written instructions that enables the computer to process a particular application. Thus, the instruction is the fundamental component in program preparation. Like a sentence, a machine instruction prepared in a *basic form* consists of a subject and a predicate. The subject, however, is usually *not* specifically mentioned; it is, instead, some *implied* part of the computer system that is directed to execute the command that is given. For example, if a teacher tells a student to "read the book," the student will interpret this instruction correctly even though the subject "you" is omitted. Similarly, if the machine is told to "ADD

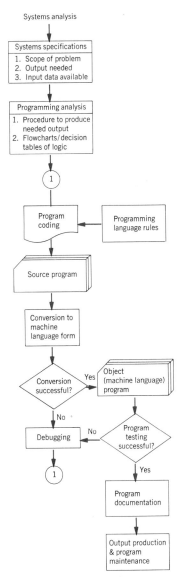

Systems analysis

Systems specifications
1. Scope of problem
2. Output needed
3. Input data available

Programming analysis
1. Procedure to produce
   needed output
2. Flowcharts/decision
   tables of logic

1

Program
coding

Programming
language rules

Source program

Conversion to
machine
language form

Conversion
successful? Yes Object
(machine language)
program

No

Debugging No Program
testing
successful?

1

Yes

Program
documentation

Output production
& program
maintenance

FIGURE 9-1
Programming process.

0184," the control unit may interpret this to mean that the arithmetic-logic unit is to add the contents of address 0184 to the contents of the accumulator.

In addition to an implied subject, every basic computer instruction has an explicit predicate consisting of at least two parts. The *first* part is referred to as the *command,* or *operation;* it answers the question "what?"; i.e., it tells the computer what operation it is to perform. Each machine has a limited number of built-in operations that it is capable of executing. An *operation code* is used to communicate the programmer's intent to the machine. Operation codes vary from one machine line to another.

The *second* explicit part of the instruction, known as the *operand,* names the object of the operation. In general terms, the operand answers the question "where?"; i.e., it tells the computer where to find or store the data or other instructions that are to be manipulated. Thus, an operand may indicate:

1 The location where data to be processed are to be found.
2 The location where the result of processing is to be stored.
3 The location where the next instruction to be executed is to be found. (When this type of operand is not specified, the instructions are taken in sequence.)

The *number* of operands and therefore the structure or format of the instruction *vary* from one computer to another. Up to this point we have dealt only with instructions having a *single* operand. But in addition to the *single-address* format there are also *two-* and *three-address* command structures (see Figure 9-2).

The number of commands that may be executed also varies from less than 50 to more than 200 depending on the computer make and model. These commands may be classified into (1) I/O, (2) data movement and manipulation, (3) arithmetic, (4) logic, and (5) transfer of control categories. *Input/output* instructions are required to permit communication between I/O devices and the CPU. *Data movement and manipulation* commands are used to copy data from one storage location to another and to rearrange and change data elements in some prescribed manner. An example of a data movement command is shown in Figure 9-2*(b).* If the programmer of a two-address processor wishes to preserve the number in address 0184 for future use, he or she may need to copy the number in another location prior to the add instruction. *Arithmetic* commands to permit addition, subtraction, multiplication, and division are, of course, common in all digital computers. *Logic* instructions are available to permit

Command			Explanation
Code	**Meaning**	**Operand**	
(1) XX	(CLA)	0184	Three steps are used to perform an addition and a storage
(2) XX	(ADD)	8672	operation. The accumulator is cleared of previous data, and
(3) XX	(STO)	1273	the number in address 0184 is then put in that register (1). The
			number in address 8672 is added to the first number. The result
			is now in the accumulator (2). The result in the accumulator is
(a)			stored in address 1273 (3).

Command				Explanation
Code	**Meaning**	**First Operand**	**Second Operand**	
(1) XX	(ADD)	0184	8672	The number in address 8672 is added to the number in location
(2) XX	(MOVE)	0184	0185	0184. The result may automatically be stored in address 0184
(3) XX	(ADD)	0184	8672	by the computer circuitry. Of course, this erases the original
				number contained in 0184, so if that number is to be saved, it
				must be duplicated elsewhere *prior* to the add instruction.
				Instructions (2) and (3) show how this could be done. Instruc-
				tion (2) duplicates the contents of 0184 in 0185 prior to the
(b)				addition order (3).

Command					Explanation
Code	**Meaning**	**First Operand**	**Second Operand**	**Third Operand**	
(1) XX	(ADD)	0184	8672	1273	The number in address 8672 is added to the number in 0184,
(c)					and the result is stored in address 1273.

FIGURE 9-2

Command structures: (*a*) single-address, (*b*) two-address, (*c*) three-address.

comparison between variables. *Transfer of control* instructions may then be used to branch or change the sequence of program control, depending on the outcome of the comparison. Of course, some transfer instructions are not based on the outcome of comparisons. As you know, transfer commands may be *conditional* or *unconditional*. If the change in sequence is based on the outcome of a test or comparison, then it is a conditional transfer; if not, it is an unconditional branch.

LANGUAGES FOR COMPUTERS

You taught me language; and my profit on't
Is, I know how to curse. The red plague rid you
For learning me your language!

William Shakespeare

In writing program instructions, the programmer must use a language that can be understood by the computer. Let us now look at several language categories that have been developed.

Machine Languages

Early computers were quite intolerant. Programmers had to translate instructions directly into the machine language form that computers understood—a form consisting of a string of numbers that represented the command code and operand address. To compound the difficulty for programmers, the string of numbers was often not even in decimal form. For example, the instruction to ADD 0184 looks like this in the IBM 7040 machine language:[1]

000100000000000000000000000010111000

In addition to remembering the dozens of code numbers for the commands in the machine's repertoire, a programmer was also forced to keep track of the storage locations of data and instructions. The initial coding often took months, was therefore quite expensive, and often resulted in error. Checking instructions to locate errors was about as tedious as writing them initially. And if a program had to be modified at a later date, the work involved could take weeks to finish.

Symbolic Languages

To ease the programmer's burden, *mnemonic* command codes and *symbolic* addresses were developed in the early 1950s. The word *mnemonic* (pronounced *ne-mon-ik*) refers to a memory aid. One of the first steps in improving the program preparation process was to substitute letter symbols for basic machine language command codes. Each computer now has a mnemonic code, although, of course, the actual symbols vary among different makes.[2] Machine language is *still* used by the computer in the actual processing of the data, but it first translates the specified command code symbol into its machine language equivalent.

---

[1] In this case, the last 8 bits represent 0184.

[2] For example, erasing old data in the accumulator and then adding the contents of an address to it is a common command. The mnemonic code used in some computers is ZA (Zero and Add). In other machines the symbol for the same operation may be CLA (CLear accumulator and Add) or RAD (Reset accumulator and ADd). Some examples of symbolic programming languages are IBM's Assembler Language and Honeywell's Easycoder.

The improvement in the writing of command codes set the stage for further advances. It was reasoned that if the computer could be used to translate convenient symbols into basic commands, why couldn't it also be used to perform other clerical coding functions such as assigning storage addresses to data? This question led to *symbolic addressing;* i.e., it led to the practice of expressing an address, not in terms of its absolute numerical location, but rather in terms of symbols convenient to the programmer.

In the early stages of symbolic addressing, the programmer initially assigned a symbolic name and an actual address to a data item. For example, the total value of merchandise purchased during a month by a department store customer might be assigned to address 0063 by the programmer and given the symbolic name of TOTAL. Also, the value of merchandise returned unused during the month might be assigned to address 2047 and given the symbolic name of CREDIT. Then, for the remainder of the program, the programmer would refer to the *symbolic names rather than to the addresses* when such items were to be processed. Thus, an instruction might be written "S CREDIT, TOTAL" to subtract the value of returned goods from the total amount purchased to find the amount of the customer's monthly bill. The computer might then translate this symbolic instruction into the following machine language string of bits:

011111	011111111111	000000111111
Operation or command code	2047	0063
(S)	(CREDIT)	(TOTAL)

Another improvement was that the programmer turned the task of assigning and keeping track of instruction addresses over to the computer. The programmer merely told the machine the storage address number of the *first* program instruction, and then all others were automatically stored in sequence from that point by the processor. If another instruction were to be added later to the program, it was not then necessary to modify the addresses of all instructions that followed the point of insertion (as would have to be done in the case of programs written in machine language). In such a case, the processor automatically adjusted storage locations the next time the program was used.

Programmers no longer assign actual address numbers to symbolic data items as they did initially. Rather, they merely specify

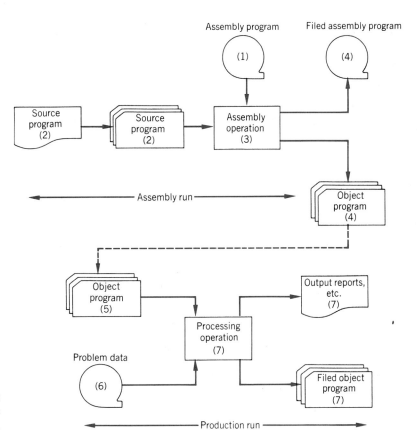

FIGURE 9-3
Converting symbolic language to
machine language.

where they want the first location in the program to be, and an
assembly program then takes it from there, allocating locations for
instructions and data. The *assembly program* translates the programmer's symbolic language instructions into the machine code of
the computer. The following steps (numbered in Figure 9-3) take
place during the *assembly* and *production* runs:

1 The *assembly program* is read into the computer, where it has
   complete control over the translating procedure.
2 The *source program* written by the programmer in the symbolic
   language of the machine is recorded on an input medium such
   as punched cards.
3 During the assembly the source program is treated as data and
   is read into the CPU an instruction at a time under the control of
   the assembly program.

4 The assembly program translates the source program into a machine language *object program,* which is recorded on tapes or cards as the output of the assembly run. It is important to remember that *during the assembly run no problem data are processed.* That is, the source program is not *being executed;* it is merely being converted into a form in which it *can* be executed. After the assembly run, the assembly program is filed for future use.

5 The object program is read into the CPU as the first step in the *production run.*

6 Problem data, recorded on a suitable input medium, are read into the CPU under object program control.

7 The application is processed, the information output is properly received, and the object program is filed for future repetitive use.

Symbolic languages possess *advantages over machine languages.* Much time is saved; detail is reduced; fewer errors are made (and those that are made are easier to find); and programs are easier to modify. But there are *limitations.* Coding in symbolic language is still time-consuming. Also, symbolic languages are *machine oriented;* i.e., they are designed for the specific make and model of processor being used. Programs might have to be recoded if the organization acquired a different machine. Furthermore, the programmer writing instructions in a machine's symbolic language must have an intimate knowledge of the workings of that processor. Finally, the earlier assembly programs produced only *one* machine instruction for each source program instruction.

High-Level Languages

To speed up coding, assembly programs were developed that could produce a *variable* amount of machine language code for *each* source program instruction. In other words, a single *macro instruction* might produce *several* lines of machine language code. For example, the programmer might write "READ FILE," and the translating software might then automatically provide a detailed series of previously prepared machine language instructions which would copy a record into primary storage from the file of data being read by the input device. In spite of significant advances, however, assembly programs were still machine oriented; they were still written to meet the requirements of a specific equipment line.

The development of mnemonic techniques and macro instructions led, in turn, to the development of *high-level languages* that are often oriented toward a particular class of processing problems. For example, a number of languages have been designed to process problems of a scientific-mathematic nature, and other languages have appeared that emphasize the processing of business applications.

Unlike symbolic programs, high-level language programs may be used with *different makes of computers* with little modification. Thus, reprogramming expense may be greatly reduced when new equipment is acquired. *Other advantages of high-level languages are:* (1) they are easier to learn than symbolic languages; (2) they require less time to write; (3) they provide better documentation; and (4) they are easier to maintain. Also, a programmer skilled in writing programs in such a language is not restricted to using a single machine.

Naturally, a source program written in a high-level language must also be translated into a machine-usable code. The translating program that performs this operation is called a *compiler.* Compilers, like advanced assembly programs, may generate many lines of machine code for each source program statement.[3] A *compiling run* is required before problem data can be processed. With the exception that a compiler program is substituted for an assembly program, the procedures are the same as those shown in Figure 9-3. The production run follows the compiling run.

Which Language to Use?

As you have concluded by now, a number of languages are generally available that will permit the programmer to write instructions to control the computer during the processing of an application. Which of these languages should be used? Obviously, a selection must be made prior to program coding, but several factors may combine to make language selection difficult. However, obtaining answers to the following questions will generally help in the selection process:

1 *Are company programmers familiar with the language?* In many cases, the language used is simply the one that is best known to the programmers. If a language is not familiar, can it be learned quickly? Is it easy to use?

---

[3]Some use the word *statement* to refer to a line of code in a high-level language and the word *instruction* to refer to a line of machine or symbolic language code that will produce a single machine operation.

2   *What is the nature of the application?* Does the language perform well in applications of this type?

3   *Is satisfactory translating software available?* There is an important distinction, for example, between a language and a compiler. A language is a humanly convenient set of rules, conventions, and representations used to convey information from human to machine, while a compiler is a translator written by one or more programmers. It is entirely possible that a good language, when used with an inefficient compiler, will yield unsatisfactory results.

4   *How frequently will the application be processed?* A symbolic language program usually has a shorter production run time than does a program of the same application written in a high-level language. If the job is run frequently enough, the value of the operating time saved may be more than enough to offset the cost of additional time spent in program preparation. For limited-life jobs, however, the faster the possible programming time is (with high-level languages), the more economical the approach.

5   *Will the program be changed frequently?* The ease of program modification varies with different languages. A high-level language is typically easier to modify than a symbolic language.

6   *Is a hardware change anticipated during the life of the application?* Conversion of high-level language programs is easier and faster; machine-oriented programs may have to be completely rewritten.

PROGRAM CODING WITH HIGH-LEVEL LANGUAGES

All the soul in rapt suspension
All the quivering, palpitating chords of life
   in utmost tension,
With the rapture of creating!
         Henry Wadsworth Longfellow

Coding is the actual writing of the computer program of instructions. It follows the system design and programming analysis stages (see Figure 9-1). Regardless of the language used, the programmer must follow strict rules with respect to punctuation and statement structure. Special *coding forms* are used with several languages to (1) help the programmer comply with language rules, (2) help reduce clerical errors, and (3) make the job of card punching easier.

In addition to presenting examples of these coding forms in the sections that follow, we shall also consider the *development* of several popular high-level languages. We shall then briefly examine

(1) the general structure of, and (2) some of the basic characteristics of each language.

FORTRAN

In 1954, an IBM-sponsored committee headed by John Backus began work on a scientific-mathematic language. The result of this effort was FORTRAN (FORmula TRANslator), which was introduced in 1957. Since its introduction, FORTRAN has been widely accepted and has been revised a number of times. The overwhelming majority of all computers now in use have FORTRAN capability. Because of this widespread acceptance, the forerunner of the American National Standards Institute (ANSI) began work in 1962 on FORTRAN standard languages. These standards were approved in 1966.[4]

All high-level languages must be structured in such a way that they permit the (1) I/O, (2) data movement/manipulation, (3) arithmetic, (4) logic, and (5) transfer of control operations mentioned earlier. In other words, by following the rules of a specific language it must be possible to direct the computer to *read the input data, process* (i.e., perform calculations, move, and manipulate) *the data, compare values, transfer program control, repeat the input/processing operations* as needed, and *transmit the output results.*

A FORTRAN source program is composed of *statements* that will direct the machine to perform these necessary operations. The example program in Figure 9-4 shows the coding required to process Professor Shirley A. Meany's grade-averaging application discussed in the last chapter and presented in a flowchart in Figure 8-5. This program, of course, utilizes statements from the basic categories. The first line of code in Figure 9-4, for example, is a READ statement that is used to enter *input* data from an input device into primary storage, and the fifth line of code is a WRITE statement that is used to transfer output information from primary storage to an output device. Input and output statements are accompanied by FORMAT statements (lines 2 and 6 in Figure 9-4) that supply *data movement/manipulation* information to the processor. The *arithmetic assignment* statement found in Figure 9-4 that computes a student's

---

[4]There are two published standards. The ANSI Basic FORTRAN version is a subset of the "full" FORTRAN standard and does not have some of the additional features of the more extensive version. They do not differ, however, in their structure. The ANSI Basic FORTRAN standard is similar to FORTRAN II; ANSI FORTRAN corresponds to FORTRAN IV.

FORTRAN Coding Form

X28-7327-6 U/M050 Printed in U.S.A.

PROGRAM: AVERAGE OF TEST SCORES
PROGRAMMER: JOHN Q. PROGRAMMER
DATE: 1/26/7–
PAGE 1 OF 1

```
      READ (1,10)N,ANAME1,ANAME2
   10 FORMAT(I2,2X,2A10)
      IF(N)100,100,20
   20 ITOTAL=0
      WRITE (3,30)ANAME1,ANAME2
   30 FORMAT(10X,4HNAME,2X,2A10/)
      WRITE (3,40)
   40 FORMAT(21X,12HTEST RESULTS)
      DO 70 I=1,N,1
      READ (1,50)ISCORE
   50 FORMAT(I3)
      WRITE (3,60)ISCORE
   60 FORMAT(23X,I4)
      ITOTAL=ITOTAL+ISCORE
   70 CONTINUE
      IAVE=(ITOTAL+(N+1)/2)/N
      WRITE (3,80)ITOTAL
   80 FORMAT(122X,I5/)
      WRITE (3,90)IAVE
   90 FORMAT(5X,7HAVERAGE,11X,I4)
  100 STOP
      END
```

FIGURE 9-4

average grade[5] for the 35 exams is IAVE = (ITOTAL + (N+1)/2)/N. When this statement is executed, the average grade will be assigned to a storage area that the programmer has identified by the *variable name* IAVE.

FORTRAN programs are executed sequentially until the sequence is altered by a *transfer of control* statement. One example of an acceptable FORTRAN *unconditional* branching statement is GO TO 100, where 100 refers to a statement number in the program. And an example of a *conditional* branch statement is found on the third line of Figure 9-4. *If* N (the number of exams taken) is mistakenly entered as a *negative* value or as *zero,* program control will be transferred to statement number 100 (STOP); if N is a *positive* value, control branches to statement 20. An additional program-control arrangement that sets up a *loop* to permit a *repetitive input/processing operation* to continue as long as necessary is found on lines 9–15 of

[5]Since Shirley Meany wants a rounded average grade, the purpose of (N+1)/2 is to round off computations to the nearest whole value. In FORTRAN, the slash symbol (/) represents division; one asterisk (*) represents multiplication; and two asterisks (**) indicate exponentiation.

Figure 9-4. The DO statement on line 9 determines the number of times the steps in the operation will be performed.

FORTRAN has the *advantage* of being a compact language that serves the needs of scientists, engineers, and business statisticians very well. It is available for use with the smallest minicomputers or the largest number-crunchers. Because there are established FORTRAN standards, programs written for one computer are usually easily converted for use with another processor. *However,* it may be more difficult to trace program logic in FORTRAN code than in some other high-level languages, and it is not as well suited for processing large business files as COBOL.

COBOL

As its name indicates, COBOL (COmmon Business-Oriented Language) was designed specifically for business-type data processing applications. The group that designed the language gathered at the Pentagon in Washington, D.C., in May 1959, with the official sanction of the U.S. Department of Defense—the world's largest single user of computers. Members of the COnference of DAta SYstems Languages (CODASYL) represented computer manufacturers, government agencies, user organizations, and universities. The CODASYL Short-Range Committee, which prepared the COBOL framework, consisted of representatives from federal government agencies (the

"My son is assisting in University studies on computer languages ... dear, say something in Cobol or Fortran."

Air Material Command, the Bureau of Ships, and the Bureau of Standards) and from computer manufacturers (IBM, Honeywell, Burroughs, RCA, UNIVAC Division of Sperry Rand, and Sylvania). From June to December 1959, this committee worked on the language specifications. Their final report was approved in January 1960, and the language specifications were published a few months later by the Government Printing Office.

Since 1961, COBOL compilers have been prepared for all but the smallest commercial processors. Other CODASYL committees have continued to maintain, revise, and extend the initial specifications. An ANSI COBOL standard was first published in 1968.

COBOL is structured much like this chapter. *Sentences* (analogous to statements in FORTRAN) are written to direct the processor in performing the necessary operations. A varying number of sentences dealing with the same operation are grouped to form a *paragraph.* Related paragraphs may then be organized into a *section,* sections are grouped into a *division,* and *four* divisions complete the structural hierarchy of a COBOL program. Figure 9-5 shows the COBOL coding to process the grade-averaging application discussed in the preceding FORTRAN section.

The first entry in Figure 9-5 (page 001, line 010) is IDENTIFICATION DIVISION—the *first* of the COBOL divisions. A required paragraph identifies the program (001, 020), and additional optional paragraphs are included for documentation purposes. The *second* division is the ENVIRONMENT DIVISION (001, 060), which consists of two required sections that describe the specific hardware to use when the program is run. If the application is to be processed on different equipment, this division will have to be rewritten, but the rewriting usually presents no problem.

The DATA DIVISION (001, 140), the *third* of the four divisions, is divided into two sections. The purpose of this division is to present in detail a description and layout of (1) all the input data items in a record, and all the records in each file that is to be processed (lines 001, 150 to 001, 230); (2) all storage locations that are needed during processing to hold intermediate results and other independent values needed for processing (lines 002, 040 to 002, 081); and (3) the format to be used for the output results (lines 002, 090 to 003, 060).

The *last* COBOL division, the PROCEDURE DIVISION, contains the sentences and paragraphs that the computer follows in executing the program. In this division, *input* (e.g., 003, 091), *data movement and manipulation* (003, 160), *arithmetic* (003, 220), *transfer of control* (003, 180), and *output* (004, 090) operations are performed to solve the problem.

IBM COBOL Coding Form

SYSTEM		
PROGRAM	AVERAGE GRADE	
PROGRAMMER	BAL SHEET	DATE 10/13/1999

PAGE 1 OF 4

PUNCHING INSTRUCTIONS: GRAPHIC / PUNCH — CARD FORM #

IDENTIFICATION (73–80): AVERAGES

SEQUENCE	CONT	COBOL STATEMENT
001010		IDENTIFICATION DIVISION.
020		PROGRAM-ID. 'AVERAGES'.
030		AUTHOR. BAL SHEET.
040		DATE-WRITTEN. OCTOBER 13, 1999.
050		DATE-COMPILED. OCTOBER 13, 1999.
060		ENVIRONMENT DIVISION.
070		CONFIGURATION SECTION.
080		SOURCE-COMPUTER. IBM-360 F30.
090		OBJECT-COMPUTER. IBM-360 F30.
100		INPUT-OUTPUT SECTION.
110		FILE-CONTROL.
120		SELECT GRADE-CARDS ASSIGN TO UNIT-RECORD 2540R.
130		SELECT REPORT ASSIGN TO UNIT-RECORD 1403.
140		DATA DIVISION.
150		FILE SECTION.
160		FD GRADE-CARDS, DATA RECORD IS GRADE-RECORD
170		LABEL RECORDS ARE OMITTED.
180	01	GRADE-RECORD.
190	02	INITTALS-1 PICTURE IS A.
200	02	INITTALS-2 PICTURE IS A.
210	02	LAST-NAME PICTURE IS A(12).
220	02	SCORE PICTURE IS 999.
230	02	FILLER PICTURE IS X(63).

*A standard card form, IBM Electro C51897, is available for punching source statements from this form.
Instructions for using this form are given in any IBM COBOL reference manual.
Address comments concerning this form to IBM Corporation, Programming Publications, 1271 Avenue of the Americas, New York, New York 10020.

GX28-1464-5 U/M 050
Printed in U.S.A.

FIGURE 9-5

213

SYSTEM

PROGRAM

PROGRAMMER

PUNCHING INSTRUCTIONS — GRAPHIC — PUNCH — DATE — CARD FORM #

IDENTIFICATION: A V E R A G E S (columns 73–80)

```
SEQUENCE  CONT
002010  FD  REPORT, DATA RECORD IS PRINT-LINE
   020      LABEL RECORDS ARE OMITTED.
   030  01  PRINT-LINE PICTURE IS X(132).
   040      WORKING-STORAGE SECTION.
   050  77  ONE PICTURE IS 9 USAGE IS COMPUTATIONAL-3 VALUE IS 1.
   060  77  ACCUMULATOR PICTURE IS S9999 USAGE IS COMPUTATIONAL-3
   061          VALUE IS ZERO.
   070  77  NO-GRADES PICTURE IS 99 USAGE IS COMPUTATIONAL-3
   071          VALUE IS ZERO.
   080  77  AVERAGE PICTURE IS 999 USAGE IS COMPUTATIONAL-3
   081          VALUE IS ZERO.
   090  01  HEADING-LINE.
   100      02  FILLER PICTURE IS X(10) VALUE IS SPACES.
   110      02  FILLER PICTURE IS X(6) VALUE IS 'NAME'.
   120      02  INITIAL-P1 PICTURE IS A.
   130      02  FILLER PICTURE IS X VALUE IS '.'.
   140      02  INITIAL-P2 PICTURE IS A.
   150      02  FILLER PICTURE IS XX VALUE IS '.'.
   160      02  LAST-NAME-P PICTURE IS A(12).
   170      02  FILLER PICTURE IS X(99) VALUE IS SPACES.
   180  01  HEAD-LINE-2.
   190      02  FILLER PICTURE IS X(21) VALUE IS SPACES.
   200      02  FILLER PICTURE IS X(12) VALUE IS 'TEST RESULTS'.
   210      02  FILLER PICTURE IS X(99) VALUE IS SPACES.
```

*A standard card form, IBM Electro C61897, is available for punching source statements from this form.
Instructions for using this form are given in any IBM COBOL reference manual.
Address comments concerning this form to IBM Corporation, Programming Publications, 1271 Avenue of the Americas, New York, New York 10020.

GX28-1464-5 U/M 050
Printed in U.S.A.

FIGURE 9-5 (continued)

214

IBM COBOL Coding Form

SYSTEM		PUNCHING INSTRUCTIONS		PAGE 3 OF 4
PROGRAM		GRAPHIC		CARD FORM # *
PROGRAMMER	DATE	PUNCH		

```
SEQUENCE    A    B                                  COBOL STATEMENT                                   IDENTIFICATION
(PAGE)(SERIAL)
003010  01  DATA-LINE.                                                                                AVERAGES
   020      02  FILLER        PICTURE IS X(5)      VALUE IS SPACES.
   030      02  LABEL         PICTURE IS X(7)      VALUE IS SPACES.
   040      02  FILLER        PICTURE IS X(9)      VALUE IS SPACES.
   050      02  SCORE         PICTURE IS ZZ,ZZ9.
   060      02  FILLER        PICTURE IS X(105)    VALUE IS SPACES.
   070  PROCEDURE DIVISION.
   080  OPEN-PARA.
   090      OPEN INPUT GRADE-CARDS OUTPUT REPORT.
   091      READ GRADE-CARDS AT END GO TO TOTAL-PARA.
   100  INITILIZ-PARA.
   110      PERFORM HEADING-ROUTINE.
   111      GO TO A1.
   110  PROCESS-PARA.
   130      READ GRADE-CARDS AT END GO TO TOTAL-PARA.
   140  A1. ADD SCORE OF GRADE-RECORD TO ACCUMULATOR.
   150      ADD ONE TO NO-GRADES.
   160      MOVE SCORE OF GRADE-RECORD TO SCORE OF DATA-LINE.
   170      WRITE REPORT FROM DATA-LINE AFTER ADVANCING 1 LINES.
   180      GO TO PROCESS-PARA.
   190  TOTAL-PARA.
   200      MOVE ACCUMULATOR TO SCORE OF DATA-LINE.
   210      WRITE REPORT FROM DATA-LINE AFTER ADVANCING 2 LINES.
   220      DIVIDE NO-GRADES INTO ACCUMULATOR GIVING AVERAGE ROUNDED.
```

*A standard card form, IBM Electro C61897, is available for punching source statements from this form.
Instructions for using this form are given in any IBM COBOL reference manual.
Address comments concerning this form to IBM Corporation, Programming Publications, 1271 Avenue of the Americas, New York, New York 10020.

GX28-1464-5 U/M 050
Printed in U.S.A.

FIGURE 9-5 (*continued*)

COBOL Coding Form

IBM

SYSTEM		PUNCHING INSTRUCTIONS		PAGE 4 OF 1
PROGRAM		GRAPHIC		CARD FORM #
PROGRAMMER	DATE	PUNCH		*

SEQUENCE (PAGE) (SERIAL)	CONT	A B	COBOL STATEMENT	IDENTIFICATION
004010		MOVE AVERAGE TO SCORE OF DATA-LINE.		AVERAGES
020		MOVE 'AVERAGE' TO LABEL.		
030		WRITE REPORT FROM DATA-LINE AFTER ADVANCING 2 LINES.		
040		CLOSE GRADE-CARDS REPORT. STOP RUN.		
050		HEADING-ROUTINE.		
060		MOVE INITIALS-1 TO INITIAL-P1.		
070		MOVE INITIALS-2 TO INITIAL-P2.		
080		MOVE LAST-NAME TO LAST-NAME-D.		
090		WRITE REPORT FROM HEADING-LINE AFTER ADVANCING 0 LINES.		
100		WRITE REPORT FROM HEAD-LINE-2 AFTER ADVANCING 2 LINES.		

*A standard card form, IBM Electro C61897, is available for punching source statements from this form.
Instructions for using this form are given in any IBM COBOL reference manual.
Address comments concerning this form to IBM Corporation, Programming Publications, 1271 Avenue of the Americas, New York, New York 10020.

GX28-1464-5 U/M 050
Printed in U.S.A.

FIGURE 9-5 (continued)

" I TOLD HIM: ' WHEN THE GOING GETS TOUGH, THE
TOUGH GET GOING!'... AND HE LEFT"

One advantage of COBOL is that it can be written in a quasi-English form that may employ commonly used business terms. Because of this fact, the logic of COBOL programs may be followed more easily by the nonprogrammers in business. Thus, there may be less documentation required for COBOL programs. Also, COBOL is better able to manipulate alphabetic characters than FORTRAN, and this is important in business processing where names, addresses, part descriptions, etc., are frequently reproduced. Finally, a standard version exists; the language is relatively machine independent; and it is maintained, updated, and supported by its users. A *limitation* of COBOL, however, is that it is obviously not a compact language. (The 22 lines of FORTRAN code in Figure 9-4 will produce the same output as the 81 lines of code in Figure 9-5.) It is not the easiest high-level language for most of us to learn, and it is not as well suited for complex mathematical computations as FORTRAN. In spite of these drawbacks, however, "COBOL is the most widely used language in the world by a very wide margin, and it will stay that way at least a decade."[6]

PL/I

Developed in the mid-1960s by IBM and a committee of users for the IBM System/360 family of computers, PL/I (Programming Language

---

[6]Daniel D. McCracken, "Let's Hear It for COBOL," *Datamation,* p. 242, May 1976.

GENERAL PURPOSE CARD PUNCHING FORM

PUNCHING INSTRUCTIONS

JOB AVERAGE OF TEST SCORES		WRITTEN AS:
BY JOHN Q PROGRAMMER	DATE 1/26/78	PUNCH AS:

NOTES: PL/I

FIELD IDENTIFICATION

	1-10	11-20	21-30	31-40	41-50	51-60	61-70	71-80
	12345678901	234567890	1234567890	1234567890	1234567890	1234567890	1234567890	1234567890

```
1   AVERAGE: PROCEDURE OPTIONS (MAIN);
2   DECLARE
3    N FIXED (2),
4    NAME CHARACTER (15),
5    SCORE FIXED (3),
6    TOTAL FIXED (4),
7    AVE FIXED (3),
8    SWT FIXED (1),
9    WORK FILE,
10   NWORK FILE PRINT;
11   TOTAL = 0;
12   N = 0;
13   SWT = 0;
14   OPEN FILE (WORK) INPUT, FILE (NWORK) OUTPUT;
15   READ: GET FILE (WORK) EDIT (NAME, SCORE) (X(60), A(15), X(2), F(3));
16   ON ENDFILE (WORK) GO TO OUTPUT;
17   IF SWT = 1 THEN GO TO CONTINUE;
18   SWT = 1;
19   PUT FILE (NWORK) EDIT ('NAME ', NAME) (PAGE, X(10), A(6), A(15));
20   PUT FILE (NWORK) EDIT ('TEST RESULTS') (SKIP(2), X(21), A(12));
```

FIGURE 9-6

PAGE 1 OF 2

218

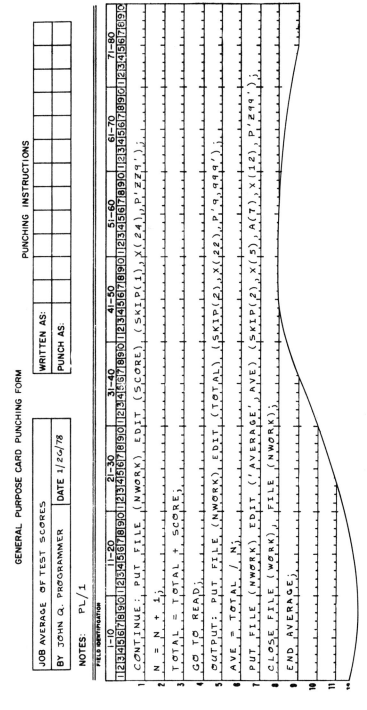

FIGURE 9-6 (continued)

219

I, where I stands for *one*) is being promoted as a universal language; i.e., it is reputed to be a single high-level language that can be used to solve all types of business and scientific problems efficiently. As a scientific language, PL/I appears to be an extension of FORTRAN; however, COBOL-type data description is also used.

The measure of success of a language, of course, is determined by its use. Although the ultimate success of PL/I remains to be determined, it is expected that its use will increase in the future because of its suitability for use in a *structured programming* environment. Although there is as yet no universally accepted definition of structured programming, it is the name given to an approach or philosophy of program preparation. *One* feature of this approach is that complex programs may be broken down into smaller *logical blocks* of statements that may be read and executed in sequence from *top to bottom* without the necessity of using statements such as GO TO to transfer program control back to something earlier. Programs are thus easier to read and understand. A *second* feature of this approach is that programs may be designed by a *chief programmer* from the *top down.* That is, the instructions to control and integrate the lower-level logical blocks are written first, and the smaller modules are then prepared and tied into this main control program.[7]

The PL/I coding for Shirley Meany's grade-averaging problem is shown in Figure 9-6. Although a general-purpose coding form is used, PL/I programs may be written in a rather *free-form* way. The basic element in PL/I is the *statement* which is concluded with a semicolon. Statements are combined into *procedures.* A procedure may represent an entire small program (as in Figure 9-6) or a "building block" or module of a more complex program. Of course, *input* (e.g., page 1, line 15 of Figure 9-6), *arithmetic* (2, 6), *transfer of control* (2, 4), *repetition of input/processing* (from lines, 1, 15 to 2, 4), and *output* (2, 5) operations may be performed in any PL/I program.

PL/I has the *advantage* of being a flexible and sophisticated language with features found in both FORTRAN and COBOL. Because of its modular structure, a novice programmer need only learn a *small part* of the language in order to prepare applications programs of a particular type. Also, modular procedure blocks facilitate the use of structured programming concepts and are efficiently handled by a processor operating in a multiprogramming environ-

---

[7]In a *bottom-up* approach, the smaller elements may be written and tested first, and then they may finally be tied together by a main control program. There is no unanimous agreement at this time on which of these construction approaches is best. For more information, see Richard G. Canning, "The Advent of Structured Programming," *EDP Analyzer,* pp. 5–13, June 1974.

ment. Finally, programmers have considerable latitude in the way they write statements, and the PL/I compiler has built-in features—called *default options*—that can detect and correct common programming errors. A *limitation* of PL/I, however, is that it is more difficult to learn in its entirety than either FORTRAN or COBOL. There is no ANSI standard version of PL/I.

BASIC

BASIC (Beginner's All-purpose Symbolic Instruction Code) is a popular *timesharing* language that has wide appeal because of its simplicity and ease of usage.[8] A problem solver with little or no knowledge of computers or programming can learn to write BASIC programs at a remote terminal in a short period of time.

BASIC was developed in 1963–1964 at Dartmouth College under

---

[8]BASIC and FORTRAN are the two most popular timesharing languages. Many other user languages are, of course, available, including PL/I, APL, and JOSS. Among the more interesting names are DDT, LAFFF, SYNFUL, FRED, and PENELOPE. One can't help but speculate about whether SYNFUL FRED and PENELOPE would be allowed alone in core together.

FIGURE 9-7

```
010 READ A,N$
020 IF A<=0 THEN 250
030 LET T=0
040 PRINT TAB(11);"NAME";TAB(17);N$
050 PRINT
060 PRINT TAB(22);"TEST RESULTS"
070 FOR I=1 TO A
080 READ S1
090 PRINT USING 95,S1
095:                            ####
100 LET T=T+S1
110 NEXT I
120 LET M1=T/A
130 PRINT
140 PRINT TAB(23);T
150 PRINT
160 PRINT TAB(6);"AVERAGE";TAB(25);M1
170 DATA 35,A.V. STUDENT
180 DATA 075,050,055,000,100,
190 DATA 100,075,100,100,050,
200 DATA 000,075,100,067,063,
210 DATA 097,063,093,057,067,
220 DATA 083,000,100,100,072,
230 DATA 075,063,087,093,075,
240 DATA 100,100,100,100,090
250 END

RUN
```

FIGURE 9-8

NAME   A.V. STUDENT

TEST RESULTS

75
50
55
0
100
100
75
100
100
50
0
75
100
67
63
97
63
93
57
67
83
0
100
100
72
75
63
87
93
75
100
100
100
100
90

2625

AVERAGE   75

the direction of Professors John Kemeny and Thomas Kurtz. The purpose of this effort was to produce a language that undergraduate students in all fields of study (1) would find easy to learn and (2) would thus be encouraged to use on a regular basis. BASIC was a success at Dartmouth on both counts. The Dartmouth timesharing system was implemented on General Electric equipment with the assistance of G.E. engineers. Recognizing the advantages of BASIC, G.E. quickly made the language available for the use of commercial timesharing customers. BASIC is now offered in some form by virtually every major computer manufacturer and by almost every independent supplier of timesharing. Users of BASIC range from public school students to aerospace engineers.

The BASIC program for Shirley Meany's grade-averaging problem is presented in Figure 9-7. As you may notice, BASIC is similar to FORTRAN. A series of statements make up a program. These program statements are all identified by a line number and are typically entered into the computer from an online terminal keyboard. The data needed to solve the problem are also entered via the terminal (see the 35 test grades scored by a Mr. A. Valiant Student in Shirley's class in line numbers 180 through 240). Processing is initiated by the system command RUN, and the output results are then transmitted back to the terminal as soon as the program has been executed. The result of processing the program shown in Figure 9-7 is presented in Figure 9-8.

BASIC has the *advantage* of being the easiest to learn of any of the languages discussed in this chapter. Entering data is easy, and the problem solver need not be confused about output formats because a usable format may be automatically provided. And if revisions are to be made in a BASIC program, it is necessary to retype only the line number(s) of the statement(s) to be changed and then supply the revised statement(s). Additions can easily be inserted into existing programs in much the same way. Libraries of BASIC programs may be stored in direct-access devices for immediate call-up by users working at terminals. By interacting with the program by following directions written into the program, the user need know only how to correctly enter the data in order to receive processed output information. BASIC is thus a "friendly" language for nonprogrammers. Finally, BASIC is available for even the smallest processors. Unfortunately, however, it is *limited* in its ability to handle large file processing applications. And there is as yet no ANSI standard version of the language.

RPG

RPG (Report Program Generator) is a *limited-purpose* language that is used for certain business-type data processing applications. It is a

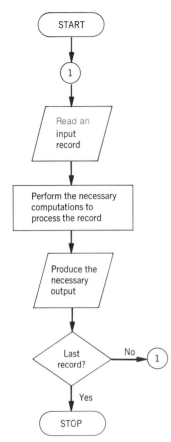

FIGURE 9-9
RPG object program processing logic.

limited-purpose language because *every* report-writing object program generated from source programs by the RPG compiler follows a basic processing cycle from which it *never* deviates. (The general form of this cycle is shown in Figure 9-9.) Since the processing logic never varies, the RPG programmer is concerned only with *file description* and with specifications about *input, calculations,* and *output.* Very detailed specification sheets are used for coding purposes. Figure 9-10 shows the coding sheets required to process the accounts-receivable penalty procedure outlined in the last chapter in Figures 8-6 (flowchart) and 8-8 (decision table). An IBM version of RPG is used here.

One *advantage* of RPG is that it is relatively easy to learn and use. Since program logic is fixed, there are fewer formal rules to remember than with many other languages. RPG is well suited for applications where large files are read, few calculations are performed, and output reports are created. It has been an important language of small business-oriented computers for several years. Of course, the limited purpose for which it was designed is also a *disadvantage* of the language since it therefore has restricted mathematical capability and cannot be used for scientific applications. Finally, RPG is not a standardized language and so programs written for one processor may require extensive modification before they will run on a different make of machine.

Executing Coded Programs

We have seen how the system command RUN is used in BASIC to cause a program to be executed. But how are programs in languages such as FORTRAN and COBOL executed? Thank you for your interest (?). You may recall from Chapter 2 that one of the functions of an operating system is to control the loading of programs for processing. A group of programs awaiting processing may be assembled into a *job stream* by the computer operator and fed into some input device such as a card reader. *Job control cards* are used to supply the operating system with such information as the name of the job, the user's name and account number, and the language compiler to be used. After the source program has been compiled, additional job control cards signal the end of the program and the beginning of the data to be processed by the program (Figure 9-11).[9] The codes used on these job control cards differ from one installation to another.

---

[9]Translating programs and programs to process repetitive applications are likely to be maintained on magnetic tape or in a direct-access storage device rather than on decks of punched cards.

INTERNATIONAL BUSINESS MACHINES CORPORATION
REPORT PROGRAM GENERATOR FILE DESCRIPTION SPECIFICATIONS
IBM System 360

Form X24-3347-3
Printed in U.S.A.

Date 1/26/7–

Program ACCOUNTING PENALTY PROCEDURE

Programmer JOHN Q PROGRAMMER

Punching Instruction — Graphic / Punch

Page 01

Program Identification 75 76 77 78 79 80

Line	Form Type	Filename	File Type (I/O/U/C)	File Designation (P/S/C/R/T)	End of File (E)	Sequence (A/D)	File Format (F/V)	Block Length	Record Length	L/R	Mode of Processing (K/I)	Length of Key Field / Record Address Type (I/D/T)	Overflow Indicator	Key Field Starting Location	Extension Code E/L	Device	Symbolic Device	Labels (S, N, or E)	Name of Label Exit	Extent Exit for DAM	File Addition / No. of Extents	Tape Rewind
0 1 0	F	CARD	I P													MFCM1					
0 2 0	F	OUTPUT	O													PRINTER					
0 3	F																				
0 4	F																				
0 5	F																				
0 6	F																				
0 7	F																				
0 8	F																				
0 9	F																				

IBM

INTERNATIONAL BUSINESS MACHINES CORPORATION
REPORT PROGRAM GENERATOR   INPUT SPECIFICATIONS
IBM System/360

Form X24-3350-1 U/M025
Printed in U.S.A.

Date 1/26/7–

Program ACCOUNTING PENALTY PROCEDURE

Programmer JOHN Q. PROGRAMMER

Punching Instruction — Graphic / Punch

Page 02

Program Identification 75 76 77 78 79 80

Line	Form Type	Filename	Sequence	Number (1-N)	Option (O)	Resulting Indicator	Position 1	Not (N)	C/Z/D	Character	Position 2	Not (N)	C/Z/D	Character	Position 3	Not (N)	C/Z/D	Character	Stacker Select	Packed (P)	Field Location From	To	Decimal Positions	Field Name	Control Level (L1-L9)	Matching Fields or Chaining Fields	Field-Record Relation	Plus	Minus	Zero or Blank	Sterling Sign Position
0 1 0	I	CARD	A A			0 1	2	N	C																						
0 2 0	I																				1	2	0	NDAYS							
0 3 0	I																				3	10	2	UNBAL							
0 4 0	I																				11	25		NAME							
0 5	I																														
0 6	I																														
0 7	I																														
0 8	I																														
0 9	I																														
1 0	I																														

FIGURE 9-10

REPORT PROGRAM GENERATOR   CALCULATION SPECIFICATIONS
IBM System/360

Date 1/26/7–

Program ACCOUNTING PENALTY PROCEDURE

Programmer JOHN Q. PROGRAMMER

Punching Instruction — Graphic / Punch

Page 03

Program Identification 75 76 77 78 79 80

Line	Form Type	Control Level (L0-L9, LR)	Indicators And Not	And Not	And Not	Factor 1	Operation	Factor 2	Result Field	Field Length	Decimal Positions	Half Adjust (H)	Resulting Indicators Plus High 1>2	Minus Low 1<2	Zero or Blank Equal 1=2	Comments
0 1 0	C						SETOF						02	03	04	
0 2 0	C						SETOF						05			
0 3 0	C						NDAYS	COMP	30					02		
0 4 0	C		02					GOTO	COMPUT							
0 5 0	C						UNBAL	COMP	200.					03		
0 6 0	C			03			UNBAL	MULT	0.03	PENLTY	5	2				
0 7 0	C			03				GOTO	PNLIZE							
0 8 0	C						UNBAL	MULT	0.02	PENLTY	5	2				
0 9 0	C						PNLIZE	TAG								
1 0 0	C						UNBAL	ADD	PENLTY	CACCNT	5	2				
1 1 0	C							SETON					04			
1 2 0	C						NDAYS	COMP	60				05	05		
1 3 0	C						COMPUT	TAG								
1 4	C															
1 5	C															
	C															
	C															
	C															

IBM

Form X24-3352-1 U/M 025
Printed in U.S.A.

REPORT PROGRAM GENERATOR OUTPUT-FORMAT SPECIFICATIONS
IBM System/360

Date 1/26/7–

Program ACCOUNTING PENALTY PROCEDURE

Programmer JOHN Q. PROGRAMMER

Punching Instruction — Graphic / Punch

Page 04

Program Identification 75 76 77 78 79 80

Line	Form Type	Filename	Type (H/D/T)	Stacker Select	Space Before	Space After	Skip Before	Skip After	Output Indicators And Not	And Not	And Not	Field Name	Zero Suppress (Z)	Blank After (B)	End Position in Output Record	Packed Field (P)	Constant or Edit Word	Sterling Sign Position
0 1 0	O	OUTPUT	D			2			01									
0 2 0	O														24		'CUSTOMER STATEMENT FOR'	
0 3 0	O											NAME			39			
0 4 0	O		D			3			02									
0 5 0	O														21		'ACCOUNT NOT INCLUDED'	
0 6 0	O		D			1			02									
0 7 0	O														2		' '	
0 8 0	O		D			2			04									
0 9 0	O														19		'BALANCE DUE $'	
1 0 0	O											CACCNT			25		' 0. '	
1 1 0	O		D			2			NO5 NO2									
1 2 0	O														2		' '	
1 3 0	O		D			3			05									
1 4 0	O														12		'ACCOUNT IS '	
1 5 0	O											NDAYS	Z		14			
1 6 0	O														27		' DAYS OVERDUE'	
1 7 0	O		D			1			05									
1 8 0	O														2		' '	
	O																	
	O																	

Card Electro Number _____

FIGURE 9-10 (continued)

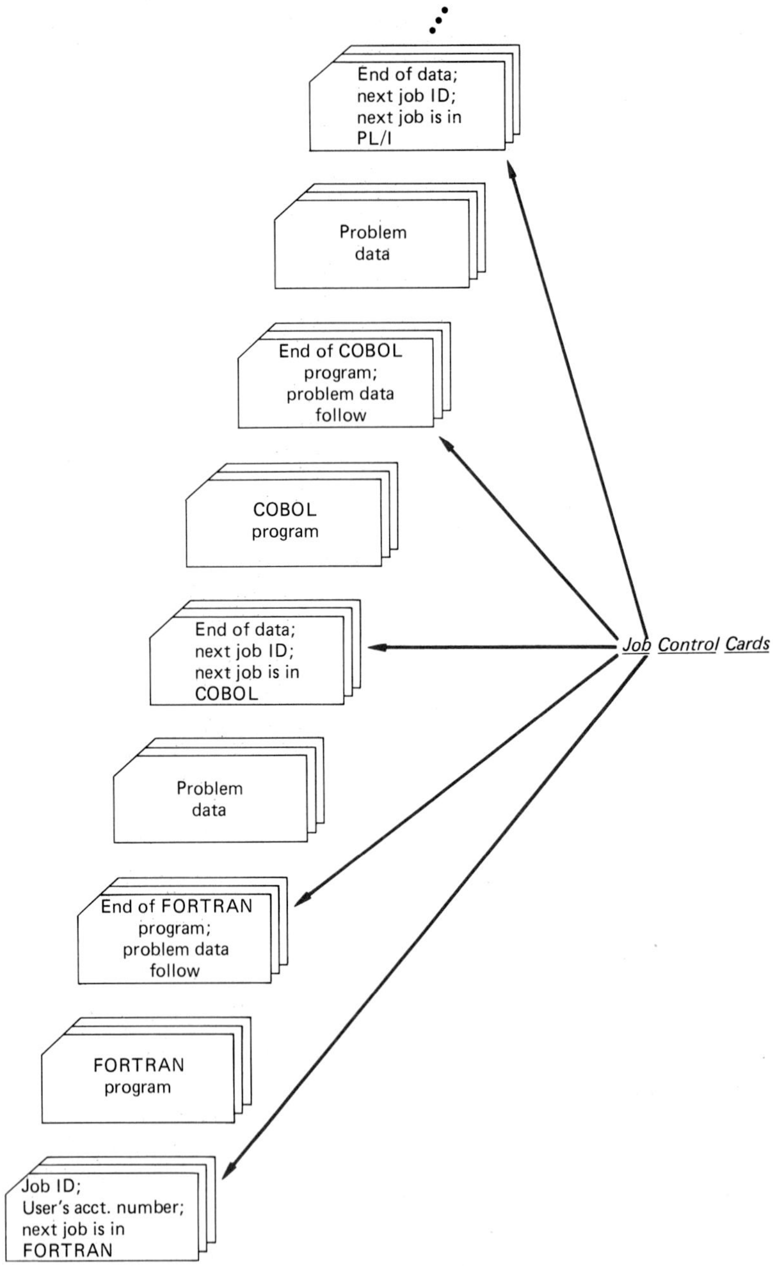

FIGURE 9-11
Job control cards in a job stream.

SUMMARY   Although computers vary with respect to the number of commands that they can execute, they are all similar in that they must ultimately receive their instructions in a machine language form. Early programmers had to code instructions laboriously into this machine language.

To ease the programmer's burden, mnemonic operation codes and symbolic addresses were developed in the early 1950s. The development of machine-oriented symbolic languages led to further programming improvement, first in the form of macro instructions and then in the form of high-level languages. Many high-level languages are directed toward either scientific or commercial problems. Some languages, e.g., PL/I, are used with both types of applications. The selection of a language, like the selection of hardware, is a complex task. Among the most popular high-level languages are FORTRAN, COBOL, PL/I, BASIC, and RPG. A brief overview of these languages has been presented in this chapter to acquaint you with the general structure of each and to introduce you to some of their characteristics. Each language has strengths and weaknesses.

REVIEW AND   **1** Identify the steps in the programming process.
DISCUSSION   **2** "Every computer instruction has an explicit predicate consist-
QUESTIONS   ing of at least two parts." Identify and explain these two parts.
                  3 Compare the command structures of single-, two-, and three-
                        address machines.
                  4 What types of commands are found in a computer's repertoire?
                  5 What are the differences among machine, symbolic, and high-
                        level languages?
                  6 (**a**) What is an assembly program? (**b**) What is a source pro-
                        gram? (**c**) What is an object program? (**d**) Explain the relation-
                        ship among these three programs.
                  7 (**a**) What is FORTRAN? (**b**) For what type of problems was
                        FORTRAN designed?
                  8 (**a**) What is COBOL? (**b**) How did it originate? (**c**) For what
                        purposes was COBOL designed?
                  9 (**a**) What is PL/I? (**b**) How did it originate? (**c**) Why is it suitable
                        for use in a structured programming environment?
                 10 (**a**) What is BASIC? (**b**) Where did it originate? (**c**) For what
                        purpose was BASIC designed?
                 11 (**a**) What is RPG? (**b**) For what is it used?
                 12 Discuss the factors to consider in language selection.
                 13 (**a**) What are job control cards? (**b**) How are they used?

10

IMPLEMENTING PROGRAMS AND SYSTEMS

229

For the last few chapters, we have been following several steps or stages in the *system development/programming life cycle.* Assuming that (1) the problem has been analyzed and a feasible system or application solution has been designed (Chapter 7), (2) the system specifications have been analyzed and broken down into the detailed arithmetic and logic operations required to solve the problem (Chapter 8), and (3) the written instructions that will control the computer during processing have been coded in a source program form (Chapter 9), the final steps remaining in the life cycle dealing with the *implementation* of programs and systems may now be considered. Of course, you should realize that *the steps in this life cycle do not necessarily follow a rigid chronological order.* Questions arising during programming analysis may make it necessary for the study team to gather additional facts and redesign the problem solution; and, as you may have noticed in Figure 9-1, an unsuccessful program test may send the programmer back to the coding sheets. In short, many of the steps that we have rather arbitrarily assigned to this chapter may have been performed concurrently with earlier phases of the system development/programming process. Certainly, for example, the program debugging, testing, and documentation of some parts of a new system may be occurring simultaneously with the coding of other parts of the same system.

It is often a hectic time for those who are installing a new application or system (and for those awaiting the results!) even when existing hardware is available to handle the job(s). But when new hardware must be acquired to implement the system, the number of details that must be considered is magnified. In the following sections we shall discuss the *debugging, testing, conversion, documentation, maintenance,* and *follow-up* activities needed to properly install *any* new application. Brief comments are· also made about some of the details that cannot be overlooked if a *new computer system* is needed. Figure 10-1 summarizes implementation activities and shows the overlapping nature of many of these tasks.

IMPLEMENTATION EFFORTS AND EARLIER ACTIONS

Many of the actions that may have been taken by thoughtful system analysts and programmers during the system design and initial program preparation stages may now pay dividends by reducing the time and effort required to implement the system. Some of these preinstallation decisions that may now prove beneficial are:

1 *Decision to use modular program design* Programs may be prepared in such a way that there is a *main-control module* that

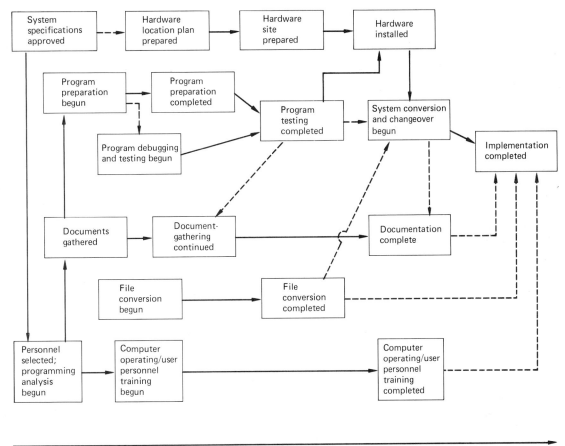

FIGURE 10-1

Implementation considerations.

specifies the order in which each of the *other* modules (or *subroutines*) in the program will be used. (A subroutine, you will remember, is a well-defined set of instructions that performs a specific program function.) In the modular programming approach, an instruction in the main-control module branches program control to a subordinate module. When the specific processing operation performed by the module is completed, another branch instruction may transfer program control to another module or return it to the main-flow program. Thus, the modules or subroutines are really programs within a program. Figure 10-2 summarizes the modular design concept. Further-

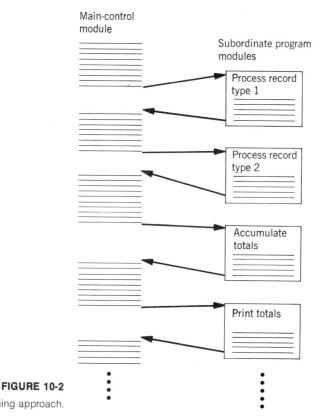

FIGURE 10-2

Modular programming approach.

more, in the *structured programming* approach to modular design, a strong emphasis is placed on simplifying the possible paths of program control. Instead of organizing the program in such a way that confusing branches to other parts of the program—both forward and backward—are permitted, the user of the structured programming approach attempts to write programs that can be read (as implied in Figure 10-2) from top to bottom without program control being transferred to earlier program elements.[1] Some of the advantages of modular design are: (*a*) complex programs may be divided into simpler and more manageable elements; (*b*) simultaneous coding of modules by several programmers is possible; (*c*) a *library* of modules may

---

[1]Thus, in the structured programming approach, the unconditional GO TO branching command is discouraged. It has been noted, however, that not even God was "GO TO free," for in Genesis He said "Go to, let us go down, and there confound their language that they may not understand one another's speech."

be created, and these modules may be used in other programs as needed; (*d*) the location of program errors may be more easily traced to a particular module, and thus *debugging and maintenance may be simplified;* and (*e*) effective use can be made of tested subroutines prepared by equipment manufacturers and furnished to their customers.

2 *Decision to use packaged programs* In addition to subroutines, manufacturers have prepared entire programs for applications that are of a general nature and that are common to the needs of many firms in an industry. For example, IBM and Honeywell have prepared programs to suit the needs of a number of businesses in the areas of banking, insurance, distribution, and manufacturing. Other manufacturers have similar packages available. These "canned" programs can reduce implementation time and expense since they are readily available and have been debugged.

3 *Decision to use software consultants* A number of independent software consulting firms have been formed to help businesses with their programming and implementation problems. The better firms can often provide their clients with specialized software that is not available from the manufacturer or that is more efficient than the software provided by the manufacturer. Consultants, for a fee, can supplement a firm's own programming staff during overload periods created by conversion to a new machine or by the installation of complex new system programs.

4 *Decision to put top priority on satisfying user needs* The best modular design approach, the most effective use of packaged programs, and the most judicious use of consultants to solve problems are of little value if the solutions do not satisfy the needs of the end-users of the processed information. It will be very expensive if it is discovered during the implementation stage that the efficient programs that have been coded or acquired have to be completely revised. Although these may seem to you to be obvious points, they have sometimes been overlooked in practice!

PROGRAM DEBUGGING AND TESTING

Sometimes he thought sadly to himself, "Why?" and sometimes he thought, "Wherefore?" and sometimes he thought, "Inasmuch as which?"
                              Winnie-the-Pooh

Clerical mistakes, and errors caused by faulty logic, are inelegantly referred to as *bugs.* Eliminating these mistakes and errors that prevent the program from running and producing correct results is appropriately called *debugging.*

Debugging

It is a tale
Told by an idiot, full of sound and fury,
Signifying nothing.
William Shakespeare

(A possible description of the first attempt to run a program.)

There are days when things never seem to go quite right. Such days may be more common for programmers than for other mortals because program bugs (or "glitches") just seem to occur even under the best of circumstances and even when matters are not being helped along by our natural human tendency to screw things up. (Of course, Murphy's laws—which state, among other things, that (1) anything that can go wrong will go wrong, (2) when left to themselves, things will always go from bad to worse, and (3) if there is the

"Oh, oh—another dropout...."

possibility that several things can go wrong, the one that will go wrong is the one that will do the most damage—may account for the distressing frequency with which bugs appear.)

It is unusual for complex programs to run to completion in the first attempt. In fact, the time spent in debugging and testing often equals or exceeds the time spent in program coding.[2] Failure to provide for a possible program path, or branch, keypunching errors, mistakes in coding punctuation, incorrect operation codes, transposed characters—these are but a few of the bugs that can thwart the programmer.

To reduce the number of clerical and logical errors, the programmer should carefully check the coding sheets before they are turned over to the keypunch operator. This *desk-checking* process should include an examination for program completeness; furthermore, typical input data should be manually traced through the program processing paths to identify possible errors. In short, the programmer attempts to play the role of the computer.[3]

After program cards are punched and again desk-checked for accuracy, an attempt is made to assemble or compile the source program into object program form. Assembly and compiler programs contain error diagnostic features, which detect (and print messages about) certain types of mistakes in the source program, e.g., undefined symbols and incorrect operation codes. Detected mistakes, of course, must be remedied by the programmer. An error-free pass of the program through the assembly or compiler run *does not* mean that the program is perfected or that all bugs have been eliminated. It usually does mean, however, that the program is ready for testing.

Testing

All real programs contain errors until proved
otherwise—which is impossible.
Tom Gilb

A program to be tested has generally demonstrated that it will run

---

[2]See Frederick P. Brooks, Jr., "The Mythical Man-Month," *Datamation*, pp. 45–52, December 1974. Professor Brooks estimates that *half* the total time of a programming project is likely to be spent in debugging and testing.
[3]On large projects, a team of programmers led by a chief programmer may be preparing the programs. In such situations, a team member often lets the others read his or her code to check for errors.

and produce results. The purpose of *testing* is to determine if the results are correct. The testing procedure involves using the program to process input test data that will produce known results. The test deck should contain (1) typical data, which will test the generally used program paths; (2) unusual but valid data which will test the program paths used to handle exceptions; and (3) incorrect, incomplete, or inappropriate data, which will test the program error-handling capabilities.

If the program passes the test, the programmer may release it for implementation. It should be noted here, however, that bugs may still remain undetected. In complex programs there may be tens of thousands of different possible paths through the program. It simply is not practical (and maybe not even possible) to trace through all the different paths during testing. For example, the flowchart in Figure 10-3 looks rather simple, but the number of different possible paths is an astounding 10^{20}. As Dr. Barry Boehm has observed, if we could somehow check out one path per nanosecond, and if we had started our testing in the year 1, we would only be about half done at the present time![4] This example explains why programs may suddenly produce nonsense months after they have been released for production use. Some unique and unanticipated series of events has produced input or circumstances that turn up a bug for the first time. The error was always there; it simply remained undetected. Very complex systems are considered to be *undebuggable* by professional programmers.

If the program does not pass the test, the programmer may do the following:

1 Trace through the program, a step at a time, at the computer console. Errors may be discovered by noting register contents after each program operation. Such an approach may be permissible with a few minicomputer and small computer systems,

---

[4]See Barry W. Boehm, "Software and Its Impact: A Quantitative Assessment," *Datamation*, p. 58, May 1973.

FIGURE 10-3
(Adapted from B. W. Boehm, "Software and Its Impact: A Quantative Assessment," *Datamation*, May, 1973, p. 58).

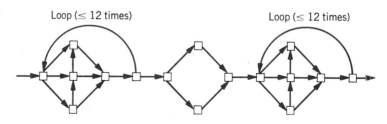
Loop (≤ 12 times)   Loop (≤ 12 times)

but it is hardly appropriate to tie up an expensive large computer for such purposes.

2 Call for a *trace program* run. The trace program prints out the status of registers after each operation and thus is comparable to console checking. However, less machine time is required.

3 Call for a *storage dump* when the program "hangs up" during a test run, i.e., obtain a printout of the contents of primary storage and registers at the time of the hangup. The programmer can then study this listing for possible clues to the cause of the programming error(s).

SYSTEM CONVERSION AND CHANGEOVER

After the program(s) appears to be running properly and producing correct results, the system conversion and changeover may begin. This conversion period is almost always a period of personnel and organizational strain. Data processing employees may work long hours and be subjected to pressure to complete the conversion. Unforeseen problems, last-minute corrections, and the disruption of data processing services to using departments, customers, suppliers, etc., may contribute to these pressures. It is at this time that cooperation is badly needed between data processing specialists and personnel of affected departments. Yet it is precisely at this time that cooperation frequently breaks down because of managerial preoccupation with technical conversion matters at the expense of proper personnel preparation.

During system conversion, current files must be changed into a form acceptable to the processor. This can be a tremendous task, and it is one that is often underestimated. Files should be consolidated and duplicate records eliminated; errors in current files must be detected and removed; and file inconsistencies must be found *before* the changeover rather than later when they can cause system

"I work better under a strain."

malfunctions. Also, new manual methods that are to be developed and new forms that are to be designed must receive attention.

There is frequently a transitional changeover or shakedown period during which applications are processed by both currently used and new procedures as a final check before the cutover to the new system occurs. A *parallel running* check involves the processing of *current* input data by old and new methods. If a significant difference appears, the cause must be located. A *pilot testing* approach is sometimes substituted for parallel running. Input data for a *previous* month's operations are processed using new methods, and the results are compared with the results obtained from existing operations. If new hardware is being acquired to implement the new system, preliminary pilot tests can be run on the vendor's equipment prior to delivery of the user's hardware. Thus, debugging and testing may be facilitated through the use of actual input data, and it may be possible to reduce the time (and costs) associated with maintaining two different systems at a later date. Regardless of the checking approach, final conversion to computer production runs comes from satisfactory performance during this shakedown period.

DOCUMENTATION AND MAINTENANCE

Consider that two wrongs never make a right but that three do. Whenever possible, put people on hold. Be comforted that in the face of all the aridity and disillusionment and despite the changing fortunes of time, there is always a big fortune in computer maintenance.

Anonymous in Deteriorata

Documentation, as stated in Chapter 8, involves collecting, organizing, storing, and otherwise maintaining a complete record of the programs and other documents associated with the firm's data processing systems. The need for documentation was explained in Chapter 8.

The documentation package for a particular program should include:

1 *A definition of the problem* Why was the program prepared? What were the objectives? Who requested the program and who approved it? Questions such as these should be answered.

2 *A description of the system* The system or subsystem environment in which the program functions should be described; system flowcharts should be included. Broad system specifica-

tions outlining the scope of the problem, the form and type of input data to be used, and the form and type of output required should be clearly stated. A *user's manual* should be prepared.

3 *A description of the program* Program flowcharts, decision tables, program listings, test decks and test results, storage dumps, trace program printouts—these and other documents that describe the program and give a historical record of difficulties and/or changes should be available.

4 *A recitation of operator instructions* Among the items covered should be computer switch settings, loading and unloading procedures, and starting, running, and terminating procedures.

5 *A description of program controls* Controls may be incorporated in a program in a number of ways. For example, programmed controls may be used to check on the reasonableness and propriety of input data. A description of such controls should be a part of the documentation.

If schedules begin to slip during program preparation and debugging (and they often do), there may be a tendency to slight the documentation activity. But time made up at the expense of good documentation is likely to be a very temporary gain; it will be lost at high cost in a later period when programs must be tested and when program corrections and changes must be made.

Production-run programs are continuously being modified and improved. Sometimes the object program can be patched to include small modifications so that a compiling run is not necessary. (A danger of this approach, however, is that the small changes may not be incorporated in the supporting documents.) Program *maintenance* is an important duty of the programmer and may involve all steps from problem definition through analysis, design, and program preparation. It is not unusual to find a programmer spending 25 percent of his or her time on this activity. In some installations there are programmers who do nothing but maintain production programs.

HARDWARE IMPLEMENTATION MATTERS

If additional processing capacity is needed to implement a problem solution, it is possible that an existing computer can be upgraded by the addition of new *modular* hardware elements. That is, it may be possible to attach additional I/O and storage units to the original CPU as the need arises, just as additional freight cars can be hooked onto a freight train. Or, it may be possible for the user of a smaller model computer in a *compatible family* of machines to move up to a larger-capacity model. In either of these approaches, the acquisition of new hardware generally does not produce conversion difficulties because proven and satisfactory older application programs will generally run with little or no modification on the upgraded equipment. But if existing hardware is no longer adequate, and if the decision is to acquire a larger computer that is *not* compatible with the existing machine (e.g., because it is made by another vendor), then is there any alternative to completely rewriting older applications programs? Considering the tremendous investment in such programs, the answer, fortunately, is yes. The transition from an old system (computer O) to a new one (computer N) can be made less painful by the use of the following techniques, which permit existing programs to run on computer N without the necessity for initial reprogramming:[5]

1 *Writing programs in a machine-independent language* As discussed earlier, if computer O programs have been prepared in a higher-level standardized language that is essentially machine independent, computer N will have translating software available to accept existing programs directly with a minimum of reprogramming needed.

2 *Using translation techniques* The machine-level language of a particular computer is a collection of all the acceptable instructions it can understand and execute. The machine-level languages of different computers may vary because of design and technology changes. Several special programs have been developed to translate the "foreign" machine language of machine O into the machine language of computer N. The new machine language program produced can be used thereafter without reference to the original program.

3 *Using emulation techniques* Emulation involves software features and the use of a special-purpose read-only storage device. The contents of this special storage element may sometimes be altered by mechanical or other means, but unlike other storage devices it generally will not accept input data and instructions from applications programmers. Computer O program instructions are channeled through this *emulator,* which interprets them, converts them into computer N equivalent instructions, and thus permits their execution by computer N. This process (see Figure 10-4) is repeated each time the program is run. Computer N is thus made to act like computer O.

---

[5]On frequently used programs some subsequent reprogramming will likely be necessary to realize the full potential of computer N, but the conversion pace need not be so frantic.

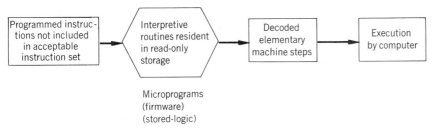

Microprograms
(firmware)
(stored-logic)

FIGURE 10-4

Computer Site Preparation

The cost of site preparation can range from a very modest figure for a minicomputer to hundreds of thousands of dollars for a large system. Some of the *factors that must be considered during site planning and preparation are:*

1 *Location* From an economic standpoint, the computer location should probably be chosen for its accessibility to those company departments that will be closely associated with computer operations. Consideration must also be given to the physical security of the hardware/software in determining the proper location.

2 *Space and layout* The physical dimensions of the equipment to be housed; the location and length of power and connecting cables; the storage room needed for I/O media, supplies, spare parts, and maintenance equipment; and the number and size of work areas, offices, and conference rooms—all these factors must be considered in determining the space requirements and the layout of the site.

3 *Air conditioning* Air conditioning is needed for employee productivity and for dust, temperature, and humidity control.

4 *Power and lighting* Hardware electrical requirements must be met. If rewiring is called for (and it is usually needed), the job should be done by qualified electricians in accordance with building codes and fire insurance rules. An uninterruptible power supply to eliminate the voltage fluctuations and very brief "power flickers" that computers may not tolerate is a necessity.

5 *Cable protection* Numerous cables interconnect hardware units and supply electric power. Yet attractive sites have no distasteful cables lying around on the floor to impair safety. The usual practice is to install a raised or false floor and then run the cables beneath this floor.

6 *Fire protection* Since much of the data stored on cards and

"Waddeya mean -- you think this may be the
wrong address!"

tapes may be irreplaceable, fireproof materials should be used wherever possible in the site preparation. Hardware and media fire insurance protection is available. A fireproof vault to store vital records, programs, etc., might be a wise investment. Adequate fire-alarm facilities and emergency power cutoffs should be provided.

FOLLOW-UP ON SYSTEM DECISIONS

Once the system has been implemented and is in operation, a thorough appraisal or audit should be made. This follow-up is commonly conducted by internal auditors and others who have an independent viewpoint and are not responsible for the development and maintenance of the system. Some of the questions that should be considered in the audit are presented in Figure 10-5.

SUMMARY

Among the preinstallation decisions that may reduce the time and effort required to implement a problem solution are those to (1) use modular program design, (2) use packaged programs, (3) use software consultants, and (4) put top priority on satisfying user needs. But in spite of these decisions, it is still often a hectic and frustrating time for those who are implementing a new computer application or system.

A major cause of slippage in the implementation schedule is the clerical mistakes and logical errors that crop up in coded programs. Of course, a program must be debugged as much as possible and

1 How useful is the system to decision makers? How enthu-
siastic are they about the service they receive? Do they
receive reports in time to take action?
2 Are planned processing procedures being followed? Are
all new procedures being processed on the computer?
Have old procedures been eliminated? If not, why not?
3 Are responsibilities of data processing personnel defined
and understood? Are training programs of acceptable
quality?
4 Have adequate debugging and testing procedures been
established?
5 Are system controls being observed? Is documentation
complete? Have procedures to control program changes
been established? Are these control procedures being
enforced? Are any modifications or refinements indicated
as a result of operating experience? If so, are they being
made? How are they being controlled?
6 How do operating results compare with original goals and
expectations? Are economic benefits being obtained? If
variations exist, what is the cause? What can be done to
achieve expected results?

FIGURE 10-5
System audit questions.

tested before it can be used. These activities often take as much time
as is required to perform the initial coding; sometimes they can take
much longer. After programs appear to be running properly, the
system conversion and changeover begins. Parallel running or pilot
testing approaches are often used in the final check before the
cutover to the new system occurs. The implementation phase cannot
be considered complete, however, until the total documentation
package is put in good order. Later maintenance of production-run
programs will depend heavily on this package. Implementing programs and systems may also require changes in hardware, and,
once the problem solution has been implemented, a follow-up audit
should be made.

**REVIEW AND
DISCUSSION
QUESTIONS**

1 What actions may be taken by system analysts and programmers during the system design and initial program preparation
stages that may reduce the time and effort required to implement the system?
2 (**a**) What is modular program design? (**b**) What are some of the
advantages of this design approach?

3   (**a**) What is the purpose of the debugging stage? (**b**) What techniques may be employed during debugging?

4   What steps can be taken during program testing to locate and remove errors?

5   What information should be included in a program documentation package?

6   "Very complex systems are considered to be undebuggable by professional programmers." Discuss this statement.

7   Why is the system conversion and changeover period likely to result in personnel and organizational strain?

8   Identify and discuss some of the problems that should be considered in implementing new computing hardware.

9   (**a**) What is emulation? (**b**) Discuss one way in which it may be used.

10   What factors should be considered during computer site preparation?

11   What questions should be considered during a follow-up audit of an implemented system?

COMPUTER
IMPLICATIONS
FOR MANAGEMENT

The three principal goals of this book were identified in Chapter 1. Two of those three goals have now been discussed in the preceding chapters. In the remaining pages of this book we shall concentrate on the third goal, which is to give you an insight into the broad impact that computers have had, are having, and may be expected to have on managers, on the environment in which managers work, and on the society in which we live. Chapters 11 and 12 examine some of the important managerial implications of computer usage. Chapter 13 then looks at some of the broader social implications of the business use of computers.

MANAGERIAL
IMPLICATIONS: I

A number of changes have occurred in recent years in the structure, policies, and operations of many organizations as a direct result of their use of computers. The purpose of this chapter and the one that follows is to show you some of the ways in which computer systems have affected the activities performed by managers. After briefly *reviewing these activities* at the beginning of this chapter, we shall then outline some of the effects of computer usage on the *planning and decision-making* and *organizing* activities *within* an organization. In the next chapter, we shall examine the implications of computer systems for the *staffing* and *controlling* activities *within* a company. Finally, in Chapter 13, we conclude this part of the text by considering some of the important *external* or *social issues* that have emerged, in part, as a result of the increased use of business computer systems.

MANAGERIAL ACTIVITIES

As we saw in Chapter 1, *planning, organizing, staffing,* and *controlling* are important activities because the successful achievement of organizational goals depends on how well they are performed.

Planning

The *planning* activity looks to the future; to plan is to decide in advance a future course of action. Thus, planning involves making decisions. *The steps followed in planning and arriving at rational decisions* are about the same as those followed in conducting a system study—i.e., the steps are: (1) *identifying the problem or opportunity,* (2) *gathering and analyzing relevant facts,* (3) *determining suitable alternatives,* (4) *evaluating and selecting the most appropriate alternative,* and (5) *following up on the decision(s).* Of course, administrative skill and quality information are needed during each of these planning activities.

Organizing

The *organizing* function involves the grouping of work teams into logical and efficient units in order to carry out plans and achieve goals. In a manufacturing company, for example, employees may be grouped by *type of work* (production, marketing), by *geographic area* (district sales offices), and by *product line* produced or sold. Managers at each organizational level receive formal authority to assign goal-directed tasks; they then must motivate and coordinate employee efforts if goals are to be achieved. The formal organizational (or authority) structure clarifies the formal lines of authority and the assigned role of a work group in the overall structure.

Staffing

One aspect of the *staffing* function consists of selecting people to fill the positions that exist in the organizational structure of the business. The staffing activity also includes (1) the training of employees to meet their job requirements, (2) the preparation of employees for promotion to positions of greater responsibility, and (3) the reassignment or removal of employees when such action is required.

Controlling

Unlike planning, which looks to the future, the *control* function looks at the past and the present. It is a follow-up to planning; it is the check on past and current performance to see if planned goals are being achieved. The *steps in the control function* are (1) *setting standards,* (2) *measuring actual performance,* (3) *comparing actual performance with the standards,* and (4) *taking appropriate control action* (e.g., unfavorable performance might be corrected by reorganizing work groups or adding more personnel).

The *order* of the activities presented here is a logical one, and we shall use this order to present material in the following pages. In practice, however, managers carry out these activities simultaneously, and it is unrealistic to insist on a particular sequence in all situations.

PLANNING AND DECISION-MAKING IMPLICATIONS   We can look at this broad topic from at least two viewpoints. *First,* we can examine the implications of *planning with computers,* and second, we can consider some computer-oriented *decision-making techniques* that are now being used.

Planning with Computers

Generally speaking, *the use of computers can have an impact on planning activities by:*

1 *Causing faster awareness of problems and opportunities* Computers can quickly signal out-of-control conditions requiring corrective action when actual performance deviates from what was planned. Masses of current and historical internal and external data can be analyzed by the use of statistical methods, including trend analyses and correlation techniques, in order to detect opportunities and challenges. Planning data stored online may permit managers to probe and query files and receive quick replies to their questions.

2 *Enabling managers to devote more time to planning* Use of the computer can free the manager of clerical data-gathering tasks so that more attention may be given to analytical and intellectual matters.

3   *Permitting managers to give timely consideration to more complex relationships* The computer gives the manager the ability to evaluate *more* possible alternatives (and to consider *more of the internal and external variables* that may have a bearing on the outcome of these alternatives). It makes it possible for managers to do a better job of identifying and assessing the probable economic and social effects of different courses of action. The awareness of such effects, of course, influences the ultimate decision. In the past, oversimplified assumptions would have to be made if resulting decisions were to be timely. More complex relationships can now be considered and scheduled. In short, computers can furnish managers with planning information that could not have been produced at all a few years ago or that could not have been produced in time to be of any value.

4   *Assisting in decision implementation* When decisions have been made, the computer can assist in the development of subordinate plans that will be needed to implement these decisions. Computer-based techniques to schedule project activities have been developed and are now widely used. Through the

" For lunch today, 94 students will choose hamburger
patties, 67 will pick roast beef sandwiches but
only 24 will select hot dogs and baked beans... "

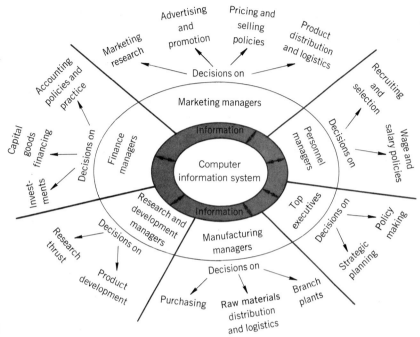

FIGURE 11-1

use of such techniques, business resources can be utilized and controlled effectively.

Computer information systems now regularly support the planning and decision-making activities of managers in a number of business areas (see Figure 11-1). In marketing, for example, data may be gathered that show consumer preferences from consumer surveys, results of market testing in limited geographic areas, and past sales data on similar products in an industry (obtained from the company's own past sales records and from subscriptions to data-gathering services). These facts may subsequently be processed by a computer to produce summary statistical measures (market percentages, arithmetic means, product rankings, etc.). These summary measures may then be analyzed by managers or by computer programs. These analyses, in turn, can be used as input to computerized statistical forecasting procedures that may be used to project sales volume into the future, given assumptions about pricing, economic trends, promotional effort, competitive reactions, and so on. Armed with this information, managers may be able to do a better job of planning marketing strategies. And in many companies, market plans become the basis for inventory acquisition plans and production plans.

Of course, provisions must also be made in a business to have adequate financial resources available to carry out marketing and production plans. The costs and revenues associated with alternative estimates of promotion plans and prices, and sales and production volumes must be analyzed to determine the financial implications. To evaluate these implications (and to determine the expected profitability of various alternatives), financial managers frequently use computer programs to make cash flow analyses, time-series financial forecasts, and loan and interest rate projections. Decisions about the advisability of making investments in new plants and equipment are often made with the help of a computer.

Decision-making Techniques

A number of quantitative managerial aids such as *network analysis, linear programming,* and *simulation* have been introduced which utilize computers to provide the framework for decision-producing analyses.

Network analysis   Both PERT (program evaluation and review technique) and CPM (critical path method) are network models which are used to plan, schedule, and control complex projects. The basic concepts of PERT and CPM are similar. In setting up a network model, all the individual activities to be performed in the project are identified, and the sequence and time required to complete each activity is determined. The *longest* sequence of events (i.e., the *critical path*) in the project is then identified to determine the total project time. The use of such a model in a construction project, for example, improves the *planning* function because it forces managers to identify *all the project activities that must be performed. Control* is also improved because attention can be focused on the sequence of activities in the critical path. Managers quickly become aware of potential problems. If a critical activity begins to slip behind schedule, steps can be quickly taken to correct the situation. By a greater commitment of resources, managers can often reduce the time required to complete certain activities in the critical path (and thus reduce total project time). The effect of a greater resource commitment, however, is often higher project cost (see Figure 11-2).

Linear programming   Linear programming models are used to find the *best combination* of limited resources to achieve a specified objective (which is, typically, to maximize profit or minimize cost). One important class of linear programming applications is in blend-

FIGURE 11-2
Reducing of project time may be possible if greater costs are acceptable.

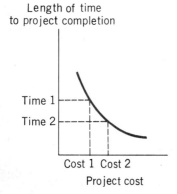

Length of time to project completion

Project cost

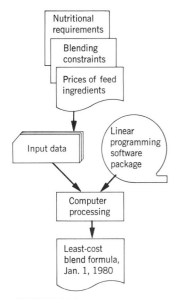

FIGURE 11-3

ing operations, where the objective is often to minimize the cost involved in the production of a given amount of blended product. For example, cattle feed may be a mixture of minerals, grains, and fish and meat products. The prices of these ingredients are subject to change, so the least-expensive blend required to achieve specified nutritional requirements is subject to variation. Linear programming can help managers quickly determine the correct blend to use to minimize cost while meeting product specifications (Figure 11-3). Thus, as this example illustrates, linear programming is a powerful planning tool that enables a manager to select the most appropriate alternative from a large number of options.

Simulation In the physical sciences, experiments may be performed in a laboratory using small models of a process or an operation. Many complex variations may be possible in these tests, and the results show the scientist what happens under certain controlled conditions. Simulation is similar to scientific experimentation. Perhaps Figure 11-4 will clarify the meaning of simulation. At its base, Figure 11-4 rests on reality or fact. In complex situations, few people (if any) fully understand all aspects of the situation; therefore, theories are developed which may focus attention on only part of the complex whole. In some situations models may be built or conceived in order to test or represent a theory. Finally, *simulation* is the use of a model in the attempt to identify and/or reflect the behavior of a real person, process, or system.

In organizations, administrators may evaluate proposed projects or strategies by constructing theoretical models. They can then determine what happens to these models when certain conditions are given or when certain assumptions are tested. Simulation is thus a trial-and-error problem-solving *approach;* it is also a *planning aid* that may be of considerable value to organizations. For example, Potlatch Forests, Inc., a producer of lumber and wood pulp products, has a corporate planning staff that has developed an overall corporate financial model. Given assumptions from top executives about economic conditions, capital expenditures, etc., for a 5-year future period, simulation runs produce estimated financial statements for each of the 5 years. Executives then analyze the simulated financial statements. If results are judged to be disappointing, executives may change variables in the model that are under their control—e.g., future capital expenditures—and the simulations are repeated. When acceptable financial results are obtained, they become the targets for planning at lower levels in the company. When feasible, lower-level plans are formulated (again, simulation models are used), and they are assembled into an overall corporate plan.

FIGURE 11-4

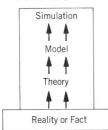

Of course, the output of simulation models is only as good as the facts and assumptions that go into the computer.[1] National economic data and assumptions about the national economy are usually an integral part of a corporate simulation model. Several organizations such as Lionel D. Edie, Data Resources, Inc., and the National Bureau of Economic Research provide extensive national economic data bases that are available to subscribers to their services. General Electric's MAP system is one that was originally developed for internal use by that organization but is now available to timesharing customers. When combined with a firm's internal information, the national economic data provided by these services may enable managers to more accurately model a firm's future.

---

[1]The U.S. Geological Survey uses a complex computer-based model to come up with estimates of the oil and gas reserves that might be found in the government's offshore tracts that oil companies bid on. In one area 50 miles off New Jersey's shore, the model "estimates that reserves in the area range from 400 million to 1.4 billion barrels of crude oil and from 2.6 trillion to 9.4 trillion cubic feet of natural gas. But oilmen in Houston irreverently call this computerized approach SWAG—for 'Scientific Wild-Ass Guess.'" See *Business Week,* p. 116, Sept. 20, 1976.

"According to our research department, our public opinion polls, our sampling of potential users, our forecasts of marketing trends, our estimates of consumer reaction, and our statistical model manipulations, we overcooked the vegetables."

© DATAMATION ®

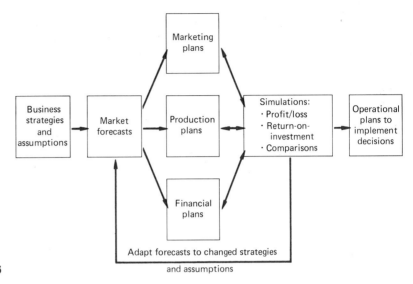

FIGURE 11-5

To summarize several of the points that have now been made, the planning and decision process followed by many business executives may resemble the one shown in Figure 11-5. The strategies, goals, economic assumptions, etc., of these executives serve as the basis for market forecasts. This expectation of *how many* items can be sold then becomes the basis for determining (1) how and when to acquire materials and make the items (the production plans), (2) how and when to have the money on hand to pay for the acquired materials and produced items (the financial plans), and (3) how and when to promote and distribute the items (the marketing plans). And these plans are then used in simulations to estimate such variables as profit and return on investment. Of course, the results of these simulations may bring about changes in established plans and/or the results may cause changes in strategies and assumptions. Once initial simulations have been concluded and high-level plans have been made, operational plans at lower levels are often needed to implement the decisions.

ORGANIZING IMPLICATIONS

As computer-based management information systems are designed and implemented, there is often a need to reconsider the answers to several important and interrelated organizing questions. Included in these questions are: (1) *Where will decision making occur?* (2) *Where will data be processed and stored?* (3) *Where will the* computer department be located? and (4) How will the computer staff be organized? As is so often the case, the "right" answers to these questions in one situation may be very wrong in another. Thus, all we will do in the following sections is look at some of the general implications of these issues.

Where Will
Decision Making Occur?

The concept of *centralization of authority*[2] refers to a concentration of the important decision-making powers in the hands of a relatively few top executives. *Decentralization of authority,* on the other hand, refers to the extent to which significant decisions are made at lower levels. In very small organizations, *all* decision-making power is likely to be centralized in the hands of the owner-manager; in larger firms, the question of centralization or decentralization *is a matter of degree*—i.e., it is a question of how much authority is held at different levels. The extent to which authority is delegated to lower levels depends, in part, on such factors as: (1) the managerial philosophy of top executives; (2) the availability of qualified subordinates; and (3) the availability of good operating controls. Since all these factors may change, it is apparent that the degree of authority centralization is subject to revision.

Before computers came along, the general trend was toward *greater decentralization* of authority. To some top managers decentralization was more a matter of necessity than of choice. They often found themselves in a position where they could (1) wait for the necessary supporting information to arrive from lower levels before making a decision (in which case company reaction time suffered and opportunities were lost), (2) place their trust in experience, intuition, and their horoscope and make the decision without proper supporting information, or (3) delegate the authority to make the decision to a lower-level manager who was closer to the situation calling for the decision and who could thus be expected to react in a prompt and more informed manner. Given these alternatives, it is understandable that as businesses grew in complexity, the third path was frequently chosen.

With the introduction of quick-response computer systems, however, information may be processed and communicated to top executives at electronic speeds; reaction time may be sharply reduced;

---

[2] *Authority* is defined here as the right to give orders and the power to see that they are carried out.

and thus the *need* for decentralization of authority may be lessened. But although new systems may make it possible to reconcentrate at the upper echelons authority and control previously held at lower levels, there is *no reason* why the information output cannot be disseminated via online terminals to lower-level managers to provide them with better support for decision-making purposes. In fact, if an organization implements the distributed processing concepts that were discussed in Chapter 5, the lower-level managers may have access to an entire hierarchy of processors that can supply them with decision-making information. Thus, the degree to which authority and decision-making powers are centralized or decentralized in an organization is now often determined more by managerial philosophy and judgment than by necessity. But the implications of the path selected for the organizational structure and for middle-level managers may be great.

Where Will Data
Be Processed and Stored?

Prior to the introduction of computers, data processing activities were generally handled by manufacturing, marketing, and finance departments on a separate and thus decentralized basis. Similarly, data were also typically stored at the using departments, although some summary facts needed to prepare companywide reports were maintained at a central site. When computers first appeared, however, the tendency was to maximize the use of the expensive hardware by establishing one or more *central processing centers* to serve the company's needs. Large centralized data bases were also established and *stored* at the *central site* on such media as magnetic tapes and disks. But in recent years, such development as (1) the rapid reduction in hardware costs and (2) the arrangement of intelligent terminals, minicomputers, and larger processors into distributed processing systems have made it feasible for businesses to use either a centralized or a decentralized approach to data *processing*.[3] Thus, many firms must now decide to what extent (if any) they will centralize their data processing activities.

The considerations in favor of the centralized processing approach are:

1 *It may permit economies of scale.* With adequate processing

---

[3]In most cases, data with corporatewide significance will continue to be *stored* at a central site, but there is no reason why local, applications-oriented files cannot be stored and maintained at the decentralized processing sites.

volume, the use of larger and more powerful computers may result in reduced operating costs.

2 *It may facilitate systems integration.* For example, achieving companywide agreement on customer code numbers is a necessary step in integrating the procedures required to process customer orders. Such agreement is more likely to occur for efficiency reasons when order processing is handled at a central point.

3 *It has certain personnel advantages.* It may be possible to concentrate fewer skilled programmers at a centralized site and thus make more effective use of their talents.

4 *It may permit better utilization of processing capability.* With a centralized operation, companywide priorities can be assigned to processing tasks. Those jobs that are of greatest importance are, of course, completed first.

Included among the possible advantages of decentralization are the following:

1 *Greater interest and motivation at division levels* Division managers in control of their own computers may be more likely to (*a*) maintain the accuracy of input data and (*b*) use the equipment in ways that best meet their particular operating needs. Greater interest and motivation, combined with greater knowledge of division conditions, may produce information of higher quality.

2 *Better response to user needs* The systems standardization typically required for centralized processing may not be equally suitable for all divisions. With decentralization, special programs can be prepared to meet exact divisional needs. In addition, although a smaller machine will probably be slower than the centralized equipment, it should be remembered that central machine time must be allocated to several users. Information considered important by one division may be delayed because higher priority is given to other processing tasks. Thus, the fact that a smaller machine allows for prompt attention to a given job may lead to faster processing at the division level.

3 *Reduced downtime risks* A breakdown in the centralized equipment or the communications links may leave the entire system inoperative. A similar breakdown in one division, however, does not affect other decentralized operations.

There is no general answer to the question of where *should* data be processed and stored. Small organizations have usually opted for

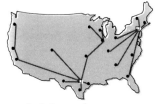

□ Central processing
  complex

• Intelligent terminal/satellite
  minicomputer

FIGURE 11-6
A distributed processing compromise approach.

central computers because their departments often do not have sufficient volume to justify separate machines. Very large organizations have often achieved a greater degree of centralization by establishing several regional data processing and storage centers. Some executives who have chosen to follow the centralized processing/storage route have retained a decentralized decision-making structure by giving operating managers online terminals with which to obtain the necessary support information. And still other executives are following a distributed processing compromise approach to the centralization-decentralization issue by combining larger central computers (and centralized data files) with small processors, minicomputers, and intelligent terminals at operating levels. The central processor(s) serves the local processors by managing large data bases and by executing those jobs that require extensive computations (see Figure 11-6).

Where Will the Computer Department Be Located?

Each business must determine the proper location for its main computer department. What is "proper" depends, in part, on the size of the company, the jobs to be processed, the degree of systems integration achieved and sought, and the importance attached to information systems by top executives. Three possible locations for the main computer department are designated in Figure 11-7. Let us look at each of these arrangements.

FIGURE 11-7
Alternative computer department locations.

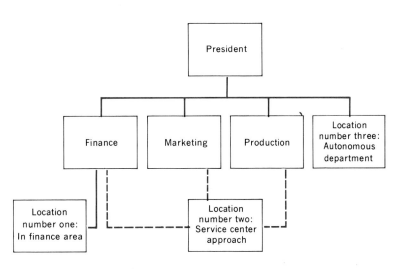

Location number one   Historically, the accounting department was often the first to see that a computer could be used to process large-volume applications such as customer billing. Since most of the early applications were of a financial nature, the computer was most often placed under the control of financial managers. It still remains in this location in many businesses. But there may be several possible drawbacks associated with this finance-area location:

1   *Possible lack of objectivity in setting job priorities* Computer-department personnel may tend to concentrate on accounting applications at the expense of important nonfinancial jobs.
2   *Possible limited viewpoint* The computer department may continue to be staffed and managed by people whose viewpoint is limited primarily to accounting.
3   *Possible lack of organizational status* Organizational status and authority are lacking when the top computer executive is interred several echelons down in one functional area of the business.

Location number two   One approach which can avoid the lack of objectivity in setting job priorities is to establish a company "service center" to handle the various tasks. Each department may be charged its proportionate share of center costs. While the center manager may report to a neutral top-level executive or an executive committee, the service center basically occupies a position that is on the periphery of or outside the main organizational structure.

The main limitation of this type of organizational arrangement for business data processing is that the center manager generally has little status or authority outside his or her own department. Thus, little attempt is made to initiate systems improvements or develop integrated systems; a fragmented, every-department-for-itself approach may be expected.

Location number three   In order to realize the full potential of the computer a large number of managers have established an independent computer department as shown in location three of Figure 11-7. Their reasoning is that this location:

1   *Reflects the broad scope of information.* Independent status is needed to give impartial service to all organizational units that receive processed information. An interdepartmental viewpoint is required of data processing personnel.
2   *Confers organizational status.* The top computer executive should have a strong voice in determining the suitability of new and existing applications, should probably set processing prior-

ities, and should study and make necessary changes in corporatewide systems and procedures in order to achieve better integration. To perform these duties, the information manager must have the cooperation of executives at the highest operating levels. In the event of significant change, such cooperation may not be received unless the information manager occupies a position that is no lower in the organization than the highest information-using department. Furthermore, in the event of a dispute, the information manager should report to an executive who is at a higher level than any of the disputing parties.

3 *Encourages innovation.* Personnel of an independent department can be encouraged to recommend improvement and change whenever and wherever the opportunity arises. They may also be encouraged to introduce, for the greatest total benefit, fresh ideas that may upset certain conventional approaches.

How Will the Computer Staff Be Organized?

The composition of a computer department depends on the scope and magnitude of the data processing work that must be performed and the extent to which this work is carried out by the particular department. It is usual, however, to include the activities of system analysis and design, program preparation, and computer operation in the department. Although other logical arrangements are possible, Figure 11-8 provides us with an organizational framework from which combinations or further subdivisions of activities may be made as needed.

FIGURE 11-8
Possible composition of computer department.

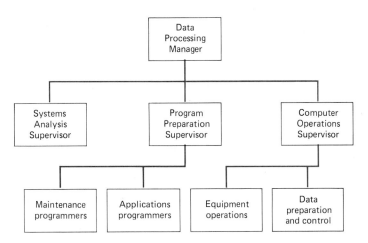

System-analysis section   Because of the close cooperation that must exist between programmers and system analysts, it is generally desirable that both groups report to the same executive to minimize friction. The system-analysis section acts as the vital interface between outside operating departments and the other sections in the computer organization. Some large firms with centralized computer centers locate system analysts in their operating divisions.

Program-preparation section   There is no reason why a single supervisor could not be in charge of both system analysis and program preparation. In medium-sized and large organizations, however, a separate supervisor is frequently found. The programming function is sometimes subdivided into (1) the preparation of new applications and (2) the maintenance of existing programs. Authority may also be given to one or more individuals to make sure that proper standards and documentation levels are maintained. In order to fix total responsibility for the design, implementation, and maintenance of a system application, it is often desirable to establish a *project group* of analysts and programmers. Under this type of organization, the project leader might report to a manager of system analysis and programming.

Computer-operations section   The function of this section is to prepare the input data and produce the output information on a continuing production basis. Multiple shifts may be required. The control of equipment time and the scheduling of processing activities are an important part of the duties of the operations supervisor. Controls must also be established to make sure that input data are accurate. Computer operators, operators of peripheral equipment, keyboard operators, and media librarians are found in this section.

Regardless of how the organizing questions that have now been considered are answered, it is likely that work groups may be realigned; tasks formerly assigned to operating departments may be eliminated, farmed out to outlying units, or consolidated in a few central areas; and existing departments may be eliminated, the scope of their operations may be curtailed, or they may be expanded. There are likely to be a number of staffing implications associated with these possible organizational changes as we shall see in the next chapter.

SUMMARY   To achieve organizational goals, managers must perform the activities of planning, organizing, staffing, and controlling. The information produced by a computer-based system can have an impact on *planning* by (1) quickly identifying problems and opportunities, (2) supporting problem analysis and selection of alternatives, (3) influencing the choice of the most appropriate option, and (4) supporting decision implementation. Computers can also be used to apply decision-making techniques such as PERT/CPM, linear programming, and simulation to problems.

In addition to these planning implications, computer usage also raises a number of questions which have organizing implications. Although there are no general right or wrong answers that apply in every situation, executives must consider such questions as: (1) Will decision making be centralized or decentralized? (2) Will the data processing and storage activities be centralized or decentralized? (3) Where will the computer department be located within the company? and (4) How will the computer department itself be organized?

REVIEW AND DISCUSSION QUESTIONS

1 (**a**) What is involved in the planning function? (**b**) What steps must be followed in planning?

2 Explain what is involved in (**a**) the organizing function and (**b**) the staffing function.

3 Identify and discuss the steps in the control function.

4 (**a**) How may computer usage have an impact on the planning activities of managers? (**b**) Give examples of the use of computers for planning and decision making.

5 (**a**) Identify and explain the purpose of three computer-based decision-making techniques. (**b**) What are the managerial implications of these techniques?

6 (**a**) What is meant by centralization of authority? (**b**) What factors determine the extent to which authority is delegated to lower management levels?

7 "An organization may be centralized in one sense of the term and not in others." Discuss this statement.

8 (**a**) What developments have made it possible to centralize data processing activities? (**b**) What are the advantages of centralized data processing? (**c**) What are the possible advantages of decentralized data processing?

9 (**a**) Identify and discuss three possible organizational locations for the computer department. (**b**) What reasons can be given to justify the establishment of an independent computer department?

10 What activities are usually included in the computer department?

MANAGERIAL
IMPLICATIONS: II

LEARNING OBJECTIVES   After studying this chapter and answering the discussion questions, you should be able to:

Discuss the possible implications of computer usage on noncomputer personnel.

Briefly summarize the job functions of computer personnel and the approaches used in training these employees.

Describe how computer systems help managers control business operations.

Explain what is meant by internal control and what information system failures may result from poor internal control.

Outline the significance of organizational separation of duties in maintaining internal control.

Discuss the relationship that exists between data integrity, data security, and the right to privacy.

In this chapter we continue our study of the *internal* effects of computer usage on business organizations by examining some of the *personnel/staffing* and *controlling* implications of computer-based information systems. In the next chapter, we shall consider some of the important ways in which business computer systems may be exerting an influence on *society as a whole.*

PERSONNEL/ STAFFING IMPLICATIONS

We saw in the last chapter how computers may change the organizational structure of a business. And as computers change an organization, they are bound to touch the lives of its members. The nature of this influence will depend on decisions consciously made, and on the indirect and perhaps unintentional effects of the application of computing tools. Let us now look at some of the *possible effects* of computer systems *on noncomputer personnel* and then consider some of the *staffing issues related to the computer department.*

Possible Effects on Noncomputer Personnel

Computer-based systems can affect noncomputer personnel by changing their *job duties* and/or their *employment status.* Naturally, employees may be expected to offer *resistance to some of these possible changes.*

Changes in job duties   Individuals may *benefit* from changes in job duties. For example, computer usage can relieve *lower-level supervisors* of many of their clerical duties so that they can give greater attention to the needs of their employees. Some *middle-level managers* can also turn over many of their clerical control activities to the computer, secure in the knowledge that the computer can signal with a "triggered" report whenever actual performance begins to vary from what was planned. The time thus saved has enabled these managers to devote more attention to the challenging activities of planning and motivating subordinates. And company *scientists* conducting research into areas that could not be considered without computers; *salespersons* with less paperwork to do and with better inventory information available to serve customers and to thus improve their own performance; *clerical workers* whose job duties have changed from routine, repetitive operations to more varied and appealing tasks—all these individuals can benefit from computer usage.

Unfortunately, however, some company personnel have been the *victims* of job changes. In some cases, middle managers whose decisions were highly structured and repetitive have found that those decisions were programmable on a computer. The information system has therefore taken over those duties, and the need for as many administrators to perform the remainder of the job duties has been reduced. In some organizations, those who were not displaced found their jobs less challenging because, although they retained the duties that required less judgment and skill, their other tasks that required the skilled interpretation of system information were moved upward in the organization or were taken over by the information system staff.

Changes in employment status   The use of computers has created hundreds of thousands of new jobs, and many of these employees are currently working in challenging and satisfying positions. But many clerical employees have also been displaced by computers. It should be noted, however, that displacement and unemployment are not the same. *Unemployment* refers to the total number of people involuntarily out of work. *Displacement* occurs when the jobs of individual workers are eliminated as a result of technological change. *If* these displaced workers cannot find similar jobs elsewhere and *if* they cannot find work in other occupations, then there is, indeed, an increase in the unemployment figures. But has the development of the computer caused a larger number of people to be unemployed than would otherwise have been the case? In other words, have computers reduced the total number of jobs available in the total labor market? Many economists are of the opinion that, although computers do cause displacement and some displaced workers become unemployed, unemployment may not be created in the sense that more people are out of jobs than would have been if computers had not been used. Why? Because there are those who owe their jobs to computer usage, and there are probably many more who might have joined the jobless if new technology had not been used to maintain a competitive level of productivity with other countries of the world.

Regardless of the ultimate effects of computers on total employment, to the employee being displaced today the future consequences are of secondary importance. The displaced victim is likely to be in sympathy with the famous economist who noted wryly that "in the long run we are all dead." *The extent to which displacement actually occurs depends on such factors as:*

1   *The rate of growth of the firm and the economy*   If the company is growing rapidly so that more work must be done to handle the expanding business, then there may be little or no effect on the

"THIS ONE HELPS ME FIGURE OUT HOW TO
KEEP MY JOB ="

number of clerical workers employed. The use of a computer enables workers to be more productive, but increases in the demand for a company's output can prevent a layoff problem.

2 *The objectives sought* Is the company introducing a computer system for processing purposes that could not otherwise be considered? Is the goal to do more work with present employees? Or is it to save money by eliminating existing jobs? Objectives obviously play a part in determining the degree of displacement.

3 *The care in planning and preparation* Business executives should give careful thought to the displacement problems that they are likely to encounter. It should be remembered that fear of displacement is a cause of resistance to change. If displacement is not expected, employees should be so informed; if jobs are to be eliminated, plans should be made to protect present employees as much as possible. Employees in departments where reductions are expected can be given the first chance to fill vacancies occurring elsewhere in the company.

4 *The type of occupations threatened* Up to the present time, most of the jobs that have been eliminated have been of a *clerical* nature and have usually been held by young women who can be transferred to other departments without too much difficulty. When the affected jobs are *not* of the clerical type, the displacement problem is likely to be much more severe. Attrition and turnover in these situations may not be of much help. The affected workers may be older employees or lower-level managers whose skills are no longer needed. They are not likely to quit, but they may find it difficult to retrain for jobs at an appropriate level. In some *production-oriented occupations,* for example, displacement is occurring as a result of the installation of computer-controlled machines (e.g., certain machine tools and typesetting machines). Employees in these occupations are protected to some extent by union contract agreements, but the demand for their skills is declining.

Resistance to change   In view of the ways in which computer usage has damaged some employees, it is not surprising that resistance to systems change is often the rule rather than the exception. Resistance may appear *in many forms*. At one extreme employees may temporarily feel threatened by a change, but after a brief adjustment period they resume their previous behavior. At the other extreme, reaction may be evidenced by open opposition and even destruction. Between these extremes may be found such symptoms as (1) withholding data from the system, (2) providing inaccurate data, and (3) showing an indifferent attitude and a lack of cooperation.

As we saw in Chapter 2, there are likely to be those in an organization who are motivated to seek change because of their dissatisfaction with the status quo, and because of their desire to create and be a leader in the use of new techniques. But the changes sought by some may appear to others to be a threat—a threat that may take one or more of the following paths:

1   *The threat to security*   Computers have a reputation for replacing people; therefore, there is the understandable fear of loss of employment and/or of reduction in salary.

"All these specifications done by computer! Next thing,
they'll have computers to set up these machines!"
© DATAMATION

2 *The reduction in social satisfaction* The introduction of a computer system often calls for a reorganization of departments and work groups. When change causes a breaking up of compatible human relationships and a realigning of personnel, it also causes a reduction in social-need satisfaction. Resistance to such a proposed change may be anticipated.

3 *The reduction in self-esteem and reputation* Individuals need to feel self-confident; but self-confidence may be shaken by the lack of knowledge about and experience with a computer system. The equipment is strange to them, and they may fear that they will be unable to acquire the skills necessary to work with it. In short, their self-esteem may suffer as a result of the change; therefore, the change may be resisted. Egoistic needs relating to the reputation of the individual are also threatened by change. Fear of loss of status and/or prestige is an important reason for resistance by both managers and employees.

In short, then, *nonsupervisory employees* may resist change because they fear they will (1) lose their jobs or be downgraded, (2) be transferred away from their friends, (3) be unable to acquire the needed new skills, and/or (4) lose status and prestige. A greater obstacle to successful computer operations, however, may be *managerial* resistance to change.[1] Although administrators may suffer economic losses because of the change to computer processing, the more usual motivating force behind their resistance is the threat of a reduction in ego-need satisfaction. For example, a department manager may oppose a change because to admit that the change is needed may imply that he or she has tolerated inefficiency—an admission that can hardly enhance his or her reputation.

Although there is no simple formula that prevents resistance and ensures successful computer usage, *there are some guidelines—developed as a result of practical experience and social research—which may, when used with care, help to reduce the level of organizational resistance.* Included in these guidelines are suggestions to:

---

[1]Of course, there are some managers who don't fear change because of an outlook which may be summarized as follows:

Yea, though I walk through the valley
Of the shadow of death
I shall fear no evil,
Because I'm the meanest son-of-a-bitch in the organization.

See Thomas L. Martin, Jr., *Malice in Blunderland,* McGraw-Hill Book Company, New York, 1973, p. 109.

1 *Keep employees informed.* Information relating to the effects of the change on their jobs should be periodically presented to personnel at all levels. Topics discussed should include loss of jobs, transfers, the extent of necessary retraining, the reasons for (and the benefits of) the change, the effect on various departments, and what is being done to alleviate employee hardships.

2 *Seek employee participation.* Employees are more likely to support and accept changes that they have a hand in creating. Psychologists tell us that *participation has three beneficial effects. First,* it helps the employee satisfy ego and self-fulfillment needs. *Second,* it gives the employee some degree of control over the change and thus contributes to a greater feeling of security. And *third,* the fear of the unknown is removed.

Staffing the Computer Department

An obvious staffing implication of computer usage is the need to recruit, select, and train computer personnel.

Selecting employees for computer department jobs   The positions created by computer usage can be classified into the following categories: (1) *information system management,* (2) *system analysis and design,* (3) *program preparation,* (4) *data-base administration,* and (5) *computer operation.*

The *information system manager* performs the administrative duties of all managers. Furthermore, the manager selected should understand the organization's purpose and goals and its data processing procedures; should be able to motivate people; and should possess the poise, stature, and maturity to command the respect of other administrators as well as information processing personnel.

Although there are often several grades of *system analyst* (senior, junior, etc.), the job basically consists of (1) examining the basic methods and procedures of current information systems and (2) modifying, redesigning, and integrating these existing procedures into new system specifications as required to provide the needed information. Typically, the analyst must know a great deal about the particular organization as well as about the uses and limitations of computers.

The job of the applications *programmer* is to take the system designs of the analyst and transform these specifications into machine instructions or programs. In most cases the programmer will work very closely with the analyst during the system-design phase. In smaller organizations, the system analysis and program preparation functions are often combined.

FIGURE 12-1

A recruitment and selection process.

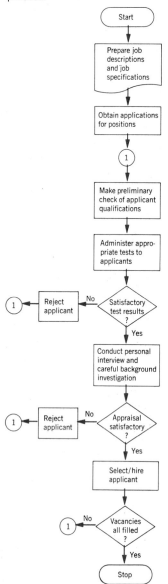

The *data administrator* may not yet exist in many computer installations, but the function of data-base administration is becoming increasingly important as more organizations seek to develop broader systems. Some of the activities of the data administrator are to (1) establish and control data definitions and standards, (2) act as a file-design and data-base consultant to others in the organization, and (3) design the data-base security system to guard against unauthorized use.

The duties of the *computer operator* include setting up the processor and related equipment, starting the program run, checking to ensure proper operation, and unloading equipment at the end of a run. Some knowledge of programming is needed.

To fill the jobs described above, it is necessary to *recruit* potential candidates, and then to *select* from among those candidates the right people for the jobs. Figure 12-1 summarizes the general recruitment and selection process.[2] The chosen candidates may then need to be trained to prepare them for their new duties.

Training computer department personnel Extensive training must be given to those selected to be system analysts, data administrators, and programmers. In addition to having a *knowledge of the organization and its environment,* the system analyst must also understand the *techniques of system analysis and design.* There is lack of uniformity at the present time in the methods used to train (*educate* is probably a better word) analysts to meet the latter requirement although the Association for Computing Machinery (ACM) has recommended college undergraduate and graduate curricula for programs in system analysis and design. Consulting firms, private institutes, and other educational organizations conduct system-analysis seminars on a limited basis. An in-house system training program utilizing senior analysts as instructors has proved to be effective.

A third requirement of analysts is that they possess a *general understanding of computer hardware and software.* The formal training given to analysts in this area may parallel or be identical with the formal training received by programmers.

The data administrator needs the skills of an analyst combined with the very detailed knowledge of hardware and software possessed by a good programmer. This "superhuman" member of the data processing community is a specialist in the system-analysis group in some organizations.

---

[2]For more details on recruitment and selection, see Donald H. Sanders, *Computers in Business,* 3d ed., McGraw-Hill Book Company, New York, 1975, pp. 495–502.

"You're hired! I like your looks!"

©DATAMATION

Programmer training is a continual, lengthy, and expensive process. To the surprise (and dismay) of many administrators, it has been found that *at least 6 months* is generally required before programmers attain a *minimum* level of proficiency. Training costs per programmer may run into the thousands of dollars. In addition to the training available from vendors and through in-house activities, programming skills are also taught by consultants, professional organizations, colleges and universities, and vocational schools.

Equipment manufacturers and vocational schools also offer brief courses to train operators of peripheral equipment. On-the-job training is often the only preparation required.

CONTROLLING IMPLICATIONS

There are numerous controlling implications associated with the use of computer-based information systems that are of concern to (1) *managers* and (2) *auditors and computer personnel.*

Concerns of Managers

A primary concern of managers is that they have ready access to a good information system in order to control the business operations for which they are responsible. In addition to this *managerial control* consideration, however, executives are also vitally interested in—and responsible for—maintaining the necessary *internal control over the information system itself* so that the system is operating efficiently, and so that the integrity and security of data, records, and other business assets are preserved. Let us now look at a few of the implications of computer usage for these managerial and internal control responsibilities.

Managerial control implications   You will recall that the general control procedure consists of several steps: (1) the establishment of predetermined goals or standards, (2) the measurement of performance, (3) the comparison of actual performance with the standards, and (4) the making of appropriate control decisions.

The information output of the computer can help the manager carry out this procedure in many ways. First of all, better information can lead to better planning and the creation of *more realistic standards.* Computer simulation can assist managers in setting goals by showing them the effects of various alternative decisions when certain conditions are assumed; and computer-based network models such as PERT and CPM can improve planning (and therefore control) by forcing managers to identify all project activities that must be performed.

Computer processing systems can also help managers control by gathering, classifying, calculating, and summarizing *actual performance data* promptly and accurately. Once performance data are read into the computer, it is possible for the machine to *compare* the actual performance with the established standards. Periodic reports showing this comparison can be prepared. In some systems, triggered reports, based on the *principle of exception,*[3] may be furnished to the manager only when variations are outside certain specified limits.

It is also possible to program the computer so that it signals when *predetermined decisions* should be carried out. For example, a program may specify that when the inventory of a certain basic part falls below a given level, an output message signals the need to reorder and indicates the reorder quantity. By thus relieving people of many of the routine operational control tasks, the computer frees them to devote more time to (1) planning future moves and (2) leading the all-important human resources of the organization. Such a human/machine relationship, in other words, makes it possible for people to concentrate more of their attention on the heuristic area of intellectual work—an area in which they are far superior to the machine—while the machine is permitted to take over the well-structured control tasks. Figure 12-2 illustrates the place of a computer system in the overall control process.

Internal control responsibilities   Managers are responsible for *internal control;* that is, they are responsible for the controls needed to (1) safeguard assets against theft and destruction, (2) check on

---

[3]In chapter 18 of Exodus, Jethro gives good advice when he tells Moses to delegate some of his routine leadership duties to subordinates and concentrate his attention on the more important exceptions, which the subordinates are unable to handle. This idea is called *"the principle of exception"* in management literature.

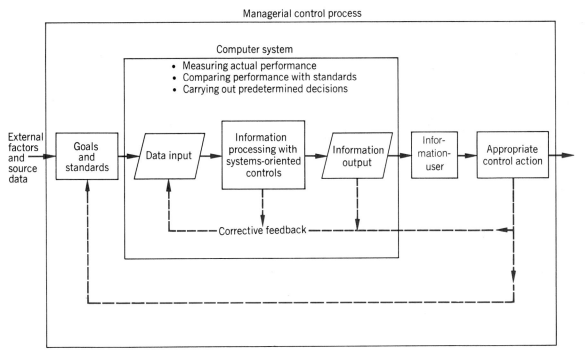

FIGURE 12-2

Control and the computer.

and maintain the accuracy and security of company data, (3) promote operating efficiency, and (4) encourage compliance with company policies and procedures. Some managers have been surprised to learn that the introduction of a computer system often requires a reexamination of internal control procedures. Why? How thoughtful of you to ask. A review is required because in noncomputer systems the data processing activities are typically separated into several departments, with a number of employees being responsible for some portion of the total activity. For example, in the processing of a customer order, credit approval may come from one location, control of the inventory of ordered items may reside in another department, customer billing may be handled by a third department, and receipt of payment for items shipped may be in a fourth location. Thus, the organizational structure separates those who authorize and initiate the order from those who record and carry out the transaction. And both of these groups are separated from those who receive payment for the order. Such a division of data processing activities makes it difficult for fraud to go undetected since several people from different departments would have to be a party to any deception. Also, personnel in each organizational unit can check on the accuracy of others in the course of their routine operations. Thus, internal control has been achieved by the reviews and cross-checks made by people at separate points in the company. In other words, *internal control was employee-oriented.*

But computer usage may make it possible for processing steps to be consolidated and integrated so that these steps may all be performed by only one or two departments. With fewer departments involved, however, and with the likelihood that fewer people are cross-checking data, it *may appear* that, even though source documents originate outside the computer department, the use of computer systems results in a reduction of internal control. Responsible managers have sometimes been distressed to learn that such a reduction *can occur* in an *inadequately controlled* computer department and can produce the following related and unhappy results:

1 *Failure to safeguard assets* Knowledgeable employees (or even a skilled outsider) can steal data and/or programs and sell them; they can acquire and use them intact to support an ongoing fraud or embezzlement; they can add, subtract, or substitute transactions in the data for fraud or embezzlement purposes; and they can do these things at the computer site or at a remote terminal hundreds of miles away. Thieves have become interested in computerized financial records because the job of accounting for the assets of many organizations has now been entrusted to computer systems, and the moves by the banking industry in the direction of EFTS will simply hasten this trend. In the past, paper money was introduced and thieves used presses; now, plastic money (credit cards) and magnetic money (money cards with magnetic strips, computer tapes and disks) are used and thieves are using embossers and computers. And they are making big "hauls." The average computer embezzlement loss suffered by organizations is reported to be between $500,000 and $1 million—5 to 10 times higher than the average manual system loss. A widely discussed example of a "computer crime" is the case involving the chief teller at a Union Dime Savings Bank branch in New York City who was charged with stealing about $1.5 million from the bank's accounts. Hundreds of legitimate accounts were manipulated; money was transferred to fraudulent accounts and then withdrawn; and false information was fed into the bank's computer so that when quarterly interest payments were due the legitimate accounts appeared intact. And all this was done by a person who did not have direct access to the computer. Other techniques used by computer-wise thieves include (a) deducting a few cents in

excess service charges, interest, taxes, or dividends from thousands of accounts and writing themselves a check for the total amount of the excess deductions and (b) reporting inventory items as broken or lost and then transferring the items to accomplices.[4] In short, it has been estimated that losses suffered by organizations as a result of fraud and embezzlement now exceed those caused by robbery, loss, and shoplifting—and the computer is playing an active part in an increasing number of theft cases.

2 *Failure to maintain the security of the computer site* The very existence of some organizations would be threatened by the physical destruction of the files and software that may now be concentrated at a *single* site. Among the possible hazards are *fire, flood,* and *sabotage.* Thousands of military records were destroyed by fire at the Army Records Center in St. Louis; numerous computer centers were flooded in the mid-Atlantic states by the rains that accompanied tropical storm Agnes; and cases of disgruntled employees changing programs to sabotage records and using magnets to ruin tapes containing programs and data have been reported. Several computer centers were also destroyed by bombs during the antiwar period of the late 1960s and early 1970s.

3 *Failure to maintain data integrity* If input data are accurate and complete when they *enter* the computer system; if they are *classified, sorted,* and updated properly when necessary; if they do not become inaccurate through subsequent errors of omission or *calculation;* and if they are not distorted or lost through system malfunctions or operating mistakes, then a manager can be confident about the *integrity* of the data. Unfortunately, the internal control procedures in many businesses have sometimes failed to maintain a high degree of data integrity.

4 *Failure to maintain data security* As Figure 12-3 indicates, a modern computer system is vulnerable to attack and penetration at many points and from many people both inside and outside the organization. Programmers, operators, and maintenance personnel usually have the opportunity to penetrate systems security, and they may do so for personal grudges or for personal gain—e.g., for a bribe from an outsider. Operators, for example, can make duplicate copies of master tapes for outsiders in a few minutes, and programmers can insert code into an

---

[4]For additional techniques and examples see Brandt Allen, "Embezzlers' Guide to the Computer," *Harvard Business Review,* pp. 79–89, July–August 1975.

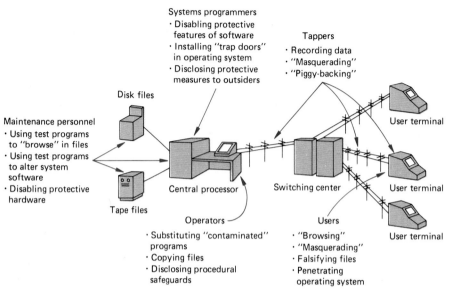

FIGURE 12-3
(*Source:* Tom Alexander, "Waiting
for the Great Computer Rip-off,"
Fortune, p. 144, July 1974.)

operating system in such a way that it provides a "trap door" for
penetration at any convenient time in the future.[5] But even without help from within an organization, unscrupulous outsiders
may gain access to the secrets and confidential records stored
in an organization's computer system. Among the techniques
employed against online systems are "masquerading" and "piggybacking." Penetrators obtain the passwords of legitimate
users by wiretapping or other means and then use these passwords to masquerade as authorized users in order to get access
to the system and to other people's files. The piggybacking
approach is similar in that a small computer or "bootleg" terminal is attached to a tapped communications line where it may
intercept and modify legitimate messages. In summary, then,
those with motivation, financial resources, and access to computer skills may find that, as one authority has stated, penetrat-
ing today's computer system is about as difficult as solving the
crossword puzzle in a Sunday paper.

---

[5]For further information on this penetration technique, see Richard G. Canning,
"Protecting Valuable Data—Part 2," *EDP Analyzer,* pp. 1–3, January 1974.

5 *Failure to protect privacy rights of individuals* Unlike the information stored in older systems, files maintained in large, integrated computer data banks may be more complete, less subject to deterioration, and therefore more worthy targets for unscrupulous persons bent on ferreting out information of a private and confidential nature. Seemingly innocent data recorded and stored at one time may be retrieved and correlated quickly and inexpensively by the computer (perhaps through the use of social security numbers) with other data collected from different sources and at different times to reveal information about individuals that might be damaging to them. It has only been in recent years that some managers have recognized the importance of safeguarding the privacy rights of those whose records are stored in their computer systems.

In spite of the possible dangers inherent in an inadequately controlled computer system, however, *there is no reason why a company should have less internal control because of computer usage.* On the contrary, there is no reason why *system-oriented controls,* in the form of computer programs, cannot be substituted for the employee-oriented controls of manual systems. Also, there is no reason why the separation of duties and responsibilities cannot be maintained *within* the computer department to safeguard the integrity of the system-oriented controls. In fact, there is no reason why a firm cannot achieve better control because of (1) the computer's ability to follow policies and execute processing procedures uniformly, (2) the difficulty of changing and manipulating, without detection, proper programmed systems controls, and (3) the computer's inherent accuracy advantage when given correct input data. Of course, top executives expect auditors and computer personnel to be sensitive to, and knowledgeable about, internal control arrangements that will avoid negative consequences. In the following section we shall consider some procedures that can be used to control the negative impact.

Interests of Auditors and Computer Personnel

Some auditing considerations Auditors may either be employees of the organization *(internal auditors)* or be independent certified public accountants employed by the board of directors *(external auditors).* Periodic examinations or *audits* are performed by these auditors to evaluate the existing internal control arrangements.

In studying these arrangements, auditors check to see if there is an *organizational separation of activities* within the computer department between those who design and prepare the new systems and those who prepare the input data and operate the equipment. In other words, analysts and programmers should design, maintain, and make necessary changes (according to specified procedures) to programs, but they *should not* be involved with day-to-day production runs; equipment operators, on the other hand, should not have unrestricted access to completed computer programs, nor should they be involved with making changes in data or programs.

In addition to their concern about a proper separation of duties that can help safeguard assets, auditors are also concerned about whether adequate controls have been created to maintain data integrity and security. Thus, during the audit attention is turned to the *audit trail* to monitor systems activity, and to determine if security and integrity controls are effective. The audit trail begins with the recording of all transactions, winds through the processing steps and through any intermediate records which may exist and be affected, and ends with the production of output reports and records. By selecting a representative sample of previously processed source documents and following the audit trail, the auditor can trace these documents through the data processing systems to their final report or record destinations as a means of testing the adequacy of systems procedures and controls.

Test data may be used in the examination by the auditor. Just as the programmer uses simulated input data to check programs during the debugging and testing stage, so, too, may an auditor use test decks to check on program integrity and security controls. Both valid and invalid transactions are included in the test data. Of course, the fact that a program passes the auditor's test does not mean that the tested program always receives accurate input data or is always the one that is used during processing. Reasonable but incorrect input data may be supplied, and a fraudulent patch may be inserted into the program during subsequent processing runs.

Some data processing considerations The overwhelming majority of computer personnel appreciate the need for internal control and are as concerned as auditors and managers in maintaining it. In particular, data processing people consider it very important to:

1 *Maintain data integrity* The data processing steps that must be carried out properly if data integrity is to be maintained are originating-recording, classifying, sorting, and calculating.

Some of the problems associated with the *originating-recording* step that computer system employees try to steer clear of are (*a*) gathering data that are not needed, (*b*) using gathered data in ways not originally intended, (*c*) entering inaccurate and/or incomplete data into the system, and (*d*) setting up input procedures that confuse and mislead those supplying the data. Data processors are also interested in establishing codes to identify and arrange data items with like characteristics into groups so that the people and machines that must *classify* and *sort* the data will do so in a common and *standardized* way with as few errors as possible. And finally, data processors seek to set up controls to prevent program bugs and other human/machine errors from producing faulty *calculations* on correct input data.

2 *Maintain data security* Computer system personnel know that in addition to maintaining data integrity, they must also maintain the security of the data if adverse effects are to be eliminated. In other words, the data processing steps of *summarizing, communicating, storing, retrieving,* and *reproducing* must also be controlled if negative consequences for organizations and for people are to be avoided. It does not help an organization if its secret product data that fall into the hands of a competitor are accurate. And it does not help much for people to know that the information relevant to them that has been summarized and stored in a data bank is accurate and complete if they also know that the information is *not secured* and protected against theft, fraud, accidental or malicious scrutiny, manipulation, and/or destruction.

3 *Maintain privacy of records* Both data integrity and security are needed to protect an individual's legitimate right to *privacy*— i.e., to protect the legitimate right of an individual to limit the access to personal and often sensitive information to persons authorized to use it in the individual's best interests. To illustrate this point, consider the following rather extreme example:[6] A computer dating service keeps poor records of its past and present customers and then sells its list of female clients to a publishing organization that prints and sells through local newsstands lists of "Girls Who Want Dates." Try and tell these women (some of whom are now married) that their privacy hasn't been invaded! In summary, data integrity, data security, and personal privacy are interrelated as shown in Figure 12-4. The security and privacy issues have been very much on the minds of data

---

[6]An actual case very similar to this hypothetical one has been reported.

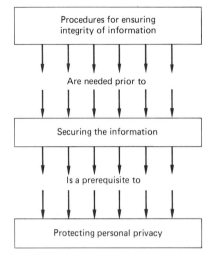

FIGURE 12-4

processors in recent years because (as we shall see in the next chapter) past control failures in these areas have led to legal and social pressures for improvement.

SUMMARY
Some of the implications for staffing and controlling that result from the use of computer-based information systems have been presented in this chapter. In the personnel/staffing area, we have seen that computer systems have changed the job duties and employment status of some noncomputer managers and workers. And since some of these changes have threatened or damaged employees, it is not surprising that resistance to systems change has been common. In addition to considering these possible implications for noncomputer personnel, however, we have also looked at the types of employees that must be recruited, selected, and trained to staff the computer department.

Several controlling implications associated with the use of computer systems that are of concern to managers, auditors, and computer personnel have been presented in the preceding pages. We have seen, for example, that information produced by computer systems can help improve managerial control over business operations. But we have also seen that the introduction of a computer can have a significant effect on the internal control of the information system itself. In some cases, the control procedures that have replaced the numerous employee-oriented checks used in a manual system have been poorly designed. Several system failures resulting from poor internal controls were presented in the chapter. Of course, managers, auditors, and data processors are concerned about these failures and are working to develop and preserve system-oriented controls that will safeguard assets and maintain the integrity and security of the system. Several of these control procedures are discussed in the next chapter.

REVIEW AND DISCUSSION QUESTIONS

1 (**a**) How may individuals benefit from changes in job duties resulting from computer usage? (**b**) How may their job duties be adversely affected?

2 What changes in employment status may result from computer usage?

3 (**a**) What is the distinction between displacement and unemployment? (**b**) What factors influence the significance of the displacement problem when computer systems are introduced into businesses?

4 (**a**) Identify an industry that has come into existence in the last 10 years. (**b**) What factors account for the creation of this industry? (**c**) Did the creation of this industry cause displacement elsewhere? (**d**) Would jobs have been lost to foreign producers if the industry had not been created? (**e**) What is your estimate of the net effect of this industry on total employment?

5 (**a**) Why do managers resist change? (**b**) Why do employees resist? (**c**) How may resistance to change be reduced?

6 Explain the job functions of the following data processing personnel: (**a**) Information system managers (**b**) System analysts (**c**) Programmers (**d**) Data administrators (**e**) Computer operators.

7 How can computer systems help managers control business operations?

8 (**a**) What is internal control? (**b**) Why is it needed?

9 Identify and discuss the types of information system failures that can result from poor internal control.

10 Of what significance is organizational structure in maintaining internal control?

11 (**a**) What is the audit trail? (**b**) Why is it needed?

12 "Data integrity, data security, and personal privacy are interrelated." Define these terms and discuss this statement.

13

SOCIAL IMPLICATIONS

In addition to affecting the planning, organizing, staffing, and controlling activities within an organization, computer usage is also exerting a significant influence on society as a whole. Of course, it is not possible in this brief chapter to present a full discussion of the social impact of computer usage.[1] But it is also not possible to conclude this Part of the book dealing with "computer implications for management" without considering some of the broader social implications of the business use of computers. Therefore, in the pages that follow we shall look at some of the *beneficial* and *negative* influences that business computers may have on a changing society. We shall then look at a few approaches that businesses can use to *control the negative impact* of their computer systems.

POSSIBLE BENEFICIAL IMPLICATIONS

We should never lose sight of the important fact that computer usage has already had a positive influence on (and will continue to offer countless benefits to) large segments of society in general and many individuals in particular. For example, most of us have probably been disturbed by the way prices have increased for many of the goods and services that we buy. However, what we may perhaps fail to realize is that, to the extent that businesses have avoided waste and improved efficiency and productivity through the use of computers, the prices we now pay may be less than they would otherwise have been. Edmund Berkeley, editor of *Computers and People,* has

---

[1] For more information on this general topic, see Donald H. Sanders, *Computers in Society,* 2d ed., McGraw-Hill Book Company, New York, 1977.

"You say it will cut our work in half? Good, bring us another one!"

estimated that "the use of computers on a large scale has made prices lower by 10 to 30 percent and often much more, than they would be without computers."[2]

In addition to possibly having an impact on the prices we pay *to* businesses, computers may also play a role in improving the quality of the services we receive *from* them. Computer processing techniques, for example, make possible the shortening of customer waiting lines at airline ticket offices and at the reservation desks of hotels, motels, and car-rental agencies; the use of credit cards as a convenient means of handling purchase transactions; and the efficient control of inventory in retail outlets so that popular items are reordered in time to avoid many of the out-of-stock situations that frustrate consumers.

Some other benefits which private individuals may receive from business organizations as a result of computer usage are:

1 *The possible benefits of EFTS* We have seen in earlier chapters that financial and retailing organizations are very interested in the use of electronic funds transfer systems (EFTS). But how can these systems benefit individuals in our society? (Once again you have asked the right question!) Although EFTS are still in the formative stages and the fully developed version(s) will be shaped by intense competition and government regulation, their general shape is clear enough for us to identify certain advantages for individuals. In a *checkless payment system,* for example, authorized credits to specified individuals from an employer, pension fund, etc., are recorded on magnetic tape along with the name of the recipient's bank and his or her bank account number. The tape is delivered to the paying organization's bank. This bank sorts out its own customers, deposits the payment amounts to their accounts, and then transfers the remaining names to an *automated clearing house* (ACH) facility. An ACH computer sorts the remaining names according to their banks and then notifies these banks of the amounts to be deposited in the specified accounts. A benefit of this EFTS approach is that it eliminates the fear of theft of checks. Millions of people are now receiving direct-deposit social security payments in lieu of mailed checks. As one recipient living on Chicago's South Side has noted, "It's better for (the check) to be in the bank than to

---

[2]Edmund C. Berkeley, "How Do Computers Affect People?," *Computers and People,* p. 6, April 1975.

take the chance of having it in your mailbox."[3] Another way in which EFTS may benefit individuals will involve the use of terminals conveniently located anywhere that substantial numbers of nontrivial financial transactions occur. Point-of-sale *cash terminal systems,* for example, have been tested and found to be technologically feasible. When such systems are fully developed, you might present your plastic "currency" or "debit" card (which uses, perhaps, a magnetic stripe to supply the necessary account information) to make a request at a store's terminal for an electronic transfer of funds to pay for a purchase. The terminal would then send a message to your bank asking for approval of the transfer. If your account has the necessary funds (or if you are eligible for sufficient credit), the bank's computer would (1) send a message approving the transaction to the merchant's terminal, and (2) see to the transfer of the payment funds to the merchant's account. This EFTS approach would give individuals the benefits associated with completing transactions for cash (speed, lack of "red tape," etc.) without the possible dangers associated with carrying large amounts of cash. Of course, you and the merchant may use different banks and so one or more ACH facilities would be used in the transaction to switch and process messages. Fully developed cash terminal systems will depend on a strong national network of ACHs. But a National Automated Clearing House Association (NACHA) has been formed, and other ACH facilities are being developed throughout the nation (Figure 13-1).

2 *The possible benefits of UPC* Merchants selling products coded with the Universal Product Code (UPC) symbols discussed in Chapter 5 expect to receive the benefits of greater efficiency and reduced costs. But their customers may also find that a UPC system (1) reduces their waiting time and gives them faster service at checkout counters, (2) reduces the chances for human error at checkouts, and (3) provides them with an *itemized* sales receipt rather than just a tape with a column of numbers.

3 *The possible recreational benefits* Some organizations are using computers for the sole purpose of amusing and entertaining individuals. For example, the computer of Recreational Computer Systems, Inc., Atlanta, Georgia, is used for just this purpose. In one application, image enhancement technology developed for the Mariner spacecraft project has been used to

---

[3] *Wall Street Journal,* p. 15, Nov. 18, 1975.

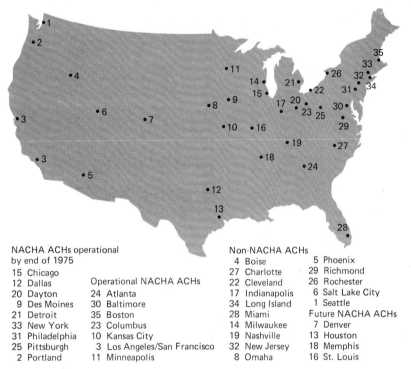

NACHA ACHs operational
by end of 1975

		Non-NACHA ACHs	
15 Chicago		4 Boise	5 Phoenix
12 Dallas	Operational NACHA ACHs	27 Charlotte	29 Richmond
20 Dayton	24 Atlanta	22 Cleveland	26 Rochester
9 Des Moines	30 Baltimore	17 Indianapolis	6 Salt Lake City
21 Detroit	35 Boston	34 Long Island	1 Seattle
33 New York	23 Columbus	28 Miami	Future NACHA ACHs
31 Philadelphia	10 Kansas City	14 Milwaukee	7 Denver
25 Pittsburgh	3 Los Angeles/San Francisco	19 Nashville	13 Houston
2 Portland	11 Minneapolis	32 New Jersey	18 Memphis
		8 Omaha	16 St. Louis

FIGURE 13-1
Operational and planned automated clearinghouses. (*Source:* Linda Flato, "Checking on EFTS," *Computer Decisions*, p. 25, May 1975.)

convert a small customer photograph into a 12- by 12-inch mosaic of computer printer characters (Figure 13-2).[4] In addition to those organizations that are using computers to entertain customers, there are other concerns that are manufacturing sophisticated games containing microprocessors that may be attached to television sets. The possibilities in this area are discussed in the next chapter.

POSSIBLE NEGATIVE IMPLICATIONS

It should be apparent by now that computer systems have taken on increasingly responsible tasks in many organizations and are now performing vital functions in our society. Thus, it is essential that in the data processing steps performed by computers *vital and relevant data are not lost or stolen, errors are not introduced into the data, and data are not stored, retrieved, modified, or communicated*

---

[4] The original 12- by 12-inch mosaic in Figure 13-2 obviously had to be reduced to fit on the page. Unfortunately, the computer could do nothing to enhance the features of the subject of the photograph.

FIGURE 13-2
Computer-produced mosaic from customer photograph (courtesy Recreational Computer Systems, Inc.).

without proper authorization. Unfortunately, however, some businesses have used questionable data processing practices that have had adverse effects on the private lives and records of individuals.

Data Integrity Issues

We have seen that the data processing steps that must be carried out properly if data integrity is to be maintained are originating-recording, classifying, sorting, and calculating. Let's now look at some of the possible ways in which the insensitive and/or thoughtless performance of these steps may lead to undesirable social results.

Data originating-recording matters A staggering volume of information of a highly personal nature has been (and is being) gathered and recorded by businesses (e.g., credit bureaus) and by governmental agencies. One fear arising from this development is that an unscrupulous person could be tempted by existing technology and the availability of mounds of computer-accessible data on individuals to misuse the data in ways not originally intended. Facts about age, sex, income, marital status, health, spending habits, lifestyle, etc., could be analyzed in a trial-and-error fashion just to see what might happen. In summary, as Frank T. Cary, chairman of the board of IBM, has observed:

> In the past you had to be famous or infamous to have a dossier. Today there can be a dossier on anyone. Information systems, with a seemingly limitless capacity for storing and sorting information, have made it practical to record and transfer a wealth of data on just about anyone. The result is that we now retain too much information. The ambiguous and unverified are retained along with legitimate data. . . . One way of preventing misuse of personal information is to discourage its collection in the first place.[5]

---

[5]Quoted by Hanna Shields and Mae Churchill in "The Fraudulent War on Crime," *The Nation,* p. 655, Dec. 21, 1974.

"Miss Bradley, I have a clean desk and a free afternoon. Bring me everything we have on somebody."

© DATAMATION ®

In addition to the widespread general concern about the seemingly uncontrolled collection of personal information on individuals, some more specific problems associated with the originating-recording step are:

1   *Gathering data without a valid need to know*   When he was Vice President, Gerald Ford wrote that it was the responsibility of all who use computers to "assure that information is not fed into the computer unless it is relevant. Even if it is relevant, there is still a need for discretion. A determination must be made if the social harm done from some data outweighs its usefulness."[6] And former New York Representative Bella Abzug, chairperson of the House Government Information and Individual Rights Subcommittee, noted that the general result of the federal government's information policies is "an ever-increasing monopoly control over access to and production of information, statistics and a wide variety of data—some necessary, some unnecessary, some gathered legally, some illegally in violation of fundamental constitutional rights."[7]

2   *Gathering inaccurate and incomplete data*   More "computer errors" may be attributed to inaccurate and incomplete data input than to either hardware failure or incorrect software. *Unintentional mistakes* in filling out input forms, keying records, coding accounts, etc., are common enough in any record-keeping system. But the consequences may be more serious in a computer-based system because there may be fewer individuals to catch errors and the speed with which inaccurate information is made available to system-users may be much faster than the speed with which errors are detected and corrected. The author, for example, had a check to a major oil company "bounce" because that particular check had been encoded with an incorrect account number by a clerk at his bank. Although in time the bank wrote letters of apology and a new check was issued to the oil company, there is still the possibility that in some credit bureau data bank there may be a negative entry in his dossier that has not been corrected. Additional problems can result from cases of *mistaken identity*. Good, bad, and indifferent input data prepared by grantors of credit usually find their way into credit bureau data banks. If your name is not

---

[6]Gerald R. Ford, "Individual Privacy and Databanks," *The Internal Auditor*, p. 14, July/August 1974.
[7]"Newsdata," *Computer Decisions*, p. 6, May 1975.

keyed correctly, if your address has changed, if you have a common name, or if you are not consistent in the way you use your first name and initials, you may be confused with some other individual (and with your luck it would be a "deadbeat" rather than a millionaire). Thus, as Robert L. Patrick has observed:

> Despite all the programming done by all the clearing-houses to date, these mistaken identities do occur, they are troublesome, and they are one of the primary reasons why credit reporting agencies treat individuals unfairly.[8]

Unfortunately, in addition to the unintentional mistakes that occur in credit bureau input data, *deliberate* errors have also been introduced into these data banks that are so important to individuals. "In one credit bureau, investigators have admitted to falsifying computer input data because they feel their case loads are too heavy to allow them time to gather all the details called for by the system."[9]

3 *Problems of confusion and bewilderment associated with data gathering* There have been several verified cases of frustrated individuals actually firing bullets into computers. And the number of such incidents would probably be much larger if individuals confused and bewildered by computer data input procedures had followed their initial impulses. A significant cause of this confusion, of course, is that people affected by an information system are often not informed of what the system does or how it works. And the result of this confusion may be the belief on the part of individuals that they have been tricked or deceived by the system. Credit application forms, for example, may not indicate that the supplied data are going to be entered into third-party data banks and used in rather secretive ways. Innocent errors in filling out one form may be considered as highly suspicious discrepancies in a consolidated data bank. Individuals may also find it confusing to operate the computer input devices that are replacing more familiar forms and procedures. Automated voting systems, for example, have confused voters and have produced questionable tallies. Finally, people have

---

[8]Robert L. Patrick, "Privacy, People, and Credit Services," *Datamation,* p. 49, January 1974.
[9]Frederic G. Withington, "Five Generations of Computers," *Harvard Business Review,* p. 107, July–August 1974.

been bewildered by the use of the deposit slips with magneti-cally encoded account numbers that banks supply to customers. It is reported that in at least one case a man distributed his encoded deposit slips about the lobby of a bank where they were used by bewildered depositors who wrote their names and account numbers on the slips. Since the names and handwritten numbers were ignored by the bank's MICR equipment, however, the deposits were credited to the account number encoded on the slips. The following morning our resourceful swindler closed out his $67,000 account and proceeded on his way.

Classification-sorting matters   Classifying and sorting input data according to some commonly defined and consistently organized coding scheme can lead to more *standardized* information systems. And the standardization now taking place in organizations may result in economies and increased efficiency. But standardization may also lead to unwanted *depersonalization*. As an individual comes in contact with an increasing number of computer systems, the use of numerical codes for identification purposes may also be expected to increase. Although individuals may understand that

‹ DATAMATION ›

"I baptize thee, 345-26-4155 . . ."

their being treated as numbers can lead to standardized and efficient computer usage by organizations, they may wish that it were not so. Instead of being numerically coded and molded to meet the computer's needs, they might prefer that the computer systems be designed so that they would be treated as persons rather than as numbers. *This is not likely to happen.* Depersonalization is something that individuals are likely to have to submit to more often in the future. Of course, as standardization spreads, individuals may need to remember fewer code numbers—e.g., their social security numbers may be substituted for several different codes. In fact, the social security number is now being used as the personal identifier in a number of large data systems. The Internal Revenue Service, the U.S. Army, colleges and universities, state driver's license departments, insurance companies, banks, credit bureaus—these and many other organizations may know you as 353-27-4765. The threat of an eventual "universal identifier," of course, is that the separate data records you have established for particular purposes can easily be consolidated through the use of the common number, and the combined data can be merged into a large personal dossier.

In addition to treating individuals as numbers, standardized procedures, once established, tend to become inflexible.[10] Thus, if an individual's needs do not conform to the "norms" of the system, there may be difficulty in getting the system to deal properly with the exception. This tendency to try to force everyone into the same mold may naturally give the individual a feeling of helplessness in trying to cope with a cold, impersonal, and remote organization. A Mr. D'Unger, for example, wrote several organizations asking them to spell his name correctly. He received several replies, all telling him that it was impossible because of the equipment employed by the systems. A computer expert then looked into the matter and found that the line printers involved had the apostrophe available, but the systems did not bother to use it.

System miscalculations   Miscalculations are primarily due to human errors in preparing input data, in designing and preparing programs, and in operating the hardware. Thus, when the computer itself is blamed for some foul-up, it is frequently being used as a convenient "scapegoat" to cover up human error, carelessness, or

---

[10]This tendency toward inflexibility is *not* an inherent flaw of computer usage. Actually, computerized systems can make individual treatment possible and can cater to individuality for less cost than manual systems. But uniform and rigid treatment costs even less to provide and is thus the approach too often used by system designers.

indifference. Or, perhaps, it is being used to add credibility to false claims. For example, the Allen Piano and Organ Company of Phoenix, Arizona, advertised on a radio broadcast that its computer had made a mistake and as a result the firm was overstocked with furniture which it was now offering at bargain prices. When a local computer professional, on behalf of the Association for Computing Machinery, contacted the firm and offered to repair any malfunctioning computer hardware free of charge, he found that the company did not have a computer and did not use any computing service!

Of course, the unfortunate fact remains that people may believe such false advertising because they are aware of computer system miscalculations that actually have occurred. Since we have already seen some examples of business system miscalculations in Chapter 3, we need not belabor the point here. But perhaps it might be appropriate to conclude this section with a few pitiful examples of nonbusiness computer system "atrocities" that have had a negative impact on individuals.

1 A New York City employee failed to get his check for three pay periods after a computer payroll system was installed. Finally, after the employee had initiated legal action against the City, a program bug was discovered, removed, and Mr. Void was at last paid.
2 Individuals have been arrested for "stealing" their own cars. The sequence of events goes something like this: The car is stolen, the theft is reported to a law enforcement data bank, the car is recovered (perhaps in another jurisdiction) and returned to its owner, the recovery is *not* entered into the data bank, and the owner is then picked up while driving the recovered property. Since the arrest may also be entered into the data bank, but the final disposition may not be, the owner may wind up with an arrest record for "grand theft-auto." If you do not think this can be serious, you should consider the plight of the ex-Marine from Illinois who has been jailed several times for desertion because of incorrect information stored in the FBI's computerized National Crime Information Center.

Data Security Issues

Data security, we have seen, is dependent upon the control over the additional data processing steps of summarizing, storing, retrieving, reproducing, and communicating. That is, data security involves the protection of *summarized* and *stored* data against accidental or malicious disclosure (through unauthorized *retrieval, reproduction,* and *communication*), modification, restriction, or destruction.

Problems with the security of information systems existed before and during the time that computers first began to replace file cabinets. But the vulnerability of computer systems has increased substantially in recent years, and so the security issue has become much more important. Early computers were generally located in self-contained installations, were accessible to a relatively small number of specialists, and were employed to process batches of data in a single stream. As computer systems increased in number and became more sophisticated, however, multiprogramming and multiprocessing concepts became available, many more individuals had access to information systems, the use of shared resources and jointly used data became common, and remote access to direct interaction with a distant computer became a routine operation for even casual users. Such an environment has obviously increased the difficulty of maintaining security. But in addition to the security difficulties caused by easy systems access by many people, the vulnerability of systems has also increased because (1) the information to be found in a relatively complete and up-to-date data bank may be of sufficient value to provide the incentive for outsiders to seek access to it, and (2) an increased number of individuals have now been trained in computer science and in the skills required to program, penetrate, and manipulate computer systems.[11]

Since the security of computer systems was recognized as a significant problem only in recent years, the computer *hardware* in general use today was not designed with security provisions in mind. Thus, the security provisions that do exist are found in the software and in the organizational policies, administrative procedures, and data processing controls that may exist in the particular system.

When it comes to security, existing *software* is indeed soft. Clever individuals have had no difficulty in breaking through the security provisions of those computer operating system programs that they have sought to penetrate. In fact, a favorite activity of some bright students on college campuses has been to successfully infiltrate the college computer system. For example, two students—one a theology major!—at little Southern Missionary College in Collegedale,

---

[11]For example, a few years ago, as a part of their rehabilitation programs to provide inmates with marketable skills, several penitentiaries began offering courses in computer programming.

Tennessee, "broke through" the file-security system used in the Hewlett-Packard 2000 series timeshared computers and devised programs that decoded protected files.

Whether the invaders be theology majors who doth covet their neighbor's files for the challenge presented, or whether they be thieves, criminal manipulators, saboteurs, or spies, they have found that the computer center of an organization may be its nerve center, that it usually contains sensitive information, and that it is often vulnerable to attack. Without adequate computer security provisions, a business, as we have seen, may be exposed to danger through theft, through careless handling of records, through espionage, and/ or through sabotage. But a lack of control over data security has also led to *undesirable consequences for individuals in society.*

Individuals as well as organizations *lose money* to the computer thief. In one instance, a computer was used to send out phony invoices to individuals. The thief knew that some people pay authentic-looking bills automatically, without questioning their validity. When a phony bill was questioned, however, the thief would merely send back a form letter saying, "Sorry. Our computer made an error." In another instance, bank customers have found that several times a year small errors in favor of the bank have occurred in their statements. Some customers have complained, but since the losses are small, most people probably have not bothered. At this writing, the bank in question does not know what is happening. It is estimated, however, that the mysterious thief may be realizing about $300,000 each year from individuals. A person's finances could also become fouled up as a result of the penetration of an EFTS by an enemy or an unethical competitor. Invalid charges from organizations selected by the penetrator—e.g., insurance companies, utilities, department stores—could be entered against the individual's accounts. At best, the resulting mess would probably involve long delays and great *inconvenience* to straighten out; at worst, it could result in financial ruin.

Finally, our society expects that confidential data on individuals be preserved and used only by authorized persons for approved purposes. But a lack of control over data security can lead to the invasion of an individual's legitimate *right to privacy.* Since this is the subject of the next section, we will not dwell on it here. It should be pointed out here, however, that the majority of computer systems installed in the nation today are *not* secure enough to meet the personal data confidentiality conditions required by existing laws; nor are they secure enough to protect the privacy rights which existing laws give to individuals.

The Privacy Issue

As every man goes through life, he fills in a number
of forms for the record, each containing a number of
questions. There are thus hundreds of little threads
radiating from each man, millions of threads in all. If
these threads were suddenly to become visible,
people would lose all ability to move.

Alexander Solzhenitsyn

We know that for years private and public organizations have been
building separate files containing "threads" of information about
those with whom they come in contact. And we know that the use of
these files has led to past abuses of individuals' legitimate right to
keep to themselves (or to have kept on a confidential basis) those
facts, beliefs, thoughts, and feelings that they do not wish to divulge
publicly. But many of these older files are incomplete and poorly
maintained. Thus, the value of their contents may be such that
unauthorized persons have little incentive to snoop. But as we saw in
the last chapter, *the development of computer data banks has
changed the situation.* Up-to-date personal information files stored
on readily accessible media and devices in large consolidated data
banks may now be worthy targets for unscrupulous persons.
Thoughtful opponents of consolidated data banks are therefore concerned about the threat that they might eventually present to an
individual. This concern is perhaps best summarized in a *Saturday
Review* cartoon which shows a distressed executive listening to a
telephone message. The message is: "This is the Computer Data
Bank. Leave $100,000 in small bills in Locker 287 at the Port
Authority Bus Terminal or I'll print out your complete dossier and
send it to your wife."

There are several possible negative implications of computer
usage that are linked to the subject of individual privacy. The
following examples and speculations should be sufficient to demon-
strate how a computer system or network could be used for *surveillance* and for the creation of *a climate that can restrict individual
freedom.*

EFTS surveillance possibilities Although the EFTS being
designed and implemented by banks and other financial institutions
are not intended for surveillance, they may be easily adapted to this
purpose in the future. If all your nontrivial financial transactions were
normally to be processed through EFTS computers, a *daily record* of

much of *what* you do and *where* you do it could be prepared. Thus, the situation illustrated in a *New Yorker* magazine cartoon of a husband and wife trying to decide what movie to see and the wife asking her husband "What would look good on our dossier?" could become less amusing and more possible in the future. Furthermore, if you were to decide to use cash for a transaction that you wished to keep private, the cash acquisition might be quite conspicuous (and suspicious?). In 1971, a group of computer, communication, and surveillance experts was gathered and given the following hypothetical problem: As advisers to the head of the KGB (the Russian Secret Police), they were to design an *unobtrusive* surveillance system to monitor the activities of all citizens and visitors inside the U.S.S.R. As Paul Armer testified in congressional hearings:

> That exercise . . . was only a two-day effort. I am sure we could add some bells and whistles to increase its effectiveness somewhat. But the fact remains that this group decided that if you wanted to build an unobtrusive system for surveillance, you couldn't do much better than an EFTS.[12]

Of course, EFTS proponents in the financial community maintain that adequate laws can be passed to prevent surveillance abuse. But critics are not so sure. They point out that existing check authorization systems, and systems such as BankAmericard, Master Charge, and American Express, can "flag" individual accounts so that if a "flagged" individual tries to cash a check or make a purchase someone (police perhaps?) can be notified of the individual's exact location. And they are fearful that future operators of EFTS networks would be unable to resist the pressures from government organizations to allow the EFTS to be used for surveillance purposes.

Freedom restrictions   Consider the following facts:

1 At this writing, computerized records are being used by the Department of Health, Education, and Welfare to track down fathers who have deserted children on welfare. This operation, officially called the Parent Locator Service (and unofficially referred to as "Dadnet"), has legal access to the "confidential" master files of the IRS, the Social Security Administration, the Pentagon, and the Veterans Administration.

---

[12]See Paul Armer, "Computer Technology and Surveillance," *Computers and People*, p. 11, September 1975.

2 At this time, thousands of law enforcement officers and bank, employment agency, and credit company clerks have easy access to networks containing information on millions of people. Many of these officers and clerks without any real "need-to-know" may while away the time browsing through the records of friends and acquaintances just to see what they can uncover.[13]

The awareness of such facts and such uses of large computerized data banks tends to have a sobering effect on individuals—it tends to restrict their freedom, and it tends to have a chilling effect on their actions even when the data are accurate, even when the use of the data is authorized by law, and even when controls on the use of the data are imposed. You may agree that runaway fathers should help support their children if possible, but you may also begin to wonder if a future system might not be designed to "track" you down; and you may be in favor of the use of computers to curtail crime, but you

---

[13]A bored deputy sheriff in Massachusetts spent one night running his family through the FBI's National Crime Information Center. The results: "His mother was listed because, when she was 18, neighbors complained of a noisy sorority party (no arrests). His stepfather, a respected businessman, was listed because he complained to the police that he had *received* a bad check." In all, 10 out of 11 of the deputy's family were listed. See Francis W. Sargent, "The National Crime Information Center and Massachusetts," *Computers and Automation*, p. 8, December 1973.

"Let's go somewhere where we can talk."

may also resent being listed with felons in an unsecured data bank. In short, you may now tend to behave differently (and less freely) than you once would have because of your increasing awareness that what you say and do may become part of some computer record.

CONTROLLING THE NEGATIVE IMPACT

What *integrity, security,* and *privacy controls* have been devised in the attempt to counter the negative effects of computer usage? What a coincidence that you should ask. . . .

Integrity Controls

To be assured that a system will provide accurate, complete, and reliable information, auditors should periodically check to see that (1) all *input* data are correctly recorded; (2) the *processing* of all authorized transactions is accomplished without additions or omissions; and (3) the *output* of the system is distributed on a timely basis and only to those who are authorized to receive it.

Input controls The purpose of input controls is to make sure that (1) *all* authorized input transactions are identified, (2) these transactions are *accurately recorded* in a machine-usable form at the *right time,* and (3) *all* these transactions are then sent to the processing station. Among the control techniques that may be adopted are:

1 *The use of prenumbered forms* Whenever possible, a simple and effective control is to use serially numbered forms so that documents may be accounted for. A missing number in the sequence signals a missing document.

2 *The use of control totals* When batch processing is used, certain totals can be computed for each batch of source documents. For example, the total dollar-sales figure may be computed on a batch of sales invoices prior to, perhaps, keypunching. The same calculation can be made after keypunching to see if the figures compare. Control totals do not have to be expressed in dollars. They can be the totals obtained from adding figures in a data field that is included in all source documents being considered. A simple count of documents, cards, and other records is an effective control total. For example, the number of cards processed in the computer-operating department can be compared with the count of the number of cards that are delivered for processing.

3 *The use of programmed checks on input* Program instructions can be written to check on the reasonableness and propriety of data as they enter the processing operation. For example, program checks can be written to determine if (*a*) certain specified limits are exceeded, (*b*) the input is complete, and (*c*) a transaction code or identification number is active and reasonable. When online processing is used, lockwords or passwords may be required from remote stations before certain files can be made accessible.

4 *The use of structural check* A test of the transactions to be processed can be made to determine whether the debits and credits called for represent acceptable combinations. Transactions with unacceptable debit and credit combinations are rejected.

Processing controls   These controls are established to (1) determine when data are lost or not processed and (2) check on the accuracy of arithmetic calculations. These controls may be classified into *hardware* and *software* categories. Important hardware controls include parity checks (i.e., checks that test whether the number of digits in an array is odd or even) and the use of dual reading and writing heads in I/O equipment. Software or programmed controls include:

1 *The use of record count* As a check against a predetermined total, the computer can be instructed to count the number of records that it handles in a program run.

2 *The use of tape labels* The *external* labeling of magnetic tapes should be carefully controlled. These outside labels may give those interested such information as the tape contents, program identification number, and length of time the contents should be retained. *Internal* header and trailer control labels may also be recorded on the tapes themselves. The first (or *header*) record written on the tape gives the program identification number and other information. Before actual processing begins, then, a programmed comparison check may be made to make sure that the correct tape reel is being used. The last (or *trailer*) record contains a count of the number of other records on the tape.

3 *The use of sequence check* In batch processing, the records are in some kind of sequence, e.g., by employee number or stock number. Programmed checks to detect out-of-sequence and missing cards and records prevent a file from being processed in an incorrect order.

Output controls   These controls are established as final checks on the accuracy and propriety of the processed information. Among the output control methods that may be employed are:

1   *The use of control totals*   How do the control totals of processed information compare with the input control totals? For example, is there agreement between the number of records that were delivered for processing and the number of records that were actually processed? A basic output control technique is to obtain satisfactory answers to such questions.
2   *The review of interested parties*   Feedback on a regular basis from input-initiating and output-using departments points out errors that slip through in spite of all precautions. Follow-up action must be taken to correct any file inaccuracies that may be revealed.
3   *The use of systematic sampling*   Internal auditors can check on output by tracing randomly selected transactions from source documents through the processing system to the output destination. This should be done on a regular and systematic basis.
4   *The use of prenumbered forms*   Certain output forms should be prenumbered and accounted for in the same manner as input documents. Blank payroll-check forms, for example, should be closely guarded.

System Security Controls

Since easy access to the computer by people with the skills needed to manipulate the system is a primary reason for the difficulty in maintaining security, an important step in achieving a more secure system is to separate the activities of those working *within* the computer department as noted in the last chapter. In addition, *system-design, programming,* and *computer-operation* controls should be enforced.

System-design controls   New systems should be designed (and documented) with audit and control considerations in mind. (It is expensive to ignore control aspects and then have to revise and rework a designed system. The participation of a knowledgeable auditor in the design phase so that proper controls may be built in is thus a wise precaution.) One of the most important controls that can be exercised over systems design is to assign authority to one or more individuals to make sure that systems and program flowcharts, decision tables, manuals, etc., are correctly prepared *and main-*

tained. Specifically written control procedures should be established for this purpose.

Programming controls A procedure should be formulated to handle *program changes.* Changes should be made only after written approval is given by someone in a position of authority, e.g., the manager of the affected department. It is sometimes a good policy to postpone making a number of minor changes until the end of an accounting cycle so that data handling remains consistent throughout the accounting period. Changes in programs should be made by authorized programmers and not by computer-operating personnel. All changes should be charted and explained in writing; when completed, they should be reviewed and cleared by someone other than a maintenance programmer. All documents related to the change should be made a part of the permanent program file.

Computer-operation controls Some of the operating controls that may be established are:

1 *Control over console intervention* It is possible for computer operators to bypass program controls. They have the ability to interrupt a program run and introduce data manually into the processor through the console keyboard. With organizational separation of program preparation and computer operation and with operators having access to object programs and not source programs, it is unlikely that an operator will have enough knowledge of the program details to manipulate them successfully for improper purposes. But the possibility of unauthorized intervention should be reduced in a number of ways. Since, for example, the console typewriter may be used to print out a manual intervention, the paper sheets in the typewriter can be prenumbered and periodically checked. Other approaches using locked recording devices may be employed. Additional control techniques include rotating the duties of computer operators (or others in sensitive positions).[14]

2 *Control over physical security* Definite controls should be established to safeguard programs and data from fire and water damage or destruction. Duplicate program and master file tapes

---

[14]Managers should be alert to the risk inherent in having employees who never take vacations, who refuse promotion or rotation, who have access to the premises when no one else is present, and who are always around when the books are closed at the end of an accounting period.

may have to be kept at a location away from the computer site. A waste-disposal procedure to destroy carbon papers and other media containing sensitive information should be followed.[15] Only authorized personnel should be allowed access to the computer site.

3 *Control over terminal usage* Control procedures to identify authorized users of the system should obviously be given special attention. Such identification is typically based on something that users *know* (e.g., a password), on something they *have* (e.g., a card with a magnetically coded identification number), on some *personal characteristic* they possess, or on some combination of these elements. Passwords are most commonly used, but when used frequently (and carelessly) these words lose their security value. A better approach, perhaps, would be to have the computer provide the user, each day, with a different word or code that the user could then modify by following a secret procedure in order to gain access to the system. For example, "The computer might send a five-digit password. The user then adds today's date to it, and then sends back the second and fourth digits of the sum."[16] Once an authorized user has been identified and has gained access to the system, various techniques employing cryptography—that is, "hidden writing"—are available to thwart those who would intercept the messages traveling between the computer and the remote terminal.

Privacy Controls

An individual's "right" to privacy has been discussed at various times in this book, but privacy is not one of the rights specifically

---

[15]Almost $1 million in telephone equipment was stolen from Pacific Telephone & Telegraph Company by a clever thief who, at the age of 16, found in the telephone company trash cans information on Bell System operating procedures, manuals on system instructions, and a guide book called "Ordering Material and Supplies." Catalogs and authority code numbers were also acquired from trash cans! The thief obtained a special input device and then accessed the Bell System computer to input coded order and authority numbers. The ordered equipment was then picked up by the thief at a company warehouse (he had also bought a used telephone company van for the purpose). See Leo Anderson, "This Man Stole Almost $1 Million from a Telephone Company," *Telephony,* pp. 36–38, Nov. 17, 1972. (After being caught and paying his debt to society, the thief started a consulting service called EDP Security, Inc.)

[16]Richard G. Canning, "Protecting Valuable Data—Part 2," *EDP Analyzer,* p. 8, January 1974. This is a good source for further information on securing online terminals.

mentioned in the Bill of Rights of the Constitution. (In fact, the word "privacy" does not appear anywhere in the Constitution.) Furthermore, what one person may consider to be a privacy right may be in direct conflict with one of the rights that *is* explicitly mentioned in the Constitution. For example, if a newspaper reporter unearths the fact that a member of Congress has put a number of relatives on the government payroll for no good purpose, and if the reporter then reveals this fact and prints the names and salaries of the relatives, he or she has undoubtedly infringed on their privacy. But the reporter has also used rights guaranteed in the Bill of Rights (the First Amendment's freedom of speech and freedom of the press) to perform a public service. Thus, there may be legitimate rights operating against privacy in some situations. In short, since privacy is not one of the specific constitutional rights, and since a balance has to be struck between the need for privacy on the one hand and society's need for legitimate information on the other, *the extent to which individuals are given privacy protection must depend on judicial and legislative decisions.* That is, the *continuous* task of balancing human rights against basic freedoms in order to establish privacy controls is the responsiblity of the judicial and legislative branches of government.

Legal controls Recognizing that rapid advances in computer technology have given users of that technology the ability to gather and store information that (1) goes beyond the legitimate information needs of society and (2) can lead to excessive and unnecessary intrusions into an individual's personal privacy, lawmakers have been busy in recent years in the effort to restore some balance in favor of privacy. The result has been that federal statutes and dozens of state bills have been passed over a brief time span to control the invasion of privacy.[17]

Some *examples of existing privacy laws* are:

1 *Fair Credit Reporting Act of 1970* This federal law gives individuals the right to know what information is kept on them by credit bureaus and other credit investigation agencies. Individuals also have the right to challenge information they consider to be inaccurate and to insert brief explanatory statements into the records in disputed cases.

---

[17]And at this writing, over 125 additional bills with privacy provisions are being considered by various lawmaking bodies.

2 *State "Fair Information Practice" laws* The California Fair Information Practice Act of 1974 spells out the rights of individuals when dealing with state government data banks. Individuals have the right (*a*) to know what information is kept on them in the various state computer data banks; (*b*) to contest the "accuracy, completeness, pertinence, and timeliness" of the stored data; (*c*) to force a reinvestigation of the current status of personal data; and (*d*) to resolve disputes in ways spelled out by the law. The Minnesota Privacy Act (and acts passed by other states) contains similar provisions.

3 *Privacy Act of 1974* This important privacy legislation was passed by Congress late in 1974 and signed into law by President Ford on January 1, 1975. It became effective late in September 1975. The act is aimed at some of the uses and abuses of federal government data banks. Some of the provisions of this law are: (*a*) With the exception of classified files, Civil Service records, and law enforcement agency investigative files, individuals have the right to see their records in federal data banks; (*b*) they may point out errors in their records, and it these errors are not removed they may ask a federal judge to order the correction; (*c*) when federal agencies request personal information, they must tell individuals whether their cooperation in supplying the information is required by law; and (*d*) no federal, state, or local government agency can design a *new* information system based upon the use of the social security number. A Privacy Protection Study Commission was also established to monitor enforcement of the law and to study issues that will have to be resolved in the future. For example, the Commission is specifically given authority in the act to examine personal information activities in the medical, insurance, education, employment, credit and banking, credit reporting, cable television, telecommunications and other media, travel and hotel reservations, and EFTS areas. The Privacy Act of 1974 is aimed only at selected federal agencies, thus, even before it went into effect, legislation was being drafted by some lawmakers to remedy what they felt were its deficiencies and oversights. At this writing, it appears likely that additional laws will eventually be passed to expand the scope of the Privacy Act to include the data banks maintained by federal, state, and local law enforcement agencies, state and local governments, and businesses.

Business responsibilities Business managers need to exercise social restraint in order to resist further abuses of personal privacy rights. If the potential privacy implications are considered prior to the design of any new systems, if system designers are motivated to create new procedures that are more private and personalized, and if employees and supervisors who handle personal information will protect that information and treat it with the respect it deserves, then there will be fewer violations of the privacy rights of individuals.

SUMMARY Computer usage has had a positive influence on (and will continue to offer benefits to) large segments of society in general and many individuals in particular. For example, the prices we now pay to businesses for some goods and services may be less because of computer usage than they would otherwise have been, and the possible benefits of EFTS and UPC would not have been feasible without computers. Furthermore, in nonbusiness areas governmental agencies use computers to control air and water pollution, prepare better weather forecasts, and provide more efficient law enforcement; and health care organizations use computers to provide faster and more thorough testing to detect and identify disease.

Unfortunately, however, some businesses have used questionable data processing practices that have had adverse effects on the private lives and records of individuals. Data are sometimes gathered without a valid reason and are too often inaccurate and/or incomplete. Also, some people have felt themselves to be the relatively helpless victims of a cold, impersonal, and remote system that classifies, sorts, and treats them as depersonalized numbers. And we have probably all read accounts in newspapers of people being victimized by computer system errors and miscalculations.

A lack of control over data security in some business information systems has also led to undesirable consequences for individuals in society. And this lack of security, combined with the development of large integrated data banks, has raised serious questions about the possible threat to an individual's right to privacy.

Fortunately, the possible negative implications discussed in the chapter are now receiving thoughtful study. A few of the approaches used to control the negative impact have been outlined in the later pages of the chapter.

**REVIEW AND
DISCUSSION
QUESTIONS**
1 How may business computer usage benefit society?
2 (**a**) What are the possible benefits of EFTS for individuals?
  (**b**) What are the possible benefits of UPC?
3 "Some businesses have used questionable data processing practices that have had adverse effects on the private lives and records of individuals." Discuss this statement.

4   (**a**) How may a lack of control over data originating-recording lead to undesirable social results? (**b**) How may computer system classifying and sorting practices lead to the same results?

5   What are the primary causes of computer system miscalculations?

6   How may a lack of control over data security lead to undesirable consequences for individuals in society?

7   Why has the creation of integrated computer data banks increased the possible threat to an individual's right to privacy?

8   How may a computer system be used (**a**) for surveillance, and (**b**) to create a climate that can restrict individual freedom?

9   (**a**) Into what categories may integrity controls be classified? (**b**) Give some examples of integrity controls.

10   (**a**) Into what categories may system security controls be classified? (**b**) Give some examples of system security controls.

11   Discuss some controls that are available to restore some balance in favor of privacy.

COMPUTERS
AND THE
FUTURE

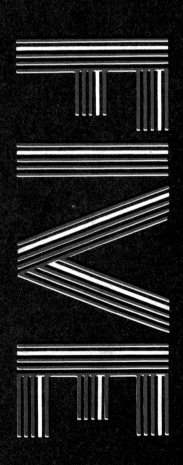

In this final Part, we shall briefly consider the future outlook for computer technology and for information systems. In addition, we shall look at the future effects of computer systems on society. Are we about to enter the utopian period envisioned by optimists, or is George Orwell's *1984,* with its eerie visions of a society controlled by a fictional "Big Brother," just a few years away in fact as well as in fiction? Turn to Chapter 14 and make your own judgments.

THE CHAPTER INCLUDED IN PART FIVE IS

TOMORROW'S OUTLOOK

LEARNING OBJECTIVES Unlike preceding chapters that were primarily concerned with factual material and established procedures, this chapter deals with speculations about computer-related developments in the next few years. Nevertheless, after reading this chapter and answering the discussion questions, you should be able to:

Describe how microprograms may be used.

Outline some developments in hardware, software, and information systems that you expect in the next 5 years.

Present the optimistic and pessimistic views about the future impact of computer systems.

CHAPTER OUTLINE

THE TECHNOLOGICAL OUTLOOK
Computer Hardware □ Computer Software

THE INFORMATION SYSTEMS OUTLOOK
Quick-Response Systems □ Broader Systems □ Some Possible Applications of Computer Systems

THE OUTLOOK FOR SOCIETY
The Optimistic View □ The Pessimistic View □ A Final Note

SUMMARY

In spite of the profound warning contained in an old proverb ("Prediction is difficult, particularly when it pertains to the future"), in this final chapter we shall attempt to summarize briefly some of the computer—and computer-related—developments that may be expected in the next few years. The topics to be considered can be classified as (1) the *technological outlook,* (2) the *information systems outlook,* and (3) the *outlook for* society.

THE TECHNOLOGICAL OUTLOOK

Computer Hardware

Numerous changes may be expected in the next few years in *I/O devices* and *central processors.*

I/O equipment   There will likely be little change in the performance of *punched card* equipment in the next several years. Efforts will be made to improve the reliability of card punches and readers, but the total demand for these devices will probably decline. In fact, Frost and Sullivan, a New York research organization, predicts that by 1984 keypunches will be supplanted by *keyboard-to-disk* storage devices for data entry purposes. Impact *printers* will not change significantly in speed or cost in the next few years. But there should be some cost reduction in *magnetic tape* drives and their controllers, and there should be a doubling in transfer speeds as the amount of data packed in an inch of tape doubles. Substantial cost reductions (50 percent or more in some cases) are expected in *OCR readers,* and this reduction will increase their use. Significant price declines are also likely in *COM* technology.

Direct-access storage devices will be developed to provide virtually unlimited online secondary storage at a very modest cost. *Storage hierarchies* will continue—i.e., the fastest auxiliary storage utilizing the latest technology will be more expensive and have less storage capacity than slower and less expensive alternatives. Mass storage approaches (in various stages of research and development) that are being considered by equipment designers include:

1   *Higher-density direct-access systems* Recording techniques using magnetic disk (and tape) surfaces that will significantly increase the density of data storage on a given surface are expected to be developed.
2   *Magnetic bubble systems* Free of the mechanical motion required with disks and drums, bubble devices are expected to be much more reliable and lower in cost. Storage density will be very high (over a million characters may be stored on a square inch of positively magnetized film). The "bubbles" are simply

negatively magnetized regions in this film. The presence of a bubble represents a binary 1, and the absence of a bubble represents a binary 0. Reading and writing operations are under the control of magnetic and electric fields.

3 *Optical direct-access systems* Information may be stored on a special light-sensitive plate by modulating electric pulses onto a *laser* light beam that is directed to a given area on the plate surface. A negative image of the varying light pattern—called a *hologram*—is etched on the plate surface and storage is thus accomplished. To retrieve information (without erasing it), a less intense laser beam is directed to the appropriate hologram to project the image onto sensors that will convert the light into electrical representations of the stored information. A single beam of light can cause the immediate transfer of a "page" of data. Theoretically, storage density and I/O speed are very high. Also, reliability is enhanced because of the absence of moving parts.

Sales of online *terminals* will more than double in the next few years, and terminals may represent over 25 percent of total hardware expenditures by 1984. Hundreds of thousands of *general-purpose typewriter* and *visual display* terminals will be installed each year in the 1980s, with visual display units being the most popular. In addition, hundreds of thousands of *special-purpose* terminals— e.g., POS and EFTS terminals—tailored specifically for a particular industry and/or application will be produced. The prices of the *intelligent terminals* discussed in Chapter 5 may rapidly decline as the costs of electronic components drop sharply. And as prices fall, increased demand for the intelligent devices will make possible an increase in production volumes which will further reduce costs and prices. By 1984, many more organizations will be (1) using stand-alone, intelligent terminals to carry out autonomous operations using the terminal's minicomputer, assorted peripherals, and secondary storage, and (2) utilizing a central computer to serve the terminals by managing large data bases and by executing those jobs that require extensive computations. In short, many more online terminals may be satellite minicomputers in a *distributed intelligence network* serviced by one or more central processing complexes.

Central processors There will continue to be substantial reductions in the *size* of electronic circuits. Tiny chips capable of storing 8,000 binary digits will give way to chips of about the same size that may have 8 times the storage capacity. Processors with more computing power than medium-sized and large machines of just a few

Peripheral devices

Central processor (top unit only)

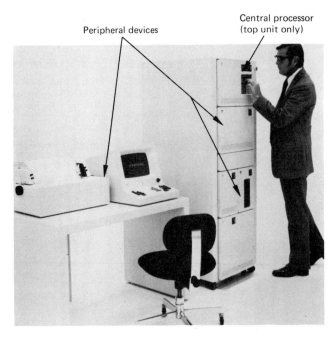

FIGURE 14-1
Series/1 minicomputer (courtesy IBM Corporation).

years ago are already dwarfed by their peripherals (Figure 14-1), and they will become much smaller in the future.

Along with further size reductions will come greater *speed*. Logic and storage circuits in 1984 will likely have switching speeds 10 to 50 times faster than those in use today; however, the total computer system may be "only" 5 times faster. Furthermore, circuits capable of performing at the same level as those in use today in larger systems may be available in just a few years at only one-tenth the present *cost*. Even now, complete central processor kits are available with case, power supply, a variable amount of storage, and other features (including the ability to accept programs written in high-level programming languages) for just a few hundred dollars.[1]

Semiconductor primary storage circuits will remain dominant during the late 1970s and early 1980s. Superconductive cryogenic devices operating at close to absolute zero temperatures have been found to be 100 times faster than any transistor circuit now in use, but

---

[1] At a recent meeting of electronic engineers, Lester Hogan, an executive of Fairchild Camera & Instrument Co., displayed a Fairchild microprocessor chip that he claimed had the processing power of the IBM 701 that was valued at $1 million in 1953. Hogan then casually tossed 18 of the chips into the audience and thus threw away the 1953 equivalent of $18 million in computer processing power!

FIGURE 14-2

Procedure for customizing a computer with microprograms.

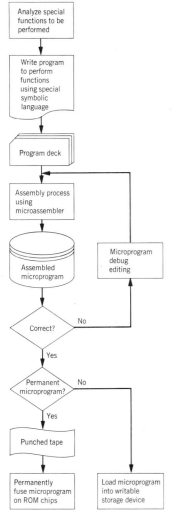

such devices are not likely to appear in commercial equipment in the next few years.

In Chapter 10, and in Figure 10-4, we saw that a special read-only storage unit in a CPU could be loaded with interpretative routines or *microprograms* that would permit one computer to interpret and execute instructions written for a different machine. In other words, the microprograms (also called *stored logic* and *firmware*) would analyze and decode foreign instructions into the elementary operations that the CPU is designed to execute. The usefulness of this concept extends beyond the emulation technique described in Chapter 10. It is also feasible to use various combinations of plug-in microprogrammed elements with *generalized* central processors to create custom-built systems for specific users. This "computer within a computer" approach can facilitate standardized CPU manufacturing and maintenance operations; it also makes it possible to convert critical, difficult, or lengthy software routines into microprograms that can be executed in a fraction of the time previously required. Furthermore, it is possible for vendors and users to *permanently* fuse their most important microprograms into read-only memory (ROM) chips and thus, in effect, convert important software into hardware.[2] Figure 14-2 illustrates how a computer manufacturer or user can create a customized computer system. Unlike the special-purpose computers of earlier years, however, the same processor can now be adapted to different functions by a simple change of microprograms. As Figure 14-2 indicates, if nonpermanent microprograms are desired, they may be loaded into a writable storage device that can be plugged into the CPU; if permanent firmware is needed, it may be fused onto ROM chips by a special writing device.

Computer technology will likely make much greater use of firmware in the future. By converting functions currently being performed with software into circuit elements (which are becoming less expensive), the need for some of the detailed (and very expensive) programming currently being done may be reduced. For example, in performing its functions of scheduling, control, etc., the operating system (OS) software discussed in Chapter 2 uses storage space in and the time of the CPU—space and time resources that might otherwise have been used for mathematical or data processing tasks. To reduce this OS overhead, resident microprograms operating at hardware speeds may be substituted for some of the tasks

---

[2]It has been suggested that "ROM of the Month Clubs" may spring up in the 1980s to send subscribers new applications programs written into ROM chips that can be plugged into home microcomputers.

currently being accomplished at relatively slow speeds with a series of OS program instructions. Also, specialized microprocessors and microprograms are likely to be used frequently in the future in place of software for language translation, data security, and data manipulation and control. Thus, the traditional and still very popular *uniprocessor* computer system that features single control, storage, and arithmetic-logic units will likely give way in the future to *multiprocessor* systems in all but the smallest installations. Of course, the component micro- and mini-sized processors dedicated to performing the specialized functions such as data-base management and security are likely to be smaller than those reserved to process user jobs in multiple and simultaneous streams. But future users—connected to such a multiprocessor system, perhaps, by intelligent terminals that further distribute and decentralize the computing power of the network—may expect faster, more reliable, and more secure service.

Computer Software

There are numerous technical articles being published that predict with confidence the course of hardware development over the next decade. But this confidence is not found in the few articles dealing with the future of software development. Perhaps this is due to the fact that the development of software will continue to be slower, much more expensive, and more painful than hardware because the functions performed by software are now (and will continue to be) more complex than the operations performed by hardware. Of course, as we saw in the preceding section, many of the "normal" functions now being performed by operating system software may be taken over by future hardware elements. And the future use of multiprocessor systems may *reduce* the need for complex *multiprogramming* software that permits instructions from several programs to be interleaved and executed on a single processor. In short, the total-cost trends for information systems discussed in Chapter 2 (and shown in Figure 2-4) will encourage the replacement of expensive software with cheap hardware whenever possible.

The comments just made in the preceding paragraph should not, however, be interpreted to mean that there will be no progress in software development. On the contrary, existing *languages* such as COBOL, PL/I, FORTRAN, etc., will be enhanced and improved to accommodate the *structured programming* approach to modular design discussed in Chapters 9 and 10. Subset dialects of these languages will also be developed for very small processors. Furthermore, new very-high-level languages may be developed to solve particular types of problems so that nonprogrammer users can conveniently make use of computing capabilities. Such languages may be *conversational*—i.e., the computer itself may keep track of the acceptable vocabulary of the language, and it may display permissible alternate terms and statements to users until the problem is satisfactorily formulated. The machine would then compute the answer to the problem. Thus, the users' major skill will be in their ability to state problems, and they will be assisted by a "dialogue" with the computer as it seeks to find out what they want to say.

Conversational programming is likely to be a feature of the *data-base management software* described in Chapter 2 (and in Figure 2-17). In 1974, there were only about 1,500 true data-base management systems in worldwide use. By 1984, however, there will be tens of thousands of these software systems in operation, they will be more comprehensive, they will be large and may require up to a million characters of storage to operate effectively,[3] and they will enable the end-user of the information to frequently bypass the services of applications programmers. Additional provisions to ensure the *integrity* and *security* of stored information will be incorporated into future data-base software as well as into future hardware.

Finally, *program development aids* such as structured programming will result in higher programmer productivity, shorter program development times, and more understandable and more error-free program modules.

THE INFORMATION SYSTEMS OUTLOOK

Although traditional batch processing computer installations are economical, are well suited to many types of applications, and are going to continue to account for a high percentage of the total processing work for some time, the trend is toward future systems that will be *quicker-responding* and *broader in scope* than these traditional installations.

Quick-Response Systems

As we have seen, emphasis is currently being given to the development of (1) distributed computer systems with logic and storage capability moved to the point of origin of transactions, (2) user-

---

[3]Alternatively, and quite possibly, the data-base management function may be performed by a separate dedicated minicomputer utilizing stored logic rather than by a large software package tied to the main operating system of the installation.

oriented interactive programming languages designed to enable operating personnel to get information quickly without having to wait for the help of an applications programmer, and (3) direct-access storage devices, online terminals, and multiprocessor computer configurations. And these developments, in turn, signal a definite trend in the direction of quick-response systems that will give remote users immediate access to very powerful computing facilities. *Real time processing* will become increasingly common in those applications where immediate updating of records is justifiable. When the time limitations are not so severe, *online processing,* with periodic updating of those records that affect other users of a distributed network, will be frequently used in place of traditional batch processing methods. Source data will frequently be keyed directly into the computer system, thus eliminating the need for cards and/or tapes in many applications.

With increased emphasis being placed on quick-response systems, there will obviously be greater use of *data communications* facilities. In fact, the transmission of data is expected to continue to increase by 35 percent *each year* between now and 1985. New data communications services will be established (satellites will be used), and the current services offered by data carrier organizations will be expanded to meet this demand. Data transmission line costs will be reduced by up to 50 percent by 1984.

Broader Systems

Many of the quick-response systems that will be developed in the next few years will take a broader *data-base approach* to the needs of the organization. (Given the rapid growth expected in data-base management software, this is not a surprising prediction.) The data-base approach can be flexible; that is, it may be used by organizations combining large centralized computers (and a centralized data base) with nonintelligent terminals located at operating level, it may be used by organizations with a smaller central processor to maintain a centralized data base for a network of distributed minicomputers and outlying intelligent terminals, or it may be used by organizations adopting some other alternative.

Regardless of the technical approach used, the trend in many organizations will be to define, classify, and store certain types of basic data commonly so that better integration will be possible. The development efforts to produce data banks that will replace a multitude of the independent files maintained at the present time will probably continue at a more rapid pace in spite of the potential

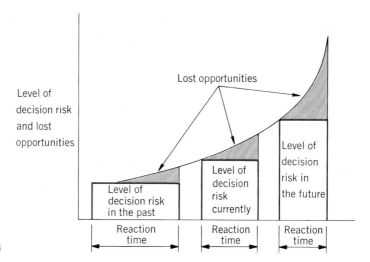

FIGURE 14-3

dangers to individual privacy. Why will this happen? It will likely happen because managers will have to respond to future changes that may occur at a much faster rate than in the past. Therefore, decision makers forced to make quicker choices involving greater risks will press for relatively complete information rather than settle for information in bits and pieces located in scattered files. As Figure 14-3 indicates, it is quite possible that as reaction time diminishes, opportunities for profitable action could be lost while preoccupied managers searched scattered files for decision-making information.

Some Possible Applications of Computer Systems

The following applications seem to be *technically* possible during the 1980s; whether they are all *socially desirable,* however, is another matter. These few applications have not been included in earlier speculations, and they have been *arbitrarily* classified into those that may affect *businesses* and those that may have an impact on *individuals in society.* Of course, the development, for the home, of new computer-controlled products by some businesses will also affect the private lives of individuals in our society.

Applications affecting businesses A few of the computer-related applications that may have an impact on businesses in the 1980s are:

1 *Computer-assisted manufacturing* By 1984, the installation of tens of thousands of micro-sized and mini-sized computers to run machine tools will have resulted in an incredible gain in the efficiency and cost effectiveness of many manufacturing operations. Only 10 programmable manipulators, or robots, were installed during 1974; by 1984, however, it is predicted that 14,000 robots will be added each year. Since computer-controlled automatic machines can be switched from the production of one item to another simply by changing the program, it will be feasible to keep equipment busy by having it produce small quantities of a number of different items. Thus, small-lot manufacturing may become nearly as economical as mass production is today. In fact, "Nathan Cook of MIT predicts that computers and robots may reduce overall costs in small-lot manufacturing by 80 to 90 percent."[4] And since the machines that will be used in future mass production operations will be produced in small lots, the net effect is that they will be relatively less expensive, and so may be the prices of the items they produce.

2 *Automatic meter reading* At this writing, many telephone companies have installed computer-controlled testing equipment to check on the condition of telephone lines. In the 1980s, gas, electric, and water meters may be connected to these telephone lines so that as the system automatically tests line condition it will also read the meters for the utility companies.

3 *Attending meetings electronically* Telephones and cable TV sets may be combined with computers to provide an integrated voice-data-picture communication system for some organizations. Ultimately (but probably not by 1984), it may be possible for many professionals such as managers, teachers, engineers, etc., to perform most of their job duties in offices located in their homes. Thus, the transmission of information may be substituted for the transportation and concentration of humans. The need to crowd together into cities may be reduced; communities of interest and interaction may be linked electronically rather than by geographic boundaries.[5]

---

[4]James S. Albus, "Automation and the Sleeping Nation," *Computer Decisions*, p. 32, August 1975.

[5]For more details on these intriguing possibilities, see Joseph Ferreira and Jack M. Nilles, "Five-Year Planning for Data Communications," *Datamation,* pp. 51–57, October 1976.

Applications affecting individuals in society   Some of the computer-related applications that could affect the lives of people at home and at play in the 1980s are:

1   *Home and hobby applications*   Microprocessors on small chips will be used to control most home appliances in the 1980s. The electromechanical controls found on washers, dryers, food mixers, etc., will be replaced by more reliable microprocessors. Television sets may also have microprocessors to perform automatic tuning and color-regulating operations. Typewriters will incorporate tiny computers for control and duplication purposes. And a microcomputer could be added to the push-button telephone to convert it into a terminal suitable for requesting and receiving stock quotations, recorded information such as emergency first-aid procedures from voice libraries, mathematical computation procedures to assist in income tax preparation, and online banking (EFTS) services. Inexpensive computers with considerable power will also be widely used for *home recrea-*

"She's charming, witty and attractive, dear,
but can she program?"

© DATAMATION ®

"Yes, Master?"

tion and *education* purposes. When connected to a TV set, the computer will provide an almost unlimited number of games. For example, small children can play with a controllable TV puppet, they can do TV picture drawing, and they can play a simple electronic organ; older members of the family can play a target-shooting game, they can play a football game or go bowling, or they can trace through a maze or make a moon landing—the list of entertainment applications is virtually endless. The computer may be reprogrammed to play different games in just a few seconds by using preprogrammed tapes and an inexpensive audio-type cassette reader. In addition to recreational applications, this computer-TV system will also be used for educational purposes. Instead of games (which can be very educational in their own right), the preprogrammed tapes can provide all kinds of test and drill applications to bring the advantages of *computer-assisted instruction* right into the home.

In addition to computer systems using TV sets and prepro-grammed tapes, there will also be, for the hobbyist, tens of thousands of home computer systems that can be programmed in high-level languages. Complete computer kits selling for less than $300 are now available. Much more powerful machines at the same cost will be available in the 1980s. Clubs of computer hobbyists are springing up across the nation to share programs and experiences.

2 *Opinion polling in the home* In some parts of the country today, TV sets receive their signals from cable connections rather than from airwaves. Cable television may expand in the future to permit subscribers to choose from a wider selection of incoming

programs. But the cable can also be used to communicate *outgoing* messages. A cable TV set might be equipped with a few buttons such as might be found on a pocket calculator. A broadcaster could then invite viewers to participate in a "personal response program." Questions could be asked, buttons could be pushed, and responses could be recorded and tabulated in computer systems. A national "town meeting" could be called in this way to provide political leaders with the electronic "votes" of citizens on important issues.

3 *Automotive applications* The family car in the 1980s will be equipped with microprocessors that will take over the functions now performed by electromechanical systems. Instruments, speed and skid control systems, ignition and fuel injection systems, engine analysis sensors, temperature control and antitheft devices, emission control and collision avoidance devices—all these components will be under computer control.

THE OUTLOOK FOR SOCIETY

The Optimistic View

The optimistic view of the future is that *greater freedom and individuality* are encouraged by the use of computers. Optimists note the individual benefits, such as those mentioned in preceding sections and chapters, and they expand and project those benefits into the future. They foresee no insurmountable problems in society's adapting to the changes brought about by increased computer utilization. The greater productivity that results from computer usage, they contend, will lead to an increased standard of living, a shorter work week, and increased leisure time. Although it will be a challenge for human beings to put aside age-old attitudes toward work and learn to use creatively the free time that they will have in the future, the optimists believe that people can learn to use their leisure in ways that are contemplative and self-fulfilling.

Also, it is argued, people will be freed from the basic struggle to maintain their existence and will have the time and resources to pursue the activities of their choice. (Since individuality has been defined as the "freedom to exercise choice according to one's own scale of preference,"[6] it will thus be enhanced.) Aristotle's prophecy that "When looms weave by themselves, man's slavery will end" is cited by the optimists. Nonhuman slaves (computers and automated tools controlled by computers) will liberate many people from the

---

[6]Robert M. Gordon, "Computers and Freedom, Individuality and Automation: Challenge and Opportunity," *Computer,* p. 30, September–October 1971.

unpleasant working conditions that have evolved from Charles Dickens's England of the 1800s and Upton Sinclair's United States of the early 1900s. No longer will people have to spend long hours at an assembly line, for example, tightening a few bolts on the monotonous widgets passing by, when a computer-directed and uncomplaining robot can do the work accurately and inexpensively.

Optimists also believe that the sophisticated computer systems of the future will permit a *more human and personalized society* that will further reduce the need for individual conformity. They argue that the complexity of our present society, the millions of people crowded into it, and the inadequacy of our present information systems act to encourage conformity and thus to restrict personalization and human freedom of choice. However, when sophisticated information systems are developed and widely used to handle routine transactions, it will then be possible to focus greater personal attention on exceptional transactions. Therefore, more humanistic attitudes will emerge. Of course, these optimistic views do not go unchallenged.

The Pessimistic View

The pessimistic view of the future is that the effects of computer usage will *not* lead to greater freedom and individuality. On the contrary, pessimists can examine many of the same applications as optimists did and come to the opposite conclusion that computer usage will (1) dominate our lives as a society and as individuals and (2) sweep us along in a tide over which we—the harassed and exposed victims of a depersonalized and dehumanized process that places greater value on efficiency than on the more noble qualities of life—shall have little control.

Critics of the effects of computer usage have evidence to show that questionable practices in originating and recording data are common; that dossiers containing incorrect, ambiguous, and unverified data on individuals are produced; that correct personal data are misused; that systems miscalculations are frequent; that stored sensitive personal data are often not secured and protected against theft, manipulation, and malicious scrutiny; and that those facts, beliefs, thoughts, and feelings that people want to keep to themselves (or have kept on a confidential basis) are repeatedly revealed and disseminated. The net effect, pessimists contend, is that individual freedom will be severely threatened by computer-usage pressures leading to greater regimentation and conformity.

On the economic front, pessimists agree with optimists that computer-assisted manufacturing will result in enormous gains in productivity. But the pessimists argue that when humans must compete with programmable robots, the humans will lose—they will lose their jobs[7] and they will lose their personal dignity. And as jobs are eliminated by machines, purchasing power is certain to decline. A monumental economic depression may result from the overproduction of machines and the decline in demand, and this could lead to a severe political upheaval and a change in our form of government.

The fears expressed in the above summary of the pessimistic view are not all new, nor are they all related solely to the future impact on individuals of computers alone. For at least 100 years people have feared that automatic machines might develop consciousness and turn on their creators. In 1872, for example, a science fiction work entitled *Erewhon* was published by Samuel Butler. Residents of Erewhon, fearing that people would some day stand in the same relation to machines as "the beasts of the field" now stand to people, attacked and destroyed nearly all the machines in Erewhon.

A Final Note

There comes a time when one asks even of
  Shakespeare,
even of Beethoven, "Is this all?"
  Aldous Huxley

Is it possible in this last section to draw any conclusions from the dozens of different viewpoints that have so often been presented in the pages of this book? Perhaps. We can conclude, for example, that there are at least three different contemporary views of computers and technological change:

1 *Computers and technology are an unblemished blessing.* This uncritical optimistic view holds that technology is the source of all progress for the individual and society, that social problems will inevitably be solved through the application of technology, and that every new technological possibility will automatically be beneficial.

2 *Computers and technology are an unbridled curse.* This pessimistic view holds that technology increases unemployment, leads to depersonalization and bewilderment, threatens an indi-

---

[7] A recent Associated Press news item quoted Bernard Sallot, executive director of the Robot Institute of America, as saying that a new programmable robot would soon replace thousands of semiskilled workers—perhaps hundreds of thousands of them—in factory jobs. A "tremendous backlog of orders" for robots now exists, Sallot added.

"You'll be all right as long as you remember it's just
another tool."

© DATAMATION ®

vidual's right to dignity and privacy, and threatens to pollute
and/or blow up the world.

3 *Computers and technology are undeserving of special attention.* This unconcerned view is that technology has been with us
for decades, and we are now better educated and more able
than ever before to adapt to the new ideas and changes which it
has brought (and will bring).

Each of these views is deficient although each probably contains
an element of truth. The optimists are correct when they conclude
that new technology often creates new opportunities for society; the
pessimists are correct when they conclude that new problems are
often created by new tools; and the unconcerned are correct when
they conclude that social institutions (e.g., schools) can, and often
do, play an important role in tempering the effects of technology.

The predictions of optimists or pessimists will become facts or fables if people make them so. We cannot know what people *will* do in the future. They *could* achieve the optimistic vision. But if in using computers they choose procedures that are impersonal and coldly efficient, they should not be surprised if the results are inhumane and inflexible. Thus, in the years ahead it will be up to concerned and informed managers and citizens who have an awareness of the potential dangers to see that the optimistic view prevails. I am confident that you will succeed.

SUMMARY

Significant developments are expected in the next few years in computer hardware and software. Some of the likely changes have been outlined in this chapter.

Future information systems will be quicker-responding and broader in scope than the average installation in operation today. Data communications services will have to be expanded to handle the rapid increase in data transmission. A network of distributed processors and a broader data-base approach will be frequently used to respond to the needs of organizations and decision makers.

The future uses of computers are viewed by some people with optimism while others believe that computers and technology are likely to be the curse of humanity. Which view—optimism or pessimism—will prevail? No one knows. Predictions of each group will become facts or fables only if people make them so. An enlightened citizenry, aware of the dangers, can help bring about the optimistic version.

REVIEW AND DISCUSSION QUESTIONS

1 What future hardware developments would support the development of distributed computer networks?

2 How are microprograms used?

3 Why might the development of multiprocessor systems reduce the need for multiprogramming software?

4 (**a**) What is conversational programming? (**b**) What is the purpose of data-base management software?

5 "Future information systems will be quicker-responding and broader in scope than traditional installations." Discuss this statement.

6 (**a**) Are you an optimist or a pessimist about the future impact of computer systems on society? (**b**) Defend your answer to 6 (**a**).

CARD
PUNCH
OPERATION

APPENDIX A

The purpose of this supplement is to acquaint you with some of the fundamentals of keypunch operation so that you may prepare the necessary cards to run short programs or make changes in existing program or data cards. The purpose is *not* to make you a highly skilled keypunch operator. Thus, only the most basic uses of the card punch are discussed here.

A card punch commonly encountered is the IBM model 29 (Figure A-1). The keyboard and functional control switches for this machine are shown in Figure A-2.

The *shaded* keys on the keyboard are used to control certain machine operations; the *unshaded* keys are used to punch the indicated characters. Depressing the NUMERIC shift key causes the character indicated on the upper portion of the key to be punched. As you will note, the alphabetic keys are located just where they would be on a typewriter.

FIGURE A-1
Model 29 Card punch (courtesy IBM Corporation).

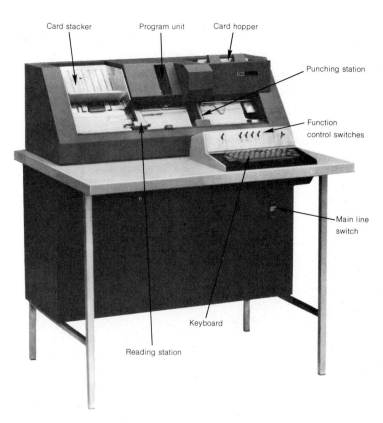

Card stacker · Program unit · Card hopper · Punching station · Function control switches · Main line switch · Keyboard · Reading station

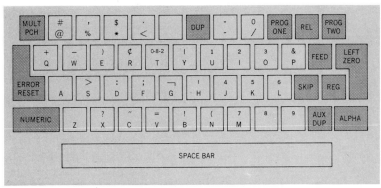

(a)

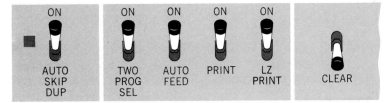

(b)

FIGURE A-2
(a) Card punch keyboard; (b)
functional control switches.

TYPICAL OPERATION TO PREPARE SHORT PROGRAMS

The operating steps in punching a typical student program may be outlined as follows:

1 Turn on the *main line switch,* shown in Figure A-1.
2 Load blank cards into the *card hopper* face forward with the 9-edge down.
3 Turn on the AUTO FEED and PRINT functional control switches, shown in Figure A-2, and switch the *program control lever* (located right below the program unit shown in Figure A-1) to the right.
4 By depressing the FEED key, you will move a card from the hopper to the entrance to the *punching station.* Pressing the FEED button a second time will drop a second card and properly align the first card at the punching station.
5 Punch the necessary data into the card.
6 If the last column punched is column 80, the completed card will be automatically advanced to the *reading station,* and a new

blank card will be positioned at the punching station. If the last column punched is *not* column 80, the card may be advanced by pressing the REL key.

7 The punched card advanced to the reading station and the following card positioned at the punching station move together—i.e., as columns 1, 2, 3, etc., of the completed card pass under the reading station, the *same columns* of the following card are being positioned under the punching station. This synchronization feature permits data to be duplicated in the second card. If the DUP key is depressed, data sensed in the completed card will be automatically reproduced in the same columns of the following card.

8 When the last card has been punched, the CLEAR function switch on the model 29 may be used to move it to the *card stacker.*

9 Turn off the main line switch.

SINGLE-CARD PREPARATION It is often necessary to add one or two cards to a deck or to replace an existing card with a corrected or undamaged one. The operating steps to follow in these situations are:

1 Turn on the main line switch.

2 Turn off the AUTO FEED switch, turn on the PRINT switch, and switch the program control lever to the right to disengage the program unit.

3 Put a blank card into the *card hopper* and press the FEED key to move the card to the *punching station.* Then press the REG key to align the card under the punches.

4 Punch the card as required and then press the REL key to release it from the punching station.

5 The card can be cleared to the stacker by depressing the CLEAR switch.

6 Turn off the main line switch.

GLOSSARY

APPENDIX B

Access time   The elapsed time between the instant when data are called for from a storage device and the instant when the delivery operation begins.

Accumulator   A register or storage location that forms the result of an arithmetic or logic operation.

Address   An identification (e.g., a label, name, or number) that designates a particular location in storage or any other data destination or source. Also, a part of an instruction that specifies the location of an operand for the instruction.

Algorithm   A set of well-defined rules for solving a problem in a finite number of operations.

Alphanumeric   Pertaining to a character set that includes letters, digits, and, usually, other special punctuation character marks.

Analog computer   A device that operates on data in the form of continuously variable physical quantities.

ANSI (American National Standards Institute)   Formerly ASA and USASI.

APL (a programming language)   A mathematically oriented language frequently used in timesharing.

Arithmetic unit   The part of a computing system containing the circuitry that does the adding, subtracting, multiplying, dividing, and comparing.

Assembly program   A computer program that takes nonmachine-language instructions prepared by a programmer and converts them into a form that may be used by the computer.

Auxiliary storage   A storage that supplements the primary internal storage of a computer.

Background processing   The execution of lower-priority computer programs during periods when the system resources are not required to process higher-priority programs.

BASIC (beginners all-purpose symbolic instruction code)   A terminal-oriented programming language frequently used in timesharing.

Batch processing   A technique in which a number of similar items or transactions to be processed are grouped (batched) for sequential processing during a machine run.

BCD (binary-coded decimal)   A method of representing the decimal digits zero through nine by a pattern of binary ones and zeros (e.g., the decimal number 23 is represented by 0010 0101 in 8-4-2-1 BCD notation).

Binary digit   Either of the characters 0 or 1. Abbreviated "bit."

Binary number system   A number system with a base or radix of two.

Bit   See *binary digit*.

Branch   See *conditional transfer.*

Buffer   A storage device used to compensate for the difference in rates of flow of data from one device to another—e.g., from an I/O device to the CPU.

Byte   A group of adjacent bits operated upon as a unit.

Cathode ray tube (CRT)   An electronic tube with a screen upon which information may be displayed.

Central processing unit (CPU)   The component of a computer system with the circuitry to control the interpretation and execution of instructions.

Channel   A path for carrying signals between a source and a destination.

COBOL   An acronym for COmmon Business-Oriented Language— a high-level language developed for business data processing applications.

Code   A set of rules outlining the way in which data may be represented; also, rules used to convert data from one representation to another. To write a program or routine.

Compiler   A computer program that produces a machine-language program from a source program that is usually written in a high-level language by a programmer. The compiler is capable of replacing single source program statements with a series of machine language instructions or with a subroutine.

Computer network   A processing complex consisting of two or more interconnected computers.

Conditional transfer   An instruction that may cause a departure from the sequence of instructions being followed, depending upon the result of an operation, the contents of a register, or the setting of an indicator.

Console   The part of a computer system that enables human operators to communicate with the computer.

Counter   A device (e.g., a register) used to represent the number of occurrences of an event.

CPU   See *central processing unit.*

CRT   See *cathode ray tube.*

Cybernetics   The branch of learning which seeks to integrate the theories and studies of communication and control in machines and living organisms.

Data administrator   The one responsible for defining, updating, and controlling access to a data base.

Data bank   See *data base.*

Data base   A stored collection of the libraries of data that are needed by an organization to meet its information processing and retrieval requirements.

Data-base management system The comprehensive software system that builds, maintains, and provides access to a data base.

Data processing One or more operations performed on data to achieve a desired objective.

Debug To detect, locate, and remove errors in programs and/or malfunctions in equipment.

Digital computer A device that manipulates discrete data and performs arithmetic and logic operations on these data. Contrast with *analog computer*.

Direct-access Pertaining to storage devices where the time required to retrieve data is independent of the physical location of the data.

Documentation The preparation of documents, during system analysis and subsequent programming, that describe such things as the system, the programs prepared, and the changes made at later dates.

Downtime The length of time a computer system is inoperative due to a malfunction.

EBCDIC An 8-bit code used to represent data in modern computers.

EDP An acronym for electronic data processing.

Executive routine A master program that controls the execution of other programs. Often used synonymously with *executive, monitor,* and *supervisory routine.*

Field A group of related characters treated as a unit—e.g., a group of adjacent card columns used to represent an hourly wage rate. An item in a record.

File A collection of related records treated as a unit.

Flowchart A diagram that uses symbols and interconnecting lines to show (1) a system of processing to achieve objectives (system flowchart) or (2) the logic and sequence of specific program operations (program flowchart).

FORTRAN An acronym for FORmula TRANslator—a high-level language used to perform mathematical computations.

Generator A computer program that constructs other programs to perform a particular type of operation—e.g., a report program generator.

Hardware Physical equipment such as electronic, magnetic, and mechanical devices. Contrast with *software.*

Heuristic A problem-solving method in which solutions are discovered by evaluating the progress made toward the end result. A directed trial-and-error approach. Contrast with *algorithm.*

Hollerith code A particular type of code used to represent alphanumeric data on punched cards.

Hybrid computer A data processing device using both analog and discrete data representation.

Information Meaning assigned to data by humans.

Information retrieval The methods used to recover specific information from stored data.

Input/output (I/O) Pertaining to the techniques, media, and devices used to achieve human/machine communication.

Instruction A set of characters used to direct a data processing system in the performance of an operation—i.e., an operation is signaled and the values or locations of the instruction operands are specified.

Interface A shared boundary—e.g., the boundary between two systems or devices.

Internal storage The addressable storage in a digital computer directly under the control of the central processing unit.

Interpreter A computer program that translates each source language statement into a sequence of machine instructions and then executes these machine instructions before translating the next source language statement. A device that prints on a punched card the data already punched in the card.

I/O See *input/output*.

A group of related characters treated as a unit. (A record is a group of related items, and a file is a group of related records.)

Job A collection of specified tasks constituting a unit of work for a computer.

Jump A departure from sequence in executing instructions in a computer. See *conditional transfer*.

K An abbreviation for kilo or 1,000 in decimal notation.

Label One or more characters used to identify a program statement or a data item.

Language A set of rules and conventions used to convey information.

Library routine A tested routine maintained in a library of programs.

Loop A sequence of instructions in a program that can be executed repetitively until certain specified conditions are satisfied.

Machine language A language used directly by a computer.

Macro instruction A source language instruction that is equivalent to a specified number of machine language instructions.

Magnetic ink character recognition (MICR) The recognition of characters printed with a special magnetic ink by machines.

Magnetic storage Utilizing the magnetic properties of materials to store data on such devices and media as disks, drums, cards, cores, tapes, and films.

Main frame   Same as *central processing unit.*

Management information system (MIS)   An information system designed to supply organizational managers with the necessary information needed to plan, organize, staff, direct, and control the operations of the organization.

Memory   Same as *storage.*

MICR   See *magnetic ink character recognition.*

Microprocessor   The basic arithmetic, logic, and storage elements required for processing (generally on one or a few integrated circuit chips).

Microsecond   One-millionth of a second.

Millisecond   One-thousandth of a second.

Minicomputer   A relatively fast but small and inexpensive computer with somewhat limited input and output capabilities.

MIS   See *management information system.*

Mnemonic   Pertaining to a technique used to aid human memory.

Monitor routine   See *executive routine.*

Multiplex   To simultaneously transmit messages over a single channel or other communications facility.

Multiprocessing   The simultaneous execution of two or more sequences of instructions by a single computer network.

Multiprocessor   A computer network consisting of two or more central processors under a common control.

Multiprogramming   The simultaneous handling of multiple independent programs by interleaving or overlapping their execution.

Nanosecond   One-billionth of a second.

Natural language   A human language such as English, French, German, etc.

Object language   The output of a translation process. Contrast with *source language.* Synonymous with *target language.*

OCR (optical character recognition)   The recognition of printed characters through the use of light-sensitive optical machines.

Offline   A term describing persons, equipment, or devices not in direct communication with the central processing unit of a computer.

Online   A term describing persons, equipment, or devices that are in direct communication with the central processing unit of a computer.

Operand   The data unit or equipment item that is operated upon. An operand is usually identified by an address in an instruction.

Operating system   An organized collection of software that controls the overall operations of a computer.

Operation code   The instruction code used to specify the operations a computer is to perform.

Patch   The modification of a routine in an expedient way.

Peripheral equipment The input/output devices and auxiliary storage units of a computer system.

Picosecond One-thousandth of a nanosecond.

PL/I An acronym for Programming Language I—a high-level language designed to process both scientific and file-manipulating applications.

Procedure-oriented language A programming language designed to conveniently express procedures used to solve a particular class of problems.

Program (1) A plan to achieve a problem solution; (2) to design, write, and test one or more routines; (3) a set of sequenced instructions to cause a computer to perform particular operations.

Program flowchart See *flowchart.*

Program library A collection of programs and routines.

Programmer One who designs, writes, tests, and maintains computer programs.

Programming language A language used to express programs.

Radix The base number in a number system—e.g., the radix in the decimal system is 10. Synonymous with *base.*

Random-access Descriptive of storage devices where the time required to retrieve data is not significantly affected by the physical location of the data.

Real time Descriptive of online computer processing systems which receive and process data quickly enough to produce output to control, direct, or affect the outcome of an ongoing activity or process.

Record A collection of related items of data treated as a unit. See *item.*

Register A device capable of storing a specific amount of data.

Remote access Relating to the communication with a computer facility by a station (or stations) that is distant from the computer.

Report program generator (RPG) Software designed to construct programs that perform predictable report-writing operations.

Routine An ordered set of general-use instructions. See *program.*

Secondary storage See *auxiliary storage.*

Serial-access Descriptive of a storage device or medium where there is a sequential relationship between access time and data location in storage—i.e., the access time is dependent upon the location of the data. Contrast with *direct-access* and *random-access.*

Simulation To represent and analyze properties or behavior of a physical or hypothetical system by the behavior of a system model. (This model is often manipulated by means of computer operations.)

Software A set of programs, documents, procedures, and routines associated with the operation of a computer system. Contrast with *hardware*.

Solid-state   Descriptive of electronic components whose operation depends on the control of electric or magnetic phenomena in solids, such as transistors and diodes.

Source language   The language that is an input for statement translation.

Source program   A computer program written in a source language such as FORTRAN, BASIC, COBOL, etc.

Statement   In programming, an expression or generalized instruction in a source language.

Storage   Descriptive of a device or medium that can accept data, hold them, and deliver them on demand at a later time. Synonymous with *memory*.

Subroutine   A routine that can be a part of another routine or program.

Supervisory routine   See *executive routine*.

System   (1) A grouping of integrated methods and procedures united to form an organized entity; (2) an organized grouping of people, methods, machines, and materials collected together to accomplish a set of specific objectives.

System flowchart   See *flowchart*.

System analyst   One who studies the activities, methods, procedures, and techniques of organizational systems in order to determine what actions need to be taken and how these actions can best be accomplished.

Throughput   The total amount of useful work performed by a computer system during a given time period.

Timesharing   The use of specific hardware by a number of other devices, programs, or people simultaneously in such a way as to provide quick response to each of the users. The interleaved use of the time of a device.

Unconditional transfer   An instruction that always causes a branch in program control away from the normal sequence of executing instructions.

Utility routine   Software used to perform some frequently required process in the operation of a computer system—e.g., sorting, merging, etc.

Virtual storage   Descriptive of the capability to use online secondary storage devices and specialized software to divide programs into smaller segments for transmission to and from internal storage in order to significantly increase the effective size of the available internal storage.

Word   A group of bits or characters considered as an entity and capable of being stored in one storage location.

Word length   The number of characters or bits in a word.